3.47

THE
PITY
PARTY

ALSO BY WILLIAM VOEGELI

Never Enough: America's Limitless Welfare State

THE
PITY
PARTY

A Mean-Spirited Diatribe
Against Liberal Compassion

WILLIAM
VOEGELI

BROADSIDE BOOKS
An Imprint of HarperCollins*Publishers*

HarperCollins books may be purchased for educational, business, or sales promotional use. For information, please e-mail the Special Markets Department at SPsales@harpercollins.com.

FIRST EDITION

Library of Congress Cataloging-in-Publication Data has been applied for.

ISBN: 978-0-06-228929-2

14 15 16 17 18   ov/rrd   10 9 8 7 6 5 4 3 2 1

FOR MY PARENTS

ACKNOWLEDGMENTS

There's a very good chance that I never would have started this book without encouragement from Adam Bellow, who became its editor. Once I did begin writing, there's an even better chance I never would have finished it without his help. I'm grateful to Adam and his colleagues at HarperCollins, in particular Eric Meyers, Broadside Books associate editor, and Tom Pitoniak. I'm equally indebted to Carol Mann of the Carol Mann Agency for her reassurance and wise counsel.

I worked on *Pity Party* to the detriment of my obligations to the *Claremont Review of Books*, and with the help of my colleagues there: Patrick Collins, Lindsay Eberhardt, Christopher Flannery, Charles Kesler, John Kienker, and Ryan Williams. I also thank Brian Kennedy, *CRB*'s publisher in his capacity as the president of the Claremont Institute, and Tom Klingenstein, the institute's chairman. I am fortunate as well to be affiliated with Claremont McKenna College's Henry Salvatori Center, and I am grateful to Mark Blitz, the center's director, and Elvia Huerta, its administrator, for their help.

My deepest debt is to Martha and Bailey, my wife and stepdaughter, the best reasons I could have to turn the computer on, day after day, and grind out more paragraphs.

This book is dedicated, with great affection, to Beverly and Robert Jones, and to Carol and the late William J. Voegeli.

CONTENTS

INTRODUCTION:
SUFFERING SITUATIONS

The accomplished actor had read better lines, but none better suited to that particular stage, audience, and moment. Eighteen years after *Superman* had made the absurdly handsome Christopher Reeve a movie star, one year after an equestrian accident had left him a quadriplegic, Reeve addressed the 1996 Democratic National Convention. The amount of federal funding for research on spinal cord injuries, he declared, was deplorably meager. More spending would give Americans afflicted by injuries like his a better quality of life, allow them to become economically productive, and even give them hope for a complete recovery. He went on to urge increased government spending for research on the causes and cures of other ailments, naming Parkinson's disease, stroke, multiple sclerosis, and AIDS, along with famous people who suffered from each. Reeve closed by invoking another man in a wheelchair, Franklin Roosevelt, telling the delegates that FDR's "most important principle" was "America does not let its needy citizens fend for themselves."[1]

Who could hear *that* speaker give *that* speech and object to the additional funding Reeve endorsed? No one, of course—which was the whole point, and the whole problem. The quality of the arguments and evidence Reeve offered was irrelevant, and any rebuttal would have been futile. The strategy of placing him in that setting before a national television audience was not to win a political debate but to preclude one. The emotional force of Reeve's speech reminds us why Aristotle examined compassion, which we treat as a moral virtue, in the *Rhetoric*, discussing it solely in terms of the power to move an audience. He does not mention the subject in the *Ethics* or the *Politics*.[2]

Reeve's appearance was perfectly consonant with the central purpose of the 1996 convention: renominating and reelecting President Bill Clinton, who had assured voters four years before, "I feel your pain." Clinton's skill set included speaking empathy fluently, which only compounded the difficulties of his less-talented vice president, Al Gore, who expressed himself in that idiom forcefully but ineptly, a speaker of a second language never mastered. Gore concluded his 1996 acceptance speech with an account of his sister's deathbed as she succumbed to lung cancer, three decades after becoming a heavy smoker. "And that is why until I draw my last breath," he told the delegates, "I will pour my heart and soul into the cause of protecting our children from the dangers of smoking."[3] As the *New York Times* put it diplomatically the next day, Gore "took a chance by speaking about his sister in such raw terms," given "the thin line in politics between poignancy and exploitation." The political risks looked even greater after the *Times* joined other publications in pointing out that in 1988, four years after his sister's death, Gore had assured a North Carolina audience that he, too, was a tobacco farmer, and had been one all his life. Gore did not stop accepting contributions from political action committees affiliated with the tobacco industry until 1990.[4]

At the 2000 Democratic convention, Gore's first act upon accepting the presidential nomination was to share with his wife, onstage before a television audience, a kiss the Associated Press described as "awkward" and "uncomfortably long."[5] Even for a notably unsubtle politician, it was a blatant signal to voters that a Gore presidency would, unlike Clinton's, spare the nation bimbo eruptions and amorous interns. What the self-defeating phoniness of

Gore's "authenticity" really made clear, however, was that Clinton had already established the outer limit of the Empathizer in Chief role, requiring his successors to try something different rather than attempt more of the same. The next Democratic president turned out to be Barack Obama, who is always effortlessly cool and measured in public. It's impossible to imagine him giving his wife an openmouthed kiss on national television.

So central is the rhetoric of compassion to modern American liberalism, however, that even a reserved politician like Obama relies on it constantly. And, like Gore, he avails himself of the principle that if an autobiographical snippet conveys a politically resonant emotional truth, the speaker has no obligation, and the audience no right, to be exacting about its literal truth. In a 2008 debate against Senator John McCain, Obama said, "For my mother to die of cancer at the age of fifty-three and have to spend the last months of her life in the hospital room arguing with insurance companies because they're saying that this may be a preexisting condition and they don't have to pay her treatment, there's something fundamentally wrong about that." A 2012 biography of his mother, Stanley Ann Dunham, revealed, however, that health insurance *did* pay for her medical care, and she argued with an insurance company about benefits from a disability policy. When asked by reporters about the discrepancy, the White House did not dispute the book's account, but took what refuge it could in the statement "The president has told this story based on his recollection of events that took place more than fifteen years ago."

Nevertheless, in a subsequent 2012 campaign video Obama attempted to have it both ways, conveying that his mother had suffered because of poor health insurance but without repeating the contentions he had made in 2008. In umentary, Michelle Obama says of her mother oped ovarian cancer, never really had good, That's a tough thing to deal with, watchi something that could have been prevented. I don't think he wants to see anyone go through that." The film's narrator then explains that Obama's personal tragedy left him sensitive to the suffering of others, and determined to alleviate it: "And he remembered the millions of families like his who feel the pressure of rising costs and the fear of being denied or dropped from coverage."[6]

Obama did not mention his mother at the White House ceremony in March 2010 when he signed into law the Patient Protection and Affordable Care Act (more commonly referred to as the Affordable Care Act or, simply, "Obamacare"). Standing next to him at the desk, however, was an eleven-year-old boy, Marcelas Owens, whose mother had died of pulmonary hypertension in 2007, at age twenty-seven. She "didn't have insurance and couldn't afford the care that she needed," Obama said. He went on to say he was also signing the bill for Natoma Canfield, whose sister was in attendance. Canfield "had to give up her health coverage after her rates were jacked up by more than forty percent," the president explained. "She was terrified that an illness would mean she'd lose the house that her parents built, so she gave up her insurance. And now she's lying in a hospital bed, as we speak, faced with just such an illness, praying that she can somehow afford to get well without insurance."[7] (As of October 2013, Canfield had gotten better but not well—she still had leukemia, but was living at home rather than in a care facility. She had also gotten insurance, not as a result of the Affordable Care Act, but through the biggest government health programs in operation prior to 2010, Medicare and Medicaid.)[8]

It was inevitable that the signing ceremony for the Affordable Care Act would present ordinary Americans whose sufferings could be attributed to defects in the health care system, ones the new law purported to fix. Such citizens, after all, were featured prominently in the campaign for the bill. A series of town hall meetings in followed the same format: a local resident who suffered from both a specific ailment and a problem with health insurance would describe those troubles, then warmly introduce the president. In one city, it was a father whose family's health insurance was nearly canceled after the costs of treating his son's hemophilia approached the policy's lifetime cap. "If you think that can't happen to you or your family, think again," Obama said. At another forum, a woman who lost her insurance after being diagnosed with cancer introduced him. Yet another event featured a woman who could not find insurance because of a preexisting condition.[9] At a Capitol Hill "Forum on What Health Insurance Reform Means for Women and Families," three women told an audience what they had endured trying to afford health care and insurance under the existing system. Mrs. Obama then praised them for recounting their experiences because "these stories are happening all over this country, not just for thousands of women—for millions of them. For two years on the campaign trail, this was what I heard from women, that they were being crushed, crushed by the current structure of our health care. Crushed."[10]

The child who would grow up to become First Lady was less than a year old in 1964, and Barack Obama was only three, when NBC canceled the television game show *Queen for a Day*. Though they could not have known about it, the show previewed the modern Democratic Party's stagecraft and statecraft. Its contestants were women who would tell the host, studio audience, and viewers at home about their travails, usually financial or medical. An applause meter would then let the studio audience "vote" on which woman had told the most affecting story, making her Queen for a Day. The winner received prizes, some selected to alleviate her particular troubles, and the other contestants also received gifts. The host closed every show by saying, "This is Jack Bailey, wishing we could make *every* woman a queen, for every single day!" In 2010, television writer and critic Mark Evanier wrote that *Queen for a Day* was "tasteless, demeaning to women, demeaning to anyone who watched it, cheap, insulting and utterly degrading to the human spirit."[11]

Be that as it may, the line between poignancy and exploitation is not only thin, but moving inexorably: expressions once condemned for exploiting are eventually hailed for their courage and candor. Elected officials like Bill Clinton and Barack Obama reflect citizens' sensibilities more than they shape them. As the disappearance of "Blue Dog" voters and politicians has made the Democratic Party increasingly liberal, liberals have turned it into the pity party, committed to doing good socially and thereby doing well politically. People have interests, of course, and a political party that promises the government will give things to them and do things for them will never lack a constituency. But people also have pride: they desire approval, including self-approval. A modern American who doubts his compassion would have as hard a time sustaining a good opinion of himself as a medieval European lacking religious faith, or an ancient Roman convinced his life and character were devoid of honor. The term "compassion"—or "empathy," or even "kindness"—is routinely used not just to name *a* moral virtue, but to designate the pinnacle or even the entirety of moral excellence. Precisely because this moral conviction is ambient, with so many Americans taking for granted that moral growth requires little else than feeling, acting, and being more compassionate, it's an important yet difficult subject to analyze. Compassion is the moral sea we swim in, which works against our awareness of it, much less efforts to chart its depths and currents.

Compassion encompasses modern American liberalism, then, not the other way around. The most important source of their political strength, however, has been liberals' ability to make compassion the political sea we swim in. It not only helps Democratic politicians win votes but also helps rank-and-file Democrats feel worthy. "I am a liberal," public radio host Garrison Keillor wrote in 2004, "and liberalism is the politics of kindness."[12] A more politically formidable analyst than Keillor has seconded that motion. In a 2013 speech President Obama quoted the late film critic Roger Ebert: "Kindness covers all of my political beliefs." And, Obama continued, "when I think about what I'm fighting for, what gets me up every single day, that captures it just about as much as anything. Kindness; empathy—that sense that I have a stake in your success; that I'm going to make sure, just because [my daughters] are doing well, that's not enough—I want your kids to do well also." This empathy is not primarily vertical, however, the noblesse oblige the world's most powerful man feels toward ordinary citizens. Rather, it works best when practiced horizontally and reciprocally, as the disposition Americans have for one another. It's "what binds us together, and . . . how we've always moved forward, based on the idea that we have a stake in each other's success."[13]

This subject has been a recurring theme throughout the president's public career. As a U.S. senator he gave a college commencement address that urged graduates "to see the world through the eyes of those who are different from us—the child who's hungry, the steelworker who's been laid off, the family who lost the entire life they built together when the storm came to town." To what end? "When you think like this—when you choose to broaden your ambit of concern and empathize with the plight of others, whether they are close friends or distant strangers—it becomes harder not to act, harder not to help." After his victory in November 2008, President-elect Obama responded to a schoolgirl who had written to him by advising, "If you don't already know what it means, I want you to look up the word 'empathy' in the dictionary. I believe we don't have enough empathy in our world today, and it is up to your generation to change that."[14]

By speaking in these terms, Obama carries on a tradition older than he is. In *The Liberal Mind*, a book published two years after Obama was born, the late Kenneth Minogue wrote that liberalism is defined by the commitment to find and then rectify "suffering situations," thereby transforming politics into "an activity not so much for maximizing happiness as for minimizing suffering." The belief there can be no neutrality in this war to rid the world of one social evil after another—if you're not part of the solution, you're part of the problem—reduces politics to "a melodrama of oppressors and victims."[15] Thus, in a 1977 speech dedicating the Department of Health, Education and Welfare's Washington headquarters, which was being named after him, Senator Hubert Humphrey said, "The moral test of government is how it treats those who are in the dawn of life, the children; those who are in the twilight of life, the aged; and those in the shadows of life, the sick, the needy and the handicapped." Those words are inscribed on the building's wall.[16]

Equally important, by making an unqualified commitment to empathy, liberals put conservatism on trial. "Which side are you on?" asked the old labor movement anthem. In the rhetoric of modern liberalism, there are only two sides, and an easy choice between them. "Divine justice," Franklin Roosevelt told the 1936 Democratic convention, "weighs the sins of the cold-blooded and the sins of the warm-hearted in different scales. Better the occasional faults of a government that lives in a spirit of charity than the consistent omissions of a government frozen in the ice of its own indifference."[17] Nineteen thirty-six was the year Thomas P. "Tip" O'Neill won his first election, at the age of twenty-three, for a seat in the Massachusetts legislature. By 1984 he had become Speaker of the U.S. House of Representatives, and the most powerful Democrat in Washington. FDR's rhetoric apparently made a lasting impression on O'Neill, who echoed it when he denounced President Ronald Reagan: "The evil is in the White House at the present time. And that evil is a man who has no care and no concern for the working class of America and the future generations of America, and who likes to ride a horse. He's cold. He's mean. He's got ice water for blood."[18] In 2013, *New York Times* columnist

Paul Krugman made similar accusations, employing the language of epidemiology rather than hematology. Conservatives take "positive glee in inflicting further suffering on the already miserable," he wrote. Denouncing House Republicans for voting to cut funds for the Food Stamps program, Krugman said they were "infected by an almost pathological meanspiritedness. . . . If you're an American, and you're down on your luck, these people don't want to help; they want to give you an extra kick."[19]

There's no need to belabor the advantages liberals secure, on Election Day and in policy debates, by contending the republic's essential choice is between the politics of kindness and the politics of cruelty. Again, however, this way of framing the question yields not only political advantages but psychological and sociological ones. Given compassion's centrality, both to the modern understanding of moral decency and to liberal politics, liberalism offers those who embrace it a reliable basis to feel good about themselves, which includes ample reason to revile those deemed compassion-deficient. On the floor of the House of Representatives, for example, Democratic congressman Alan Grayson declared in 2009 that Republican colleagues who opposed the health care proposals advanced by Democrats had a plan of their own: "Don't get sick. And if you do get sick, die quickly."[20] Following Obama's 2012 reelection, one blogger spiked the football in an open letter to Republicans, to which many websites provided a link. "Koolking83," apparently the nom de pixel of Chicagoan Steve Sanchez, gloated that the conservative campaign to "take back the country" had failed because that country, along with its moral failings, is at long last vanishing. In "your Country," the letter asserted, "Voters don't cast their ballots with the welfare of the guy or woman next to them in mind—they don't vote for universal prosperity and equality, they don't vote with a heart full of compassion and a mind with a vision for a more fair and a more inclusive Country." Mitt Romney lost because he was "the embodiment of everything that is wrong with YOUR Country," in that he was both "insatiably greedy" and "invariably self-interested."[21]

One of compassion's advantages is that the scorn for the uncompassionate it validates is all-weather gear, which can be worn during both triumphs and setbacks. Krugman's colleague, *Times* columnist Charles Blow, reacted to the 2013 House vote on Food Stamps by deploring not just "the pariahs who roam [America's] halls of power" but also "the people who put them there" for being "insular, cruel and uncaring." He lamented a public opinion survey showing a plurality of Americans believed high poverty rates persisted because excessive welfare benefits stifle initiative. "How did we come to such a pass?" Blow demands. "Why aren't more politicians—and people in general—expressing outrage and showing empathy?"

> Part of our current condition is obviously partisan. Republicans have become the party of "blame the victim." Whatever your lesser lot in life, it's completely within your means to correct, according to their logic. Poverty, hunger, homelessness and desperation aren't violence to the spirit but motivation to the will. If you want more and you work harder, all your problems will disappear. Sink or swim. Pull yourself up. Get over it.

This callousness reflects not only the deficiencies of Republican politicians, however, but the broader phenomenon that "many Americans look at the poor with disgust." Washington, D.C., is a "town without pity," he concludes, because too many Americans desire and have succeeded in making the United States a nation without pity. "If some people's impulse is to turn up a nose rather than extend a hand, no wonder we send so many lawmakers empty of empathy to Congress. No wonder more people don't demand that Congress stand up for the least among us rather than on them."[22]

Some readers who have come this far may, like Democratic politicians and *New York Times* columnists, hold these truths to be self-evident: that compassion is the essence of moral and political decency; that liberalism is fundamentally noble because it places compassion at the center of its political efforts; and that conservatism is fundamentally odious because *its* central purpose is to reject compassion in favor of selfishness, greed, and cruel indifference to suffering. Those readers should get off the train at this station, since they will find a book interrogating these propositions as pointless as one that examines whether the world is round or the sky blue.

For those of you still on board, at least for a while, I readily confirm the subtle hints given by the preceding pages and this book's title: I am indeed a political conservative, so approach the claims made for liberal compassion skeptically, not reverently. During the Reagan-Thatcher era, some conservatives felt free to dismiss such claims as the whining of collectivists who could not accept the demise of the only alternative to market economics. Electoral setbacks—only one Republican nominee (George W. Bush with 50.7 percent in 2004) has won a majority of the popular vote in the six presidential elections beginning with Clinton's victory in 1992—and well-documented demographic trends indicating future elections are likely to grow even more difficult have drained this triumphalism from the American Right. As they did when reading the first issue of *National Review* in 1955, conservatives once more stand athwart history, yelling Stop!

Especially, however, if liberals realize their hopes of dominating the landscape as they did in the 1930s, we need to examine—less for the sake of reinvigorating conservatism than for the more general imperative to advance clear thinking and good governance—what the politics of kindness means, and how it works. If American politics is becoming an ecosystem where liberalism's natural enemies are too weak to challenge it, the only remaining restraints on the politics of compassion will exert their influence from within liberalism, rather than by opposing it from the outside. But if political compassion proves to be confused, futile, or destructive in ways that neither interest nor inhibit liberals who believe that platitudes about warmhearted empathy for the least among us constitute a political philosophy, America faces dangers it needs to understand. They are what this book is about.

My argument will have this structure: Chapter One's subject is compassion's meaning in modern discourse, and how it became central to the moral outlook, not just of American liberalism, but of social and political life in general. The next two chapters take up the question raised by Barack Obama's entreaty to broaden our ambit of concern. Some liberal polemicists to the contrary notwithstanding, most people, even registered Republicans, do not really need to be shamed into empathizing with their family members, friends, or neighbors. The question, then, is not *whether* to be compassionate or indifferent to the suffering of others, but the proper scope of compassion's ambit. This issue is best examined from the outside in: Chapter Two works through the implications of empathy that stretches across international borders. Those problems explicated, in Chapter Three I consider liberal compassion within America, an ambit better suited to the theory and practice of liberalism. Even so, the politics of kindness cannot be judged a success at the national level, either in terms of making sense or making a difference for the better. *Why* liberal compassion's good intentions translate so unreliably into good results is the subject of Chapter Four, which argues that the quality of mercy is a more consequential problem than, as liberals posit, its chronically insufficient quantity. Finally, Chapter Five examines the conservative response to liberal compassion to see how it has fared, why it hasn't done more to make liberals fear that the political risks of denouncing conservatives' alleged heartlessness might exceed the rewards, and how conservatives could explain their reservations and objectives more persuasively.

THE
PITY
PARTY

Chapter 1

HOW COMPASSION DEFINES
AND ANIMATES LIBERALISM

To understand how, in order to safeguard Casey the rabbit, Marty the Magician ended up filling out a federal disaster plan with professional help, we must first understand the suffering situation of Pepper the Dalmatian and the family who owned her. Pepper disappeared from the yard of that family's house in 1965. By the time they located Pepper she was already in the custody of a "dog farm," whose owners refused not only the family's request for access, so they could identify and claim their dog, but also a request made on their behalf by their congressman, Joseph Resnick. Before Pepper's owners were able to take additional measures, the dog farm transferred Pepper to a New York hospital, which euthanized her after a laboratory experiment.[1]

Pepper's story, publicized in a *Sports Illustrated* article, motivated Resnick to introduce a bill that became the Animal Welfare Act of 1966. One of its provisions required laboratories using dogs and cats for research to have licenses for the animals. A 1970 amendment extended the requirement to "exhibitors," understood at the time to include zoos, circuses, and carnivals, but subsequently interpreted by U.S. Department of Agriculture officials to apply to solo practitioners like Marty Hahne, a magician who performs for school groups and children's birthday parties. Thus it was that in

2005, after a show at a library in Missouri, an official from the USDA approached Hahne. Did he have a license for the rabbit he had pulled out of a hat during his performance?

He does now, a USDA rabbit license granted in exchange for a forty-dollar annual fee, along with Hahne's agreement to take his exhibited animal to the veterinarian regularly and to submit to department officials' unannounced inspections of his home. The 1965 law, four pages long, has led to fourteen pages of regulations solely on the treatment of rabbits. As with many regulatory regimes, it includes a fair sampling of the arbitrary and risible. The rules don't apply to animals raised for consumption, for example, so Hahne would not need a license if Casey were destined to be part of a stew rather than a show. Nor does it cover cold-blooded animals, leaving the performer at liberty to pull an unlicensed lizard out of his hat.

In January 2013 the Department of Agriculture ruled that exhibitors needed, in addition to a license, a "disaster plan" for all animals subject to the license requirement. It announced the intention to create such a regulation in 2008, three years after pets, livestock, and lab animals were abandoned during Hurricane Katrina, some dying, others complicating already difficult efforts to relieve afflicted areas. USDA proposed that any exhibitor required to have a license for an animal must also have a written plan to keep it safe during each of many contingencies listed by the department. It posted the suggested regulation for public comments and received 997, of which 50 were endorsements. Based on that groundswell of support, USDA went ahead and announced it would begin enforcing the new requirement in 2013.

Some magicians, ignoring abundant evidence that the Department of Agriculture has an underdeveloped sense of the absurd, took a minimalist approach. "Note: Take rabbit with you when you leave" was the entirety of one's plan. Hahne, by contrast, chose to err on the side of caution, filling out thirty-two pages with the volunteered assistance of an attorney who writes disaster plans for a living. It covers how Hahne will protect Casey in response to disasters familiar from the Old Testament, such as floods and windstorms, as well as modern perils like broken air conditioners and chemical spills.

When the *Washington Post* first ran a story about Hahne's encounter with the new disaster plan regulations, a USDA spokesman praised the policy's "flexibility," but within a few hours announced that the secretary had called for its review in the hope that "common sense be applied."[2] Hahne told one reporter, "I always thought I had a fun, easy job, and I would never have to worry about the government bothering me about it. But our government has gotten so intrusive, their tentacles are everywhere."[3]

COMPASSION, DEFINED AND PROCLAIMED

Comprehending where compassion can take us requires, first of all, a clear understanding of what it is. The terms "compassion" and "empathy" have come to be used interchangeably in modern discourse. According to the *Oxford English Dictionary*, "compassion" means, literally, "suffering together with another," and is also defined, more substantively, as the "feeling or emotion, when a person is moved by the suffering or distress of another, and by the desire to relieve it; pity that inclines one to spare or to succour." The *OED* notes a subtle but significant distinction between those two senses of the term: the first is an emotion shared by "equals or fellow-sufferers," while the second "is shown toward a person in distress by one who is free from it, who is, in this respect, his superior." The earliest instances of both senses appeared in the fourteenth century. Some three hundred years later, "compassion" shows up in Shakespeare and in treatises and translations by Thomas Hobbes. "Compassionate" is now strictly an adjective, but it was also a transitive verb until sometime in the nineteenth century, used in a manner similar to "commiserate," as in, "Men . . . naturally compassionate all . . . whom they see in Distress," from a 1726 sermon. "Empathy," defined as "The power of projecting one's personality into (and so fully comprehending) the object of contemplation," first appeared in English in 1904. The term came into existence as an attempt to translate the German word *einfühlung*, used in aesthetic and psychological theory to convey the act of "feeling into" a painting or statue. I'll treat "compassion" and "empathy" as equivalents, the way most twenty-first-century Americans do in speaking or writing.

The reader with access to a search engine, newspaper, or remote control can easily add examples of the rhetoric of compassion to those I've already provided. My inclusion of one by Franklin Roosevelt from 1936 might leave the impression that compassion has been a constant, dominant force within liberalism right from the beginning of the New Deal. That isn't quite true. In 1947 Arthur M. Schlesinger Jr. expressed his confidence about America's ability to achieve "democratic socialism"—or, more disquietingly, "a not undemocratic socialism"—through the rise of the "politician-manager-intellectual type—the New Dealer," provided he is "intelligent and decisive."[4] As this stipulation suggests, mid-twentieth-century liberalism reflected a conscious effort to be, and be seen as, tough-minded rather than softhearted. Of course, the choice to undertake such a rebranding argues that at least some liberals at the time believed their ranks contained, and their cause was harmed by, a considerable number of sob sisters.

The desentimentalization of liberalism reached its apogee in the presidency of John Kennedy. His inaugural address spoke of a new American generation "tempered by war, disciplined by a hard and bitter peace," which would "pay any price, bear any burden, meet any hardship, support any friend, oppose any foe to assure the survival and the success of liberty." In a speech silent on domestic issues, the only line that invoked social justice—"If a free society cannot help the many who are poor, it cannot save the few who are rich"—came in the context of a call for aid to "peoples in the huts and villages of half the globe struggling to break the bonds of mass misery," both because it was right and in order to fortify democracy against the spread of communism. When, in March 1962, a reporter asked JFK about military reservists who resented being called for active duty as tensions in Vietnam and Berlin increased, he replied, "there is always inequity in life. Some men are killed in a war and some men are wounded, and some men never leave the country, and some men are stationed in the Antarctic and some are stationed in San Francisco. . . . Life is unfair. But I do hope that . . . these people recognize that they are fulfilling a valuable function, and . . . will have the satisfaction afterwards of feeling that they contributed importantly to the security of their families and their country at a significant time."[5]

A great irony of modern political history, to be examined in Chapter Three, is that these efforts to make liberalism tough, pragmatic, and unsentimental collapsed, immediately and decisively, upon Kennedy's assassination in 1963. That liberals so quickly redoubled their commitment to emotionalism does not prove, but strongly suggests, that the effort to purge it was misbegotten from the start. The tough liberals, that is, wanted to turn liberalism into something at odds with its fundamental character. Ever since that day in Dallas, the only reason a liberal politician or intellectual will note that life is unfair is to insist a decent society's most compelling obligation is to make it more fair. Suggesting that any inequity or suffering may lie beyond a government's capacity and rightful power to remedy is the dodge employed by mean-spirited conservatives, not compassionate liberals.

John Kennedy's younger brothers both devoted the rest of their lives to the cause of making empathy paramount over pragmatism. When Edward Kennedy eulogized Robert in 1968 he asked that his brother be remembered "simply as a good and decent man, who saw wrong and tried to right it, saw suffering and tried to heal it, saw war and tried to stop it." Most of Kennedy's speech, however, consisted of passages from those his brother had given. In one, Bobby Kennedy had said about their father, Joseph Kennedy Sr.:

> Beneath it all, he has tried to engender a social conscience. There were wrongs which needed attention. There were people who were poor and needed help. And we have a responsibility to them and to this country. Through no virtues and accomplishments of our own, we have been fortunate enough to be born in the United States under the most comfortable conditions. We, therefore, have a responsibility to others who are less well off.

Ted Kennedy then quoted more extensively from a speech his older brother had given in 1966:

> There is discrimination in this world and slavery and slaughter and starvation. Governments repress their people; millions are trapped in poverty while the nation grows rich and wealth is lavished on armaments everywhere. These are differing evils, but they are the common works of man. They reflect the imperfection of human justice, the inadequacy of human compassion, our lack of sensibility towards the suffering of our fellows. But we can perhaps remember—even if only for a time—that those who live with us are our brothers; that they share with us the same short moment of life; that they seek—as we do—nothing but the chance to live out their lives in purpose and happiness, winning what satisfaction and fulfillment they can.[6]

There are three other statements—by a politician, a journalist, and a professor—that amount to manifestos for compassion. I quote them at some length to offer grist I'll mill subsequently. The first is Mario Cuomo's keynote address to the 1984 Democratic convention, delivered during the second of Cuomo's twelve years as governor of New York. It is remembered as one of the most effective in the era of televised political conventions. Nearly four years after Ronald Reagan had been elected president, Cuomo conceded nothing in defending New Deal and Great Society liberalism:

> We [Democrats] believe . . . that a society as blessed as ours, the most affluent democracy in the world's history, one that can spend trillions on instruments of destruction, ought to be able to help the middle class in its struggle, ought to be able to find work for all who can do it, room at the table, shelter for the homeless, care for the elderly and infirm, and hope for the destitute. And we proclaim as loudly as we can the utter insanity of nuclear proliferation and the need for a nuclear freeze, if only to affirm the simple truth that peace is better than war because life is better than death. . . .
>
> We believe in a single fundamental idea that describes better than most textbooks and any speech that I could write what a proper government should be: the idea of family, mutuality, the sharing of benefits and burdens for the good of all, feeling one another's pain, sharing one another's blessings—reasonably, honestly, fairly, without respect to race, or sex, or geography, or political affiliation.
>
> We believe we must be the family of America, recognizing that at the heart of the matter we are bound one to another, that the problems of a retired school teacher in Duluth are our problems; that the future of the child in Buffalo is our future; that the struggle of a disabled man in Boston to survive and live decently is our struggle; that the hunger of a woman in Little Rock is our hunger; that the failure anywhere to provide what reasonably we might, to avoid pain, is our failure.[7]

In 2007 the *American Prospect*'s Paul Waldman wrote "The Failure of Antigovernment Conservatism." His article examined the State Children's Health Insurance Program (SCHIP), which gave federal subsidies to state programs that helped families secure health insurance for their children if the household incomes were high enough to make them ineligible for Medicaid. Having won control of Congress in 2006, Democrats advocated, and Republicans opposed, plans to make SCHIP available to a larger number of families. The dispute, reduced to what Waldman considered its basics, meant "Democrats want to give health coverage to kids, and Republicans want kids to go without health coverage." That particular policy disagreement rested on a more basic disjunction:

> Progressives believe we're all in it together, while conservatives say we're all on our own and we're all out for ourselves. Progressives think government has to do the things markets can't do—and when it does them, it ought to do them well.

Conservatives, by contrast, are so "blinded by their antigovernment ideology" that a "junior high school debater could rip apart the Republican [presidential] candidates and their outdated attacks on 'socialized medicine.'" Waldman demonstrates conservatism's appalling imbecility with a hypothetical but richly imagined suffering situation, and the Right's odious refusal to mitigate it. "[L]et me tell you about Betsy Wilson," he begins.

> She's 10, and her parents both work hard—mom is a waitress, dad is trying to build a carpentry business. But like millions of Americans, they can't afford health coverage, so Betsy doesn't get the doctor visits she needs. Now we [Democrats] want to give the Wilsons the opportunity to get health coverage for Betsy, so she can stay healthy and they won't be bankrupted if she gets sick again. But you [Republicans] say no. Did I mention that Betsy had a rare form

of cancer when she was 6? She's in remission now, thank heavens, but the Wilsons worry every day that it could come back. And those HMOs you like so much won't cover her because they think it might cut into their profits. . . . How can you look at Betsy and say, sorry, too bad—you can't have health coverage? What kind of a person says that to a child?[8]

Finally, in 2009, George Lakoff defended the nobility of empathy and its centrality to progressivism. Lakoff, a professor of linguistics at the University of California, Berkeley, attained unusual fame for an academic when his book *Don't Think of an Elephant! Know Your Values and Frame the Debate* figured prominently in the discussions about how Democrats could improve upon their disappointing performance in the 2004 election. His article five years later defended President Obama for nominating Sonia Sotomayor to the U.S. Supreme Court, rebutting critics who charged that both of them thought judges should rule according to how much they sympathized with each party to the case, rather than confine themselves to following the dictates of law and justice.

> Empathy is at the heart of progressive thought. It is the capacity to put oneself in the shoes of others—not just individuals, but whole categories of people: one's countrymen, those in other countries, other living beings, especially those who are in some way oppressed, threatened, or harmed. Empathy is the capacity to care, to feel what others feel, to understand what others are facing and what their lives are like. Empathy extends well beyond feeling to understanding, and it extends beyond individuals to groups, communities, peoples, even species. Empathy is at the heart of real rationality, because it goes to the heart of our values, which are the basis of our sense of justice.
>
> Progressives care about others as well as themselves. They have a moral obligation to act on their empathy—a social re-

sponsibility in addition to personal responsibility, a responsibility to make the world better by making themselves better. This leads to a view of a government that cares about its citizens and has a moral obligation to protect and empower them. Protection includes worker, consumer, and environmental protection as well as safety nets and health care. . . .[9]

CAN A POLITICAL PHILOSOPHY OF LIBERAL COMPASSION EXIST?

Leo Strauss, the German professor of political philosophy whose career in America made him both influential and controversial, insisted it was a grave mistake to presume to understand important political philosophers *better* than they understood themselves unless one had already completed the exertions required to understand them *as* they understood themselves. The most common form of such misinterpretations was to reduce a philosophy to an expression or rationalization of historical circumstances, economic interests, or psychological conflicts.[10]

I submit that Strauss's advice is highly useful, not just for the exegesis of classic treatises but for laymen who want to make sense of the world, and get along in it. It's a bad idea, that is, to take the position that your own reading, training, or keen intelligence equips you to see through other people's opinions, discerning the true meanings, purposes, and desires hidden even from them (or perhaps especially from them) behind the surface of their own words. Such an approach is all but guaranteed to both read and rub people the wrong way.

There's a problem, though, with attempting to understand liberal compassion exactly as its adherents do: the advocates and practitioners of this position insist there's really nothing *to* understand. Take literally President Obama's assertion that kindness covers all

his political principles, and one must conclude that the philosophers and statesmen who have labored for centuries in the belief
that politics is supremely difficult and important have been wasting
their time. Apparently, all one really needs to know about politics
can be learned in kindergarten. If, as Lakoff contends, "[e]mpathy
is at the heart of progressive thought," and the distinguishing characteristic of progressives is that they "care about others as well as
themselves," it follows that all who are neither monsters nor idiots
are empathetic progressives, and all who are not progressives are
either monsters or idiots. (Interviewing William F. Buckley Jr. in
2004, the *New York Times* asked brightly, "You seem indifferent
to suffering. Have you ever suffered yourself?" Buckley replied, "I
do not advertise adversity and would certainly not talk about visits
with psychiatrists or proctologists.")[11]

There is one significant but also highly qualified exception to this
general rule that liberal compassion is a- or even anti-theoretical.
Nicholas Kristof, yet another *New York Times* columnist imploring Americans to be more empathetic—"compassion isn't a sign of
weakness, but a mark of civilization"—cites *A Theory of Justice*, the
1971 book by John Rawls, the subject of numberless dissertations
and colloquia. (Rawls, a professor of philosophy at Harvard, died
in 2002 at the age of eighty-one.) In Kristof's summary, Rawls
urges us to organize society, and in particular the distribution of
wealth, as we would if forced to make our decisions "from behind a
'veil of ignorance'—meaning we don't know whether we'll be born
to an investment banker or a teenage mom, in a leafy suburb or a
gang-ridden inner city, healthy or disabled, smart or struggling,
privileged or disadvantaged."[12] Were we to reason and govern on
that basis, Rawls argued, we would be utterly risk-averse, making
sure that the poorest person in our society was as un-poor as possible. That standard of justice does not mandate absolute economic
equality—it may be better to have the smallest share of a larger
economic pie than an equal share of a smaller one—but does re-

quire that any inequality be tolerated if, but only if, it benefits the very poor, as might financial incentives that spur inventors or medical researchers.[13]

There is a sense, then, in which it can be said that compassionate liberals are Rawlsians. *A Theory of Justice* takes nearly six hundred pages to delineate seemingly every possible implication and application of the adage "There but for fortune go I," the Empathizer's Credo. Every liberal I've ever met, however, was a practitioner of Rawlsianism in the same way Molière's Monsieur Jourdain was a speaker of prose: it's what both had been doing all along. It is, for example, exactly how Robert Kennedy described (years before Rawls's book was published) the social conscience his father had imparted. We, the comfortable, *are* comfortable "through no virtues and accomplishments of our own." The realization by the fortunate that they could easily have wound up as the unfortunate is the basis for a social conscience and the social responsibility it impels.

As a social scientist might put it, the correlation between any given liberal's commitment to compassion and his familiarity with Rawls appears to be zero. If that empirical observation is correct, then Rawls has nothing like the influence on the politics of compassion that Karl Marx did on the politics of the Russian Revolution, Jean-Jacques Rousseau did on the French Revolution, or John Locke on the American Revolution. Mathematicians and logicians worked through hundreds of pages of Alfred North Whitehead and Bertrand Russell's *Principia Mathematica* before getting to its declaration that 1+1=2. However important or persuasive the argument, the conclusion is not one about which either readers or nonreaders were otherwise in doubt. So, too, for *A Theory of Justice* and the politics of kindness.

Modernity's Needs

Compassion, known throughout most of human history as the emotion of pity, became a virtue, in part, because of some distinctively modern ideas. Sensibilities are often more powerful than syllogisms, however, and compassion's ascendance tracks with the many ways quotidian life in advanced, prosperous societies has been altered, setting it apart from everything humans had known before. The experience and perception of suffering was, until quite recently in our history, utterly familiar and inescapable. The philosophically inclined faced it with stoic resignation, and the religiously devout beseeched God for deliverance from it, the strength to endure it, or the grace to consecrate it. We, by contrast, take for granted anesthesia, medical care that removes the deathbed from the home to the hospital, and meals served in comfortable cities and suburbs where the slaughterhouse or farmer's ax lies beyond every diner's ken. The gradual but inescapable effect of such day-to-day lives is to view suffering as an anomaly, an affront, and an outrage. Thus understood, our moral duty is to eliminate or at least mitigate suffering, rather than practice or counsel forbearance.

It does not adequately clarify the politics of compassion, however, to say it rests on our instincts, refined by life in a world where suffering is increasingly incongruous and therefore increasingly objectionable. It appears an unfortunate necessity to attempt to understand compassion better than its adherents do, rather than limit ourselves to understanding it as they do. That better understanding calls for viewing compassion in the context of Christendom's demise, which was brought about by the Reformation and Enlightenment. In the long centuries before these latter developments, European civilization possessed a moral and teleological unity. That is, men shared—or were made to share—a comprehensive, highly elaborated understanding of how to live, and what to live for.

The fact of this shared understanding was as important as its content. There was, so to speak, a shared understanding of the necessity *for* a shared understanding if a society, or civilization, was to function and be worth preserving. In this respect, Christendom was no different from any other premodern civilization. The idea that individual members of a society should be allowed to order à la carte from various beliefs, practices, and worldviews had not yet been advocated or attempted. The wars that devastated Europe through the sixteenth and seventeenth centuries were so ferocious because all the combatants, Catholic and Protestant, took for granted the absolute necessity of a moral and teleological unity, which meant that allowing the wrong one to prevail would be worse than any amount of death and destruction.

Or maybe not, people started to think. To get past all that bloodshed to a safer—saner—historical epoch required a new political orientation, which "would no longer concern itself with God's politics," in historian Mark Lilla's words, but concentrate instead on preventing men "from harming one another."[14] The exhaustion and despair brought on by unrelenting savagery left Europeans receptive to a—really the—distinctively modern idea: perhaps people *could* live together without a shared understanding. Or, to be more precise, they could scale back a comprehensive shared understanding, where every aspect of human affairs was governed by a detailed conception of how God ordered the cosmos, in favor of a sharply delimited understanding. People could, in this new dispensation, live side by side while agreeing to disagree. Such modern concepts as the separation of church and state, the freedom of conscience, and inalienable human rights flow directly from this principle. All of them seem so obviously right to twenty-first-century Americans or Europeans that people around the world who never abandoned the commitment to a comprehensive shared understanding, such as Muslim jihadists, seem, as they say of the highest mountains climbed by the Tour de France cyclists, "beyond category." Even to embark on an effort to understand these pre- or anti-moderns as they understand themselves is hopeless, since almost all moderns who try are people who have never entertained the possibility that modernity's basic precepts are anything other than self-evidently true.

In the Federalist Papers (No. 10), James Madison praises America's new Constitution as "a republican remedy for the diseases most incident to republican government." We may say, in the same sense, that modern political philosophy is animated by the quest for a modern remedy for the diseases most incident to modernity. There's no going back to Christendom, in other words, or to any other cosmologically rooted civilization. We have to make modernity work.

That may not be easy, because the diseases most incident to modernity are not inconsiderable. If we're going to agree to disagree, we're going to have to get specific. What are we agreeing to, and what are we leaving aside as things we can safely disagree about? This is the subject of the social contract, examined by many of the most famous modern political philosophers. That contract needs not only to be drawn up and accepted, however, but obeyed. Such compliance, by both governors and the governed, will be difficult absent a powerful sense of rectitude: if people abuse or cheat one another whenever they think they can get away with it, the contract will either become null and void as we descend into anarchy, or its enforcement will require a government so strong and intrusive that its powers are effectively plenary, and the contract worthless.

The rectitude that would make modernity sustainable has, historically, been part and parcel of the kind of civilization modernity seeks to replace, one united by a shared understanding of the cosmos and man's place and duties in it. Modernity guarantees freedom of religion and conscience, but in doing so privatizes religion, reducing it to the status of a pastime, shared by those who happen to enjoy it. However important faith may be to any individual, it is *not* the sea all moderns swim in, and neither is any other pastime, leaving us with limited affections for our fellow citizens.

Moreover, religion's power to encourage morality is inseparable from its ability to impart dignity and meaning to the lives of the faithful. By discarding and not replacing the world's former moral and teleological unity, we have created a modern way of life that, for all its proliferating comforts and possibilities, leaves many feeling empty and disappointed. And because of its limited ability to inspire awe and reverence, it has a limited ability to inspire the sense of duty and propriety that makes social contracts enforceable. We rejected Christendom for modernity because traumas like the Thirty Years' War were intolerable. But the passions and aspirations that caused such wars were expressions of the same ones that built cathedrals like Chartres. The taming of those human qualities turns such works from efforts to ennoble human existence by forging a connection to the sublime and transcendent into big, pretty tourist sites. As Francis Fukuyama wrote in 1989, the "end of history," the final and complete triumph of modernity, "will be a very sad time."

> The struggle for recognition, the willingness to risk one's life for a purely abstract goal, the worldwide ideological struggle that called forth daring, courage, imagination, and idealism, will be replaced by economic calculation, the endless solving of technical problems, environmental concerns, and the satisfaction of sophisticated consumer demands. In the post-historical period there will be neither art nor philosophy, just the perpetual caretaking of the museum of human history.[15]

Harold Macmillan said in 1963 that what gave him the most satisfaction when he looked back on his long career in British politics was the sight of "a line of family cars, filled with fathers, mothers, children, uncles, aunts, all making their way to the seaside."

Ten years ago most of them would not have had cars, would have spent their weekends in the back streets, and would have seen the seaside, if at all, once a year. Now—now—I look forward to the time, not far away, when those cars will be a little larger, a little more comfortable, and all of them will be carrying on their roofs boats that they may enjoy at the seaside.

Macmillan dismissed the idea that loftier pursuits were of any concern to the politician: "If people want a sense of purpose they can get it from their archbishops."[16] By 1963, of course, the moral authority of those archbishops was already greatly reduced from what it had been during Macmillan's youth in Edwardian England, and it is much weaker today than it was half a century ago.

One modern remedy for the diseases most incident to modernity is totalitarianism, which sought to give people an encompassing sense of purpose once more by tearing up the social contract about agreeing to disagree. Totalitarianism was a modern answer by virtue of being completely secular, a theocracy without a theology. Its moral and teleological unity was, instead, based on such temporal concerns as the class struggle or the prerogatives of the master race. As George Orwell wrote in March 1940, Adolf Hitler had "grasped the falsity of the hedonistic attitude to life."

All "progressive" thought has assumed tacitly that human beings desire nothing beyond ease, security and avoidance of pain. Hitler, because in his joyless mind he feels it with exceptional strength, knows that human beings *don't* only want comfort, safety, short working-hours, hygiene, birth-control and, in general, common sense; they also, at least intermittently, want struggle and self-sacrifice, not to mention drums, flags and loyalty-parades.[17]

Orwell, writing here just weeks before German troops invaded France, can be forgiven for not realizing that people would temper their taste for self-sacrifice and loyalty parades once it became clear they were part of a package deal that included concentration camps and mass slaughter.

SELF-INTEREST WELL UNDERSTOOD

One must be bitterly cynical about humans' inability to learn from experience to think that the memories of twentieth-century totalitarianism will fade so quickly that any such ideology will be tried out again soon. Totalitarian brutality did make something brutally clear, however: You want a moral and teleological unity in an age of tepid religious faith? *This* is what it looks like. You despair over a civilization whose proudest achievement is a line of family cars making their way to the seaside? We've got something *much* more exciting.

Totalitarianism revealed, in other words, that people can't have it both ways. They have to choose. Its hideousness vindicated the social contract minimalists, who also believe we can't have it both ways, and it's better to tolerate triviality and inanity than risk the terrors of fashioning something more robust. This is the classical liberal position, more popular on the Right than the Left in our time. It tells us to agree to disagree on a great many questions, because all we really need to agree on are the terms for living together without interfering in one another's lives.

Furthermore, the adherents of this position hold out the hope that people will be moral enough to uphold the social contract if it is rightly devised. The right kind of contract could provide unprecedented levels of peace and prosperity, benefits so remarkable as to dispel any nostalgia for premodern moral unity. Better still, moral flexibility might not be ruinous if we devise a civic architecture dependent on people's most common qualities, as opposed to their most admirable ones. "This policy of supplying, by opposite and rival interests, the defect of better motives, might be traced through the whole system of human affairs, private as well as public," Madison argued in Federalist No. 51. In private affairs, arranging for ambition to counteract ambition would conduce to prosperity, as the emerging discipline of political economy was arguing. In public affairs it would give mankind a better chance than ever before to overcome *the* great political difficulty: to "first enable the government to control the governed; and in the next place oblige it to control itself."

Seven years after Madison wrote those words, Immanuel Kant, in *Perpetual Peace: A Philosophical Sketch*, endorsed the same idea in similar but more expansive terms. Devising a successful republican constitution is "only a question of a good organization of the state . . . whereby the powers of each selfish inclination are so arranged in opposition that one moderates or destroys the ruinous effect of the other." In a state so organized, "man is forced to be a good citizen even if not a morally good person." Kant went on to express, in terms impossible to surpass, his confidence in the power of the right kind of constitutional order to solve political problems, "The problem of organizing a state, however hard it may seem, can be solved even for a race of devils, if only they are intelligent."

Madison was more guarded. In Federalist No. 55, after taking up and attempting to refute hypothetical questions about how the Constitution's checks and balances might prove too weak to prevent this or that abuse, Madison finally throws up his hands. Yes, the "auxiliary precautions" that make ambition counteract ambition will help sustain a republic. But, no, a nation of devils will not form a successful republic, no matter how intelligent they are or how well their state is organized. "As there is a degree of depravity in mankind which requires a certain degree of circumspection and distrust," Madison wrote, "so there are other qualities in human nature which justify a certain portion of esteem and confidence. Republican government presupposes the existence of these qualities in a higher degree than any other form."

This stance sounds more realistic than expecting domestic tranquility from a race of devils, but brings back the problem of sustaining modernity. If republican government, more than any other form, rests on the estimable and reassuring qualities in human nature, what, in turn, do those qualities rest on? This appears to be a formulation for relying on the moral residue of classical and Christian civilization. The whole point of the modern break with the European past, however, is to circumscribe that heritage. In this light, modernity begins to look like an enterprise that constantly draws down moral and civilizational inventories it does not replenish. That approach can work for as long as the inventories last, but not longer.

Alexis de Tocqueville wrote in *Democracy in America* that the Americans he had observed during his travels in the United States in 1830 had come up with the most promising, or least unpromising, solution to this modern problem, "the doctrine of self-interest well understood." Tocqueville thought the formula of making ambition counteract ambition had penetrated the democratic soul by turning "personal interest against itself," directing the passions by appealing to them. This is the logic of what we would call "deferred gratification," manifested in entreaties to kids to stay in school, or just say no to drugs, in order to get a good job and live in a nice house someday, rather than subsist poorly and precariously. Deferring is important, in other words, but gratification's status as the ultimate prize is not questioned.

The doctrine of self-interest well understood accepts that people who believe honesty is the best policy are probably not as reliably or deeply honest as those who believe lying is a mortal sin. The first formulation implies that if, at least sometimes, *dis*honesty turns out to be the best policy, then dishonesty is acceptable. But as long as honesty really is the best policy—the smart bet—people who think this way are likely to be honest enough.

Understanding the doctrine of self-interest well understood is itself a challenge, however. It could be interpreted as self-interest shrewdly understood, as it would be when evinced by those who take the long view and weigh their risks carefully. The doctrine of self-interest well understood "forms a multitude of citizens who are regulated, temperate, moderate, farsighted, masters of themselves. . . ."[18] Tocqueville's admiration for Americans' civic engagement and commitment to many kinds of associations also suggests something higher, however, such as self-interest decently or honorably understood. The self-interested person, that is, knows that the self he is interested in will necessarily live among many other selves, forming communities and a nation. Being concerned for their well-being out of a prudent regard for his own well-being makes sense. What self-interest well understood does not encompass, however, is anything like self-interest heroically or nobly understood.

Compassion as a Modern Solution for Modernity's Problems

We may, then, treat self-interest, well understood and operating in a well-structured social contract, as the second modern remedy, after totalitarianism, to the diseases incident to modernity. Compassion is the third, one put forward as a remedy for both modernity's diseases and for the defects of totalitarianism and self-interest.

The first thing to notice about liberal compassion is that its lack of a theory is not accidental. Elaborating a philosophy of compassion is not an assignment adherents of the politics of kindness haven't gotten around to completing. Rather, what draws them to compassion is that it works just fine—better, really—without being theorized. Rousseau, the philosopher who devoted the most attention to compassion, argued in his *Discourse on Inequality* that compassion's best aspect was precisely that it came naturally to those who did not let their reasoning get in its way:

> Nothing but such general evils as threaten the whole community can disturb the tranquil sleep of the philosopher, or tear him from his bed. A murder may with impunity be committed under his window; he has only to put his hands to his ears and argue a little with himself, to prevent nature, which is shocked within him, from identifying itself with the unfortunate sufferer.

No one, that is, has ever found it necessary to develop a doctrine of compassion well understood. Indeed, it is so elemental that even animals are moved by others' sufferings:

> [I]t is well known that horses show a reluctance to trample on living bodies. One animal never passes by the dead body of another of its species: there are even some which give their fellows a sort of burial; while the mournful lowings of the cattle when they enter the slaughter-house show the impressions made on them by the horrible spectacle which meets them.

It follows that those who embrace compassion as the solution to the problem of modernity—and the political problem in general of getting people to live together peaceably—think the problem less daunting than has been supposed. The nature human beings share with other sensate creatures would let us, or at least greatly help us, get along with one another if only we would heed it.

The bigger problem, in this view, is not modernity or even politics itself, but the remedies put forward for them. So, for example, the liberal commitment to compassion entails the belief that a heavy reliance on self-interest, however well or poorly understood, is less a solution to a problem than a solution in search of a problem, and even a solution that causes a problem. Unlike Marxists, who reject capitalism as an economic system, modern liberals reject it most emphatically as a belief system. In particular, since the fall of the Berlin Wall and collapse of the Soviet Union, the leftmost boundary of the liberal economic policy agenda has shifted rightward.

Liberals remain, however, unreconciled to the moral universe of capitalism, defined by Adam Smith's famous observation, "It is not from the benevolence of the butcher, the brewer, or the baker, that we expect our dinner, but from their regard to their own interest."[19] Liberals doubt the reliability and decency of the market's purported capacity to alchemize private vices into public virtues. "Selfishness is without doubt the greatest danger that confronts our beloved country today," FDR declared in 1937.[20] That liberal judgment may be safely regarded as perennial rather than situational, however. Half a century later, journalist Pete Hamill repudiated the Reagan era's "currently fashionable ideologies of greed and selfishness," which accept and even celebrate self-interest.[21] Liberals insist that such acceptance and celebration is completely irreconcilable with an otherwise attainable social unity.

The renunciation of selfishness is, of course, neither an original nor a distinctively liberal notion. "For what is a man profited," asks the New Testament, "if he shall gain the whole world, and lose his own soul?" Liberalism's brief against selfishness *is* set apart because the caring virtues are preached by and to modernity's constituents, who doubt that the idea of losing one's soul means anything in particular, or even anything at all, but are convinced it must not mean anything politically.

Liberalism is equally opposed to the psychological dividedness wrought by the theory and practice of capitalism. According to Smith, knowing that our dinner is provided us by self-interested men, "We address ourselves, not to their humanity but to their self-love, and never talk to them of our own necessities but of their advantages." We never, that is, acknowledge the self-concern that animates all our marketplace activities. We constantly address the welfare of the guy or woman next to us, but always under the pretense that we really care about them rather than about feathering our own nests. Liberals find the pervasive falsity of this nation of Eddie Haskells intolerable. They aspire to a society where we can appeal sincerely from our own humanity and to others' because of our natural empathy, which leads to the mutual recognition that, in Paul Waldman's words, we're all in this together, and that none of us is on our own or out for ourselves.

The belief that harmony among humans might be attained more easily and simply than has long been supposed also makes compassionate liberals moderns, in that they reject the need for a moral and teleological unity in favor of an agreement to disagree. On this basis liberals reject, and equate, all premodern and totalitarian conceptions of moral and teleological unity. Many liberals, including the two most recent Democratic presidents, are fond of Judge Learned Hand's celebrated maxim from a 1944 speech: "The spirit of liberty is the spirit which is not too sure that it is right. . . ." Thus chastened, that spirit strives to understand the minds of others and weigh their interests alongside one's own without bias.[22]

More recently, the New York Times interviewed its columnist Anthony Lewis, when he retired in 2001 after a fifty-year career that saw him become, in the newspaper's words, its "most consistently liberal voice." Asked about any "big conclusion" he drew from what he had seen and written over those years, Lewis offered that "certainty is the enemy of decency and humanity in people who are sure they are right."[23] This formulation reinforces the idea that liberals stand on moral bedrock. Lewis is like the woman who insisted that modern astronomy had it all wrong: the world, in fact, was a flat plate supported on the back of a giant tortoise. Challenged as to what the tortoise stood on, the woman said, "You're very clever, young man, but it's turtles all the way down." Liberals believe it's decency and humanity all the way down: these fundamental moral imperatives rest on nothing even more fundamental.

Though "altruism" is often used as a synonym for "compassion," it's important to note that the posited natural affinity among men is not exactly altruistic, a word derived from the Latin for "other." We're naturally compassionate, both in the sense of how we feel and how we respond to those feelings, for *our* sake rather than for the sufferer's. Even the Golden Rule, Rousseau argued, "has no true foundation other than conscience and sentiment."

> [W]hen the strength of an expansive soul makes me identify myself with my fellow, and I feel that I am, so to speak, in him, it is in order not to suffer that I do not want him to suffer. I am interested in him for love of myself, and the reason for the precept is in nature itself, which inspires in me the desire of my well-being in whatever place I feel my existence. From this I conclude that it is not true that the precepts of natural law are founded on reason alone. They have a base more solid and sure. Love of men derived from love of self is the principle of human justice.[24]

Rousseau's contemporary, Immanuel Kant, mapped a different path to the same destination. In *Critique of Practical Reason* he argued that morality was concerned with being worthy of happiness, as distinguished from being happy. We could be worthy of happiness, have justified self-regard, only by living in ways we would like to see made general, which requires understanding as penetratingly as we can how it would feel to be on the receiving end of our actions. This is the logic of Rawls's argument for organizing an economy as we would if we expected to be among its poorest members. This perspective is reflected, as well, in an argument Barack Obama made in *The Audacity of Hope*:

I believe a stronger sense of empathy would tilt the balance of our current politics in favor of those people who are struggling in this society. After all, if they are like us, then their struggles are our own. If we fail to help, we diminish ourselves.[25]

It follows that if we succeed in helping, we augment ourselves.

For Rousseau, then, the inducement to respond, in feelings and acts, to the suffering of others is the direct, compassionate response hardwired in humans and other creatures. We care and share because it makes us feel better, there on the spot. For Kant, the crux of the matter is self-regard, which is a little trickier: if you empathize *in order* to have a good opinion of yourself then it's hard to be completely candid and still *have* that good opinion. You've done a worthy thing, but for a less than worthy reason.

Few of us, however, are likely to be that unsparing in the secular quest to find ourselves by losing ourselves in the service of others. This is so, particularly, since acting in admirable ways reinforces the emotional gratification of compassion. It feels good to alleviate the distress I feel when confronted with your suffering, and doubly good to respond to it in a way that leaves me with a higher opinion of myself, no matter how earnestly I might try to push that consideration to the edge of my field of vision. In the David Mamet movie *House of Games*, Mike, a con man, offers his philosophy of life—"Everybody gets something out of every transaction"—to a psychiatrist who's trying to understand how and why swindlers ply their trade. But what does the mark get, the psychiatrist asks, the one who had insisted on giving money to Mike after he contrived, shrewdly but blatantly, a suffering situation? "What he gets is he feels like he's a good man."

Introducing Problems, Theoretical and Practical, with Liberal Compassion

Taken on its own account, the only reason liberal compassion hasn't solved modernity's, or even humanity's, deepest problems is that our natural sentiments, humane and decent, have been thwarted rather than liberated. There are, however, four reasons to doubt that the necessary and sufficient cure for the problems of compassion is more compassion.

First, if the natural sociability of man, attainable simply by letting compassion express itself, is true and beyond question, then it constitutes *the* solution to the political problem, successfully reconciling what we want to do for ourselves with what we need to do to get along with others. But perhaps it's not true or beyond question. Liberals, otherwise adamant about the importance of openmindedness, do not on this point (and the many others that derive from it) suffer skeptics gladly. "Though liberals do a great deal of talking about hearing other points of view," William Buckley complained, "it sometimes shocks them to learn that there *are* other points of view."[26]

Thus, formulations like those put forward by Anthony Lewis and Learned Hand make sense only if understood to be truths existing beyond politics, as opposed to propositions that can be contested within it. To argue, as did Lewis, that certainty must be rejected because it abets indecency and inhumanity is to contend that decency and humanity alone can justify a high degree of certainty. The only logical alternative, encouraging skeptical challenges to the idea that being the enemy of decency and humanity is indeed deplorable, would defeat Lewis's purpose. It follows that while people must not be sure they're right about anything else, it's wicked or stupid to be unsure whether to favor decency over indecency, and humanity over inhumanity. It is this stance that, as Buckley suggested, leaves so many conservatives with the sense that arguing about liberalism with liberals is as futile as presenting a devout worshipper with syllogisms constructed to refute his faith's central revealed truth.

Similarly, if the spirit of liberty is not too sure that it's right, then one of the things it can't be too sure about is . . . the axiomatic rejection of being too sure one is right. Though the sincerity and humility Hand expressed are undeniably attractive, his diffidence takes a hatchet to the tree branch it sits on. Skepticism that encompasses skepticism *about* skepticism, in other words, leaves open rather than rules out the possibility that doubt and deference may sometimes be the wrong course and dogmatism the right one. If, on the other hand, the spirit of liberty is absolutely sure that it's right not to be too sure *any other* contention is right, it opens a different door to the same room: the existence of one undeniable postulate means there might be others.

This hall-of-mirrors theoretical problem becomes a practical one when liberals apply the imperative to be tolerant and nonjudgmental to concrete situations. The outcomes of those exercises in applied ethics adhere to no intelligible standard, yet somehow are always congruent with the political imperative to promote cohesion within the liberal coalition while anathematizing its adversaries. The expansive souls that make us identify with others often appear to wander in response to a political orientation instead of randomly, which leads them to feel their existence in some sufferers but not others. In the liberal melodrama of clearly designated victims and oppressors, "delinquency, or even the downright nastiness, of victims is an index of the extent of their suffering," according to Minogue, while those "who fit into the stereotype as oppressors . . . are not seen as the products of their environment, for that would incapacitate the indignation which partly fuels the impulse of reform."[27]

No one, that is, finds it necessary to inquire about the effects of childhood deprivations and historical grievances when passing judgment on Wall Street carnivores or white supremacists. This command leaves liberals, sure they must not be too sure they're right, conflicted when figuring out how to be tolerant of the intolerant, as when non-Western cultures oppress women and ethnic or religious minorities. It also means practitioners of the politics of kindness lose little sleep over those whose suffering is the collateral damage of liberal policies, such as whites denied educational or career opportunities because of affirmative action programs.

Second, liberals want to have it both ways in another, related sense: they want the modern bargain of agreeing to disagree, but also keep trying to graft a moral and teleological unity onto it. Since modernity precludes one based in religion, and the experience of totalitarianism rules out trying anything like it again, the efforts to come up with something else are unfailingly vapid.

In 1949, for example, Arthur Schlesinger's *The Vital Center* called for liberals to make their cause "a fighting faith." Freedom will survive, he wrote, "only if enough people believe in it deeply enough to die for it." Schlesinger was much better, however, at conveying the urgent need for a compelling faith than he was at describing its tenets. The "savage wounds" inflicted by modern life on the human sensibility can be healed "only by a conviction of trust and solidarity with other human beings." When trying to describe the basis of that trust and solidarity, Schlesinger does no more than implore us to accept a "new radicalism" that seeks to "reunite individual and community in fruitful union."[28]

President Jimmy Carter tried, and failed, to improve upon this fighting faith in the worst address of his life, 1979's "Malaise Speech." It warned that America faced "a crisis of confidence" reflected in "the growing doubt about the meaning of our own lives and in the loss of a unity of purpose for our nation." Because we've discovered that "owning things and consuming things does not satisfy our longing for meaning," we realize that national salvation requires taking "the path of common purpose and the restoration of American values." Carter's entire account of that path was a six-point program to reduce our dependence on imported oil.[29]

Then–first lady Hillary Clinton tried, and failed, to do better than Carter in the worst address of *her* life, 1993's speech on the politics of meaning. It asserted that "we realize that somehow economic growth and prosperity, political democracy and freedom are not enough—that we lack meaning in our individual lives and meaning collectively, we lack a sense that our lives are part of some greater effort, that we are connected to one another." The solution?

> We need a new politics of meaning. We need a new ethos of individual responsibility and caring. We need a new definition of civil society which answers the unanswerable questions . . . as to how we can have a society that fills us up again and makes us feel that we are part of something bigger than ourselves.[30]

As Harold Macmillan could have warned Ms. Clinton, this business of answering unanswerable questions really is best left to archbishops.

Nothing in these gaseous fatuities can be taken seriously, much less as a fighting faith any sane person would risk his life for. Schlesinger voiced the hope that the ultimate salvation for any free society lies "in the kind of men it creates." Unfortunately, he is far more detailed and persuasive in describing how the kind of men a free society creates are likely to imperil it than they are to rescue it. Democracy

> dissipates rather than concentrates its internal moral force. The thrust of the democratic faith is away from fanaticism; it is toward compromise, persuasion and consent in politics, toward tolerance and diversity in society; its economic foundation lies in the easily frightened middle class. Its love of variety discourages dogmatism, and its love of skepticism discourages hero-worship. In place of theology and ritual, or hierarchy and demonology, it sets up a belief in intellectual freedom and unrestricted inquiry.[31]

The incongruity of a liberal intellectual regretting, like an exiled monarchist, the spurned value of dogmatism and hero worship suggests that liberals will be the last people to fight for Schlesinger's fighting faith. Skeptics don't join crusades. As historian Michael Kazin points out, all the triumphs of "liberal modernism" encourage self-expression and -discovery, not self-sacrifice and -denial: "the unchaining of sexual pleasure from procreation, the liberation of art and literature from the didactic imperative, empathy with ethnic and racial outsiders and an identification with the rougher aspects of life, space for women to choose their work and partners, the effective use of wit to skewer all that is pompous and powerful."[32] Again, expansive souls expand in some directions, not others. Liberals prize iconoclasm, but take for granted that other people's icons are the only ones that will ever get clasmed. Andres Serrano's *Piss Christ* got financial support from the National Endowment for the Arts, and its artistic merit was validated when it elicited Senator Jesse Helms's wrath. No artist has ever created, and no museum displayed, *Piss Mandela*.

Third, the specific qualities of the emotion of pity, as described by Rousseau, make it a problematic guide even for individual ethics, and a more dubious one still for political decisions affecting millions. His stipulation—it is in order not to suffer myself that I care about someone else's distress—takes us back to the dictionary's: compassion is usually a perturbation occasioned by, but distinct from, the suffering of another. The exception is if I feel your pain because it also happens to be my pain. This is, for example, the compassion within a support group of cancer patients. The rule is for me to be distressed by the awareness of your distress, which I do not experience except vicariously, and to respond, emotionally and possibly through actions, because of "the desire of my well-being in whatever place I feel my existence."

The relation between my well-being and the abatement of your suffering is complicated, however. From one perspective, humans have grown more compassionate: as the world has become more densely interconnected, we've become aware of more people and their suffering than our ancestors were. I feel my existence in more places, that is, and it may abide there to address a longer sequence of follow-on sufferings. Max Ways, a *Fortune* editor, wrote in that publication in 1971:

> At the time when St. Francis impulsively gave his fine clothes to a beggar, nobody seems to have been very interested in what happened to the beggar. Was he rehabilitated? Did he open a small business? Or was he to be found the next day, naked again, in an Assisi gutter, having traded the clothes for a flagon of Orvieto? These were not the sorts of questions that engaged the medieval mind. The twentieth century has developed a more ambitious definition of what it means to help somebody.[33]

It is not, however, an unalloyed advance to transport our well-being to more places, ones where our expansive souls assert squatting rights rather than practice drive-by empathy. The modern, more ambitious definition of what it means to help somebody may result in empathy that is hyperactive . . . but not necessarily hypereffective. The whole point of compassion is for empathizers to feel better when awareness of others' suffering causes disquieting pangs. This ultimate purpose does not guarantee that empathizees will *fare* better, however, and may be consistent with "remedial" actions that make their situation worse. Barbara Oakley, co-editor of the volume *Pathological Altruism*, defines its subject as "altruism in which attempts to promote the welfare of others instead result in unanticipated harm."[34] Accidents and unintended consequences happen, of course. The pathology of pathological altruism is not the failure to bat 1.000, but the indifference—blithe, heedless, smug, or solipsistic—to the fact and consequences of those failures, just as long as the empathizer is accruing compassion points that he and others will admire. As philosopher and economist David Schmidtz has said, "If you're trying to prove your heart is in the right place, it isn't."[35]

Fourth and finally, compassion is problematic not just because of its distinguishing emotional qualities but because of its general ones *as* an emotion. For one thing, emotions are reliably unreliable. It has been long accepted, for this reason, that moral and material progress depends at least as much on governing our emotions as on being governed by them. The Woodstock Ethic—if it feels good, do it—was, long ago now, given a test drive and rejected as a faulty basis for living an individual life. "The heart wants what it wants," Woody Allen said of his decision to end a romantic relationship with Mia Farrow in order to have one with her adopted daughter. But the heart (like other organs) can't always get what it wants, and often shouldn't try.

The Woodstock Ethic's deficiencies as a political rule are even more severe. "The Judge's 'Spirited Woman,'" by Mark Twain, tells the story of a frontier court that acquitted a man accused of murder, not because they doubted that he committed the crime, but because they found him and his situation sympathetic enough to rule out any harsher decision. Upon hearing the verdict, the murdered man's widow stood up in the courtroom, took out a pistol she had concealed, and shot the exonerated defendant dead. The court, being in session, decided that the extenuating circumstances of seeing her husband's murderer set free also compelled their sympathy, and acquitted the woman then and there before taking up a collection to help care for the orphaned children.

This, clearly, is no way to run a railroad. As journalist Mickey Kaus wrote in 1986, compassion "*is* mushy-headed" because "it provides no principle to tell us when our abstract compassionate principles should stop. We have compassion for the working poor. We have compassion for the unmotivated delinquent who would rather smoke PCP than work."

Precisely because compassion "makes few distinctions," a "politics based on mass-produced compassion leads naturally to the indiscriminate dispensing of cash in a sort of all-purpose socialized United Way Campaign."[36]

The problem is not just that compassion is an emotion, whose variability makes it inherently unsuited to be a coherent, consistent, usable political principle. It is also that compassion is *an* emotion but not *the* emotion. We have others, several of which—including romantic passion, familial love, civic pride, patriotism, religious devotion, and concrete understandings about the requirements for decent conduct and honorable lives—make *many* distinctions.

We appear to be wired more for partiality than impartiality. Liberal compassion claims to be conforming to our emotional natures, but in asking us to manifest ever more extensive, ever less discriminating empathy, it sets itself against what comes naturally to anyone you or I have ever met. Empathy "extends beyond individuals to groups, communities, peoples, even species," Lakoff insists. Other champions of compassion make similar claims, calling on us to "emotionally join a global family," or summon a "global empathic consciousness."[37]

Is any such enterprise possible? And if it is, will we admire or deplore the results? I'll start to examine those questions by considering liberal compassion at work on the broadest possible canvas.

Chapter 2

HOW EXAMINING
LIBERAL COMPASSION
IN A GLOBAL CONTEXT
REVEALS ITS ILLOGIC

Recall, from the previous chapter, Paul Waldman's imaginary cancer survivor, Betsy Wilson. I'll see his vignette and raise it. Let me tell you about Mpinga Bomboku. He's also ten, and lives with his family in the slums of Kinshasa, where he rarely receives adequate nutrition, sees a doctor, or attends school. Mpinga's desperate plight is tragically common. In the Democratic Republic of the Congo (DRC), home to Mpinga and 75 million other people, per capita gross domestic product in 2012 was about $400, according to the CIA World Factbook, making it the poorest country on the planet. Life expectancy in DRC is fifty-six years, and only 6 percent of the population is older than fifty-five.[1]

We can use World Factbook data to conduct a rough-and-ready thought experiment. It calculates "Gross World Product," the GDP of the entire planet, to have been $85 trillion in 2012, which works out to $12,700 per person. A total of 51 nations have a per capita GDP less than $3,175, one-fourth of the world average. The 1.35 billion inhabitants of these countries account for 19 percent of the world's population, but the collective output of their economies amounts to less than 3 percent of GWP. If those 51 countries united into one—let's call it Poorlandia—its per capita GDP would be $1,875. By contrast, just over 1 billion people live in Australia, Canada, the European Union's twenty-eight nations, Japan, and the United States. That 14 percent of the world's population accounts for 48 percent of global GDP, which works out to $40,700 per person, nearly three and a half times the world average, almost 22 times more than Poorlandia's, and more than 100 times greater than the Democratic Republic of the Congo's.

If the wealthy nations named above—"Richistan"—were to transfer $1.75 trillion to the poorest countries just identified, every one of the latter could be brought up to a per capita GDP of $3,175. For the sake of the argument assume, against abundant and bitter experience, this foreign aid package is all spent honestly and effectively. The number of lives that would be improved—the amount of suffering that would be alleviated—is extraordinarily large. For all that, the program is quite limited in important respects. Put simply, it would reduce but not end global poverty. For one thing, a per capita GDP of $3,175 goes only so far. Poorlandia's new standard of living would still be significantly below that of countries not widely considered prosperous, including Uzbekistan ($3,600 GDP per person), the Philippines ($4,500), and Guatemala ($5,200). Nor, relatedly, would the $1.75 trillion transfer from Richistan do anything for the hundreds of millions of extremely poor people who reside in nations such as India ($3,900 GDP per capita) and Egypt ($6,700). And while the eternal hope of foreign aid programs is that the donated money will have a catalytic effect, the history of such aid argues that the assisted economies are likely to need assisting for a very long time. The $1.75 trillion transfer, then, is more plausibly viewed as an ongoing program, likely to be repeated every year for decades to come, than as a onetime corrective.

How much would an annual $1.75 trillion transfer cost Richistan? Viewed in one way, as an amount slightly greater than

4 percent of its GDP, it sounds modest enough. That works out to about $1,750 from each Richistani, however, or $7,000 for a family of four, which need not be economically debilitating but sounds like a serious political challenge, given that all the member states of Richistan are democracies. They are not, moreover, equally prosperous. America's per capita GDP in 2012, $50,700, is 17 percent greater than Australia and Canada's, 37 percent more than Japan's, and 44 percent greater than the European Union's. Apportion the $1.75 trillion transfer to reflect those differences, and the United States winds up contributing $687 billion. This sum equals 19.4 percent of the federal government's actual outlays in 2012, and would have amounted to $2,170 per American.

The U.S. contribution, $687 billion, is also 31 times greater than the $21.9 billion the federal government really did spend on "international development and humanitarian assistance" in 2012, six-tenths of one percent of all federal outlays that year. Lest that sliver be construed to result from heartless cuts demanded by xenophobic congressional Republicans, it should be noted that the Obama administration's 2014 budget neither calls for nor anticipates outlays on such development and assistance programs exceeding $26 billion in any year through 2018, as far into the future as it casts its gaze.[2]

Alleviating suffering is central to liberalism's understanding of what politics is about—indeed, of what life is about. Given the enormity of the suffering caused by extreme poverty around the world, one might expect Democratic candidates, MSNBC hosts, and *New York Times* editorialists to devote more bandwidth to demanding massive transfers from the Global North to the Global South than to all their other crusades combined. In reality, the suffering of the wretched of the earth is material for footnotes and appendices, a subject mentioned in passing amid denunciations of those who would stifle programs intended to reduce suffering in America. A context and a purpose explain Waldman's stipulation that Betsy

Wilson's parents were a waitress and a carpenter. At the time his article appeared, Congress was arguing over whether federal assistance in securing children's health insurance would continue to be restricted to families ineligible for Medicaid and with incomes no more than twice the poverty line, as Republicans wanted, or funded at a level that would permit states to enroll families with incomes that were three or in some cases 3.5 times greater than the poverty line, the Democratic position. The savagery Waldman denounced, then, was aimed at resisting the extension of a welfare state program to families who, in one of the richest nations in the world, were making more than the median income.[3]

If Betsy Wilson's family has an income above the American average, it is even farther above the Richistan average, which puts their standard of living comfortably inside the top 10 percent of all households in the world. Assume Mpinga Bomboku's family has an income that is average for his country, which makes it low even by the standards of Poorlandia, and well below the boundary defining the poorest tenth of the global population. Indeed, the British journalist David Goodhart points out, "The poor in a rich country are, in fact, three times richer than the rich in a poor country, defined as that top 10 percent and not just the tiny number of the super-rich."[4]

Yet, according to the moral lights of Paul Waldman and Barack Obama, it is very, very important to alleviate Betsy Wilson's suffering and only slightly important to assist the more grievously afflicted Mpinga Bomboku. How can they—how dare they—look at little Mpinga—ill-housed, ill-clad, and ill-nourished—and say: sorry, too bad—you can't have more than the pittance that rich countries, which insist they have more pressing things to do, take out of their governments' petty cash drawers? What kind of a person says that to a child?

TOGETHERNESS

We behold, then, a striking incongruity. Liberals, who in most political contexts are in equal parts verbose and lachrymose when addressing the horrors of suffering and the imperatives of compassion, have surprisingly few words and sentiments to spare concerning the world's most acute human distress. How can liberals who vote with hearts full of compassion for the guy or woman next to them also vote with hearts full of indifference for the starving child in a distant country? "If all human lives are equally valuable," asks Goodhart, "how can we any longer favour our fellow national citizens over the impoverished masses of the global south? This 'post-nationalism' nags away at the conscience of many liberal-minded people."[5]

The illogic of liberals' lopsided preference for intranational over international remedies is a good place to begin examining liberalism's problems with acting on compassion's dictates. The liberal idea treats the alleviation of suffering as the most basic, and at the same time most exalted, moral imperative. The liberal project consists of identifying suffering situations and advocating measures to address them. If it is better to alleviate more suffering than less, then it is best to alleviate as much as possible. On this basis liberals favor public programs, backed by government's singular power to tax and borrow, over private charities that always disburse help less generously by virtue of operating with fewer resources.

The project is aligned with the idea, then, which means that liberalism's theoretical problems are likely to cause practical difficulties. One theoretical problem is that because there's a lot of suffering out there, we need, in a world of finite resources and capabilities, criteria for differentiating more from less urgent claims on our humanitarianism. There are, in the main, two ways to rank suffering situations: according to severity, or according to proximity. The logic of liberalism points to calibrating the severity of suffering situations, thereby giving the greatest attention to those who suffer most acutely.

The liberal sensibility, however—and the ubiquity of appeals to compassion and empathy affirms that liberals have chosen to build their house on the foundation of moral sentiment—strongly emphasizes proximity. We are *moved* to assist the afflicted more than we are *persuaded* to do so. A problem with compassion, Kant wrote in 1763, is that "there is no proportion in the result." A "suffering child . . . will fill our hearts with sadness, while at the same time we hear with indifference the news of a terrible battle in which, obviously, a considerable number of the human species must suffer undeservedly under horrible evil."[6] Compassion pulls liberalism in opposite directions: toward a moral provincialism, insofar as it wants to make political use of the instinctive sympathy we feel for the sufferer in the center of our field of view; and toward a moral universalism, insofar as it calls upon us to direct that exact sentiment to ever wider circles of sufferers, whose plights are increasingly distant and exotic.

Anyone who says "Charity begins at home" is conveying that charity should end at a point not very far from home. It's infeasible, in other words, to proceed as if the resources available to alleviate suffering were infinite, and it's indecent to allocate those finite resources as though sufferers near and dear to us deserve no more of our compassion than distant strangers. Accordingly, normal people devote greater attention and care to immediate needs than to remote ones.

An important objective of liberal rhetoric has been to make this natural desire to help those close to us, and whom we care about, an ally rather than an enemy of the liberal project. That effort will succeed to the extent it gets us to enlarge our understanding of the home where charity begins, and the family to which we belong. As Mario Cuomo said, liberals have "a single fundamental idea" regarding "what a proper government should be: the idea of family, mutuality, the sharing of benefits and burdens for the good of all, feeling one another's pain, sharing one another's blessings. . . ."

The problems with the idea of a national family are thrown into sharper relief by the concept of a global family. The disparity between how liberals regard Betsy and Mpinga suggests that the fierce urgency to comfort the afflicted stops or dramatically weakens at the water's edge. If that's so, however, can we be entirely sure compassion extends, undiminished, right up *to* the water's edge? The global "family" of 7.15 billion people is 22 times larger than the American "family" of 318 million, but the idea is not decisively crazier. The liberal argument posits an imperative for an American to constantly weaken his particularist attachment to his own spouse, children, siblings, parents, neighbors, community, coworkers, and coreligionists in favor of an increasingly encompassing, undifferentiated concern for all other Americans. The logical next step is a bigger, more ambitiously humanitarian mission: replacing the narrow attachment Americans feel for other Americans with a comprehensive devotion to all humans everywhere. The world abounds in suffering situations, after all, millions of them more acute than the ones addressed by liberals' domestic policies.

One way to rationalize liberals' lesser concern with the greater suffering found in the Global South is to emphasize the moral and political importance of reciprocity. Philosophy professor Elizabeth Anderson upholds the mutual sharing of benefits and burdens for the good of all by using a different metaphor than Cuomo's. Instead of conceiving of our nation as a family, we should emulate tight-knit religious communities. Anderson cites an Amish barn-raising, where everyone lends help in the expectation of eventually receiving the same kind of help. She could just as plausibly be endorsing the transformation of our continental republic into the United Kibbutz of America. The welfare state, Anderson argues, mediates the reciprocal relations within a commune that has members numbering in the hundreds of millions by discharging reciprocity through redistributive public programs. "In a democracy, government is nothing more than citizens acting together, through state officials functioning as their agents. It's no different in principle from the barn-raising system. It's just on a vastly larger scale that, due to its size, requires an intermediary administrative apparatus."[7]

The intermediary administrative apparatus through which Americans could share benefits and burdens with Mpinga is much weaker than the one that allows them to share with other Americans, the United Nations being much less united than the United States. Were it otherwise, global citizens could act together in a global democracy. Therein a worldwide New Deal coalition might encompass Mpinga's family, and all others similarly situated, then use its ballot-box power to elect a global parliament and prime minister whose policies redirected some of the resources currently devoted to Betsy Wilson's needs to programs designed to alleviate the suffering of the most desperately poor. It is, alternatively, conceivable that the coalition would include the Bombokus *and* the Wilsons, but any such political effort is likely to founder on the economic infeasibility of an agenda that attempts to make more than 90 percent of global voters net importers of globally redistributed wealth. Margaret Thatcher's warning about socialists running out of other people's money applies most forcefully at the global level, since by definition there can be no auxiliary resources available to help achieve the goals of a redistributive project once it encompasses the entire planet.

Furthermore, the reciprocity Cuomo and Anderson invoke is implausible on a global scale, and will not make sense to the Americans they're trying to persuade. Reciprocity amalgamates compassion to enlightened self-interest: we help those who need it *because* they need it, but also because we can readily imagine someday needing such help ourselves. The act of imagination that puts us in another's place, making his suffering vivid and distressing to us, speaks to our heads as well as our hearts. Today's benefaction, whether it's the labor I devote to building Samuel Yoder's barn or the tax I pay to subsidize Betsy Wilson's insurance, weaves those beneficiaries into a network of obligations that may well prove beneficial to me in the future.

It's far more difficult, however, to persuade a generic Richistani voter and taxpayer that if he does Mpinga's family a good turn today there will come a time when he's down on his luck and the Bombokus will be there for him. Thus, while "the hunger of a woman in Little Rock is our hunger," in Cuomo's words, the hunger of a woman in Lagos remains . . . her hunger or, at most, her fellow Nigerians' hunger. Cuomo's admonition—"the failure anywhere to provide what reasonably we might, to avoid pain, is our failure"—is doubly qualified, then. First, reasonable people, ranging from John Rawls to William Buckley, can disagree about what we might reasonably provide to avoid pain. And it is in the family of *America* that we are bound to one another, so that the failure anywhere to alleviate suffering means anywhere in America, not anywhere in the world.

Everything's Relative

There is a second way that liberal thinking about suffering and compassion rationalizes the great solicitude shown to Betsy Wilson and the meager concern given to Mpinga Bomboku. If it turns out that the suffering of a poor person in a rich country is more severe than the suffering of a poor person in a poor country—even if the poor person in the poor country is, by every objective standard, worse off than the poor person in the rich country—then it may be just, decent, and sensible to devote more concern and assistance to Betsy than to Mpinga.

Mpinga's family is worse off than Betsy's, but may *feel* better off. After all, there's hardly anyone known to the Bombokus who *isn't* ill-housed, ill-clad, and ill-nourished. As a result, they can go through their days and years without ever looking around and feeling that fate or an unjust socioeconomic system has singled them out for some special deprivation. If, from time to time, they view television programs showing life in Richistan, they might pause to reflect on the staggering differences between what they see around them every day and what appears on the TV screen. (They might even try to imagine how it is possible that there are people living unhappily in Richistan. If Mpinga ever got a chance to see, in particular, the HBO series *The Sopranos*, he could have witnessed a scene where Tony Soprano compliments Svetlana Kirilenko, a Russian immigrant hired to care for his uncle, on her cheerful attitude despite having had a leg amputated when she was a child. "That's the whole purpose of people like me," she says with sudden coldness. "To inspire people like you." When Tony protests he meant no offense, Svetlana says, "That's the trouble with you Americans. You expect nothing bad ever to happen, when the rest of the world expect only bad to happen. And they are not disappointed.") But, more probably, the Bombokus regard news or entertainment shows from the Global North the way Richistanis view science fiction movies, as depictions of radically different creatures leading utterly dissimilar lives.

By the same token, the Wilsons lead a much nicer life than the Bombokus yet may feel worse about it. We can assume they do *not* compare themselves to Kinshasa's slum residents, but to their own neighbors and friends who have healthy children, or employer-provided health insurance, or who are eligible for some public program presently closed to the Wilsons. Within that very different frame of reference, then, the Wilsons may well feel aggrieved and deprived in a way the Bombokus do not. As a result, when we conduct empathy triage and rank the severity of the various suffering situations the world presents, the Wilsons would have a stronger claim on our compassion than the Bombokus, and on the ameliorations compassion directs us to perform.

Such is the logic of liberal author Timothy Noah's rebuke to conservatives who say America's economic inequality is not a serious problem, given that economic growth and technological progress are improving the quality of life for all. The fact that even poor Americans in the twenty-first century routinely avail themselves of medications or technologies unknown to Henry VIII or Andrew Carnegie counts for little, he says, against the fact that "people do not experience life as an interesting moment in the evolution of human living standards. They experience it in the present and weigh their own experience against that of the living." The fundamental fact is "We are social creatures and establish our expectations in relation to one another."[8]

What is true across time is also true across distance. An exponent of this position was Adam Smith, in *The Wealth of Nations*:

> By necessaries I understand, not only the commodities which are indispensably necessary for the support of life, but whatever the custom of the country renders it indecent for creditable people, even of the lowest order, to be without. . . . Custom . . . has rendered leather shoes a necessary of life in England. The poorest creditable person of either sex would be ashamed to appear in public without them. In Scotland, custom has rendered them a necessary of life to the lowest order of men; but not to the same order of women, who may, without any discredit, walk about bare-footed. In France, they are necessaries neither to men nor to women; the lowest rank of both sexes appearing there publicly, without any discredit, sometimes in wooden shoes, and sometimes bare-footed. Under necessaries therefore, I comprehend, not only those things which nature, but those things which the established rules of decency have rendered necessary to the lowest rank of people.

It will be noted that the point of this discussion was taxation, not any eighteenth-century forerunner of the welfare state. Smith was not urging Parliament to enact a Shoe Stamps program, one that would have been obviated by the established rules of decency in France. His point, rather, was that taxes should do no more to encumber people of modest means than the state's fiscal circumstances require. "It must always be remembered . . . that it is the luxurious and not the necessary expence of the inferior ranks of people that ought ever to be taxed."[9] The modern tax code adheres to Smith's logic by exempting some income from taxation. For example, the federal income tax exemption, currently $3,700 per person, leaves a large portion of a poor family's income exempt from income taxes, but only a fraction of a prosperous family's. States and cities that exempt groceries and medications from sales taxes adhere to the same principle.

Clearly, however, the idea that deprivation is relative rather than just absolute lends itself to the expanded government responsibilities that include giving things to people, as well as taxing them away. A Social Security Administration researcher came up with the first "poverty line" in 1965 by calculating the cost of a spare but adequate diet for a year, then multiplying that total by three, based on Department of Agriculture studies showing that the typical family devoted one-third of its spending to food. Lyndon Johnson declared unconditional war on poverty in 1964 and the Office of Economic Opportunity, the agency he created to wage it, began using the new poverty line in 1965, four years before it became "the federal government's official statistical definition of poverty."[10] Almost from the start, however, activists and experts have called for a relative poverty line—40, 50, or 60 percent of the median income are the measures most commonly advocated—to supplement or even supplant the absolute one. A relative poverty line, according to an advocate at the Center for Economic and Policy Research, does "a better job" than any absolute measure at "capturing the change over time in broad public consensus . . . on the minimum amount of income that an American family needs to 'get along' in their local community."[11]

If the poverty that should really concern us is always relative, however, certain paradoxes become unavoidable. A relative definition, Minogue points out, can have "the perverse effect of showing poverty on the increase in times of prosperity and on the decrease in times of depression when the average goes down."[12] A family can, that is, become simultaneously better off (in absolute terms) and worse off (in relative terms) if its quality of life is improving, but improving less rapidly than the standards of the other families with which it compares itself. By the same logic, it can be said to be prospering if its situation is deteriorating more slowly than that of other families. Furthermore, a relative poverty line affects a moral amalgamation of the suffering brought about by one's own economic setbacks and the suffering caused by the gnawing awareness of others' gains. Whenever a friend succeeds, Gore Vidal once said, a little something in me dies. This is a shaky foundation on which to build a friendship, but an even worse one for governing a nation.

And, to return to this chapter's central paradox, relativizing poverty and suffering has the effect of soothing rather than prodding Americans' consciences. There is no "broad public consensus" on the minimum income a generic global family needs to get along in a generic local community. In its absence, stipulating that the suffering that truly compassionate people work to alleviate is deprivation relative to whatever the "custom of the country renders indecent for creditable people" necessarily sanctions slight regard for Mpinga's troubles by sensitive souls who lie awake at night tormented by thoughts of Betsy's.

PATRIOTISM

It remains impossible, however, to believe that any self-congratulatory liberal actually does congratulate himself on having so little empathy left over for Mpinga. The most elemental gratification of *being* a liberal, after all, is to regard oneself superior to the cold, callous bastards who are always so adept at coming up with reasons for feeling little and doing less about other people's suffering. The thought of resembling such troglodytes is intolerable.

This tension, which makes Betsy Wilson's needs more urgent than Mpinga Bomboku's while also leaving liberals with a troubled conscience about their treatment of Mpinga, could be easily resolved by making patriotism a powerful variable in the moral equations. Betsy is an American, Mpinga isn't. Therefore, Americans have no need to be defensive about making her needs a high priority and his a much lower one.

Liberals do not, however, wish to draw deeply from this well. Liberal compassion derives from a belief in human affinity beneath the skin, which could solve many problems thought insoluble if only we would let it. Any appeal to patriotism takes us, according to that logic, in the direction of greater particularism and distrust, rather than greater cooperation and empathy. Patriots—both people devoted to a particular country and, more generally, those who believe devotion to any decent regime is honorable—are challenged by liberalism to demonstrate that patriotism is different from, or does not necessarily culminate in, jingoism, imperialism, ethnocentrism, and racism. Patriots are burdened in this task by the progress liberalism has made in setting the terms of the debate, in which respect for equality and fraternity proscribes favoritism toward any subset of the race rather than embracing all as equal, valued members of the human family.

"Should we not begin to redefine patriotism?" asked the historian Howard Zinn in 2003. Zinn was the type of leftist who makes liberals uncomfortable, less because they disagreed with things he said than because his unmodulated formulations extrapolated their principles in ways they found awkward to endorse. Zinn was a hero to those columnist Ross Douthat described as "street liberals," for whom "[p]rotests and activism aren't just hobbies . . . or a chance to go slumming with the working class—they're a way of life." Zinn was *not*, by virtue of complicating their political labors and self-regard, a hero to Douthat's "parlor liberals," who "are ultimately well disposed to the world and to their privileged place in it, believing that what injustices there are can be righted without too much political upheaval and unrest. . . ."[13]

Zinn made the pacifism and globalism inherent in liberalism uncomfortably clear when he called for expanding patriotism "beyond that narrow nationalism which has caused so much death and suffering. If national boundaries should not be obstacles to trade—we call it globalization—should they also not be obstacles to compassion and generosity?" Strobe Talbott, a parlor liberal of unsurpassable respectability—veteran of *Time* magazine, deputy secretary of state under President Bill Clinton, and president of the Brookings Institution since 2002—was sufficiently cautious, when writing in 1992, to frame his hope for a world where "nationhood as we know it will be obsolete [and] all states will recognize a single, global authority," as a *prediction* about a future that would be realized by the year 2100, rather than a demand to get on with the delegitimizing and dismantling of nation-states forthwith.[14]

Still, his intent was unmistakable. It took the terrors of the twentieth century, Talbott argued, to "clinch the case for world government." That future marks the final turn away from the organized savagery that is nationalism. Validated by myths and symbols, it has defined and deformed human history:

> The forerunner of the nation was a prehistoric band clustered around a fire beside a river in a valley. Its members had a lan-

guage, a set of supernatural beliefs and a repertoire of legends about their ancestors. Eventually they forged primitive weapons and set off over the mountain, mumbling phrases that could be loosely translated as having something to do with "vital national interests" and "manifest destiny." When they reached the next valley, they massacred and enslaved some weaker band of people they found clustered around some smaller fire and thus became the world's first imperialists.[15]

Talbott's disdain for the nation-state marks no radical departure from liberal thinking. His argument, rather, is fully congruent with the worldview of Woodrow Wilson. "The Wilsonian vision," Walter Lippmann wrote in 1952, "is of a world in which there are no lasting rivalries, where there are no deep conflicts of interest, where no compromises of principle have to be made, where there are no separate spheres of influence, and no alliances. In this world there will be no wars except universal war against criminal governments who rebel against the universal order." Thus, "In the Wilsonian ideology an aggression is an armed rebellion against the universal and eternal principles of the world society." In the Wilsonian spirit, FDR's secretary of state Cordell Hull proclaimed in 1943 that the Allies, including Joseph Stalin's Soviet Union, had settled on a post–World War II framework that would hasten the day when "there will no longer be need for spheres of influence, for alliances, for balance of power, or any other of the special arrangements by which, in the unhappy past, the nations strove to safeguard their security or to promote their interests."[16]

Geopolitics is a particularly fraught enterprise for liberals, given their misgivings about patriotism as such. Assessing, in 1999, how the Clinton administration was trying after the Cold War to realize the vision Cordell Hull had embraced before it, Charles Krauthammer found it necessary to point out, "Foreign policy is not social work." Clinton, along with his advisors and admirers, had turned the most basic principles of international politics inside out, Krauthammer argued: the moral test of any foreign intervention had become how *little* it mattered to the United States. This stance followed directly from "an abiding liberal antipathy to any notion of national interest": "Indeed, in the new liberal orthodoxy, it is only disinterested intervention—in a word, humanitarianism—that is pristine enough to justify the use of force. Violence undertaken for the purpose of securing interests is not."[17]

Purely humanitarian interventions, however, are subject to the same compassion trap as are domestic policy measures: the suffering that really needs to be alleviated is the beholders', not that endured by the beheld. This was the acid judgment of German author Peter Schneider in 1995 regarding NATO's ineffectual, dithering response to Serbian atrocities against Bosnian Muslims:

> We knew from the beginning of the war what can no longer be concealed: Western threats and initiatives were meant primarily to ease the suffering of the European onlookers rather than that of the victims themselves. These initiatives followed a domestic-policy logic typical among wealthy nations: the main intent was to pacify citizens on the home front.[18]

If the true liberal is not too sure that he's right, as Learned Hand argued, then the true patriot is not too sure that his country is right. When announcing his candidacy for the 1972 Democratic presidential nomination, Senator George McGovern said, "Thoughtful Americans understand that the highest patriotism is not a blind acceptance of official policy, but a love of one's country deep enough to call her to a higher standard."[19] That formulation of the problem came naturally to McGovern, who grew up the son of a Methodist minister and enrolled in seminary himself before commencing academic and, later, political careers. There are higher truths and duties than those defined by loyalty to a particular nation.

The solution—at least in abstract terms—to the problem patriotism poses for liberals is to insist that the patriot's duty is to bring the nation he loves into closer conformity with those higher truths, rather than to acquiesce in compromising those transcendent truths for the sake of national pride or unity. To oppose an unjust war, as McGovern understood himself to be doing with respect to Vietnam, was the very opposite, then, of being a disloyal fifth columnist. When a nation conducted a misbegotten, indefensible war, it was unpatriotic to prolong it for the sake of "staying the course" or "peace with honor." Instead, the patriotic imperative was to oppose it by "call[ing] America home to the ideals that nourished us from the beginning," as McGovern said in his 1972 acceptance speech.[20]

The higher patriotism, fixed on standards above national interest, is a concept that can be traced back to the New Testament. In three of the four gospels Jesus escapes the Pharisees' efforts to "entangle" him with a question about paying tribute to Caesar by saying, "Render theretofore unto Caesar the things which are Caesar's; and unto God the things that are God's." Jesus's implication that divine obligations are distinct from and may take precedence over secular political ones is clear, but the questions of *which* things are Caesar's, which are God's, and what to do when the two conflict remain.

An extreme case of Christians turning Christ's ambiguities into absolutes is the "Declaration of Sentiments" adopted by an American peace convention in 1838 and published in William Lloyd Garrison's abolitionist newspaper, the *Liberator*. "We cannot acknowledge allegiance to any human government," it stated, because "we recognize but one *King* and *Lawgiver*, one *Judge* and *Ruler* of mankind." Thus,

> Our country is the world, our countrymen are all mankind. We love the land of our nativity only as we love all other lands. The

interests, rights, liberties of American citizens are no more dear to us than are those of the whole human race. Hence, we can allow no appeal to patriotism, to revenge any national insult or injury. The *Prince of Peace*, under whose stainless banner we rally, came not to destroy, but to save, even the worst of enemies.[21]

Garrison's higher patriotism, unlike McGovern's, explicitly obliterates all lower patriotisms—all attachments of sentiment and obligation, that is, to individual nations and their citizens rather than to the entirety of the human race. Rendering unto God what is God's means rendering nothing unto Caesar, whose legitimacy to demand any tribute Garrison rejects. Garrison was, in effect, invoking the long-lost moral and political unity of Christendom, when the church was both powerful and confident enough to make plain its opposition to "sovereign political bodies" whose "will to power" in the words of political theorist Pierre Manent, led "both princes and subjects to address their wishes to the earthly city and to set themselves up as 'independent,' to the detriment of the divine kingdom and the human vocation." For secular moderns, Manent argues, the analogue to Christian universalism is a dubious "religion of humanity," which posits "a humanity virtually unified and healed, as, beneath the separate activities of separate human groups, there is present or latent a humanity that nothing separates or distinguishes."[22]

Even if McGovern had been disposed to follow his own argument to Garrison's ultimate conclusion, his reticence on the point is understandable, since few politicians have become the leader of a country by promising to hasten its disintegration. There is another problem with McGovern's patriotism: the higher standard to which true patriots are called to make their country conform is much less clear than the standard Garrison invokes. Throughout the nineteenth and early twentieth centuries, in the words of historian Walter Russell Mead, "an aggressively proselytizing and self-confident Protestantism was the home and natural ally of the feminist, prohibitionist, peace, and antitobacco movements."[23] But over the course of the thirteen decades separating Garrison's statement from McGovern's, liberalism came to embrace a skepticism that, however selective, was reliably vigorous. Liberal relativism insists, contrary to Garrison, that conflicting value judgments cannot themselves be judged right or wrong, superior or inferior. To deny this truth is presumptuous, and lays the foundations for tyranny.

Such intellectual diffidence, however, reduces McGovern's patriotism, which discards blind acceptance of official policy in favor of calling the nation to a higher standard, into a command to be passionately devoted to one's own political preferences. Activists, partisans, and intellectuals are *already* passionately devoted to their own political ideals and agendas, however. McGovern's formulation provided them gratuitous encouragement but, more important, also offered the reassurance that simply by virtue of being politically engaged they were already as patriotic as they needed to be, and indeed as patriotic as they possibly could be.

The highest patriotism requires making the nation conform to higher standards, in McGovern's view. But to invoke high*er* standards implies that there are high*est* standards, truths from which any and all departures will lead us into error and vice rather than toward greater wisdom and virtue. To put this Platonic point another way, if there are no highest standards then there can be no intelligible basis for supposing that one standard is higher than any other. But modern liberalism's all-in bet on relativism commits it to the contradictory proposition that the only absolute truth is that there are no absolute truths. Since tolerance requires accepting different strokes for different folks, we are obliged to respect all standards, variously and idiosyncratically understood, which means conflicts among them cannot be resolved by appeals to higher standards. The lower patriotism, in this view, honored and practiced by vulgar patriots, stands revealed as blind acceptance of official policy and bloodthirsty ethnocentrism.

In their desire for moral unity and moral diversity we note, again, liberals' wish to have it both ways, desiring the piety of religion without having to traffic in the religiosity of religion. They are especially envious of religions that offer all men everywhere hope for salvation by worshipping the one true God. Universal faiths broke down the pagan power of deities worshipped and rituals practiced solely by a particular tribe, all of which reliably intensified its chauvinism. The marriage of liberal universalism and liberal skepticism proclaims the brotherhood of man while rejecting the fatherhood of God. Where religious universalism declares that the brotherhood of man rests on the most fundamental cosmological truths, however, the only nourishment liberal universalism offers is the empty calories of Rodney King's wish that we all get along.

The historical evidence shows that humans are strongly inclined *not* to get along, an inclination unlikely to be reversed by stale sanctimonies about the wickedness of clinging to national attachments rather than discarding them in favor of universal ones. The new, improved humans for whom nationhood will be obsolete and the only legitimate political authority global are clearly different from, though not clearly better than, the ones we have known to this point in the history of the species. Liberals can only reply to this mountain of historical and anthropological evidence by affirming, as Mario Cuomo put it, "the simple truth that peace is better than war because life is better than death."

IMMIGRATION

The ultimate resolution of the problem of doing right by both Betsy and Mpinga is to get beyond nationalism, making the Wilsons and the Bombokus fellow and equal citizens of a "nation" that comprises the whole human race. In it, liberals would finally wield the powers of a planetary welfare state, a mechanism adequate for assessing global needs and apportioning global resources. They would also acquire a moral clarity that presently eludes them. With the advent of Strobe Talbott's single global authority, Cuomo's "sharing of benefits and burdens for the good of all" would at last mean *all* all, not just some all. And denouncing the "failure anywhere to provide what reasonably we might to avoid pain" would apply to *any* anywhere, not just those anywheres that happen to fall on one side of a line somebody drew on a map.

That day is not at hand, however, and this book's author and readers are unlikely to be in a position to verify whether Talbott's prediction of its arrival by the year 2100 came true. Liberals must find other ways to cope with the problem in a meantime likely to last generations. Public opinion surveys always show that American voters greatly exaggerate, and greatly resent, the rounding-error amount in the federal budget representing the allocation for humanitarian foreign aid. Liberals have every reason, then, to decline the suicide mission of branding the Democratic Party as the one committed to multiplying such expenditures.

If assistance cannot be sent to where the neediest people are located, however, perhaps those people can be brought to where it is already available. Massive immigration to rich countries from poor ones is not a *policy* of planetary redistribution, exactly, but we achieve much the same result by treating such immigration as a social and economic development we have neither the practical capacity nor the moral standing to resist. Should the Bombokus relocate from Kinshasa to Kansas, American liberals will have a simple way to work around the problem of calibrating their compassion. Mpinga will now join Betsy in the ranks of sufferers whose needs demand a generous response from a decent society.

A welcoming immigration policy serves the additional, related liberal purpose of ascribing bigotry to conservatives. In the words of *Salon*'s Sally Kohn, "racial discomfort is the overwhelming motivation behind opposition to creating a path to citizenship for millions of aspiring Americans."[24] In the twenty-first century, being anti-anti-immigrant assists those keen to demonstrate they've transcended racial discomfort while condemning those who resist that spiritual progress. Restricting immigration in the twenty-first century, after all, consists largely of lighter-skinned, wealthier people asserting authority against darker-skinned, poorer ones. As a result of its melodrama of victims and oppressors, liberalism has come to incorporate the belief that in *any* dispute between individuals or groups, the darker-skinned is presumptively aggrieved and the lighter-skinned presumptively culpable.

Conservatives are unconflicted about patriotism, and disposed to believe that Europeans' (and Euro-Americans') historical transgressions against non-Europeans are not categorically different from non-Europeans' transgressions against one another, or against Europeans. In any case, they believe that getting on with moral and political life requires subjecting all such offenses to a historical statute of limitations, since purging the world of every effect of all prior exploitations and cruelties would be an eternal, impossible project. Thus inclined, conservatives approach immigration as a practical problem: How do we, the citizens of this particular country, let in the people we want to let in and keep out the people we want, and have every right, to keep out? As blogger Steve Sailer says, "In contrast to America, countries like Canada and Australia treat immigration the way Harvard treats college admission or the New England Patriots treat the NFL draft: as a way to get the talented that can benefit the institution and keep out the untalented. Here in America, we increasingly treat immigration as if it were a sacred civil right possessed by 7 billion foreigners."[25]

We do so because immigration is more complicated for liberals. Indeed, the question of whether immigration policy should be this or that presupposes the idea that some kind of immigration policy may be rightfully enacted and enforced in the first place. As Sailer suggests, however, this proposition is one of the things the immigration debate is about, not a shared premise from which it proceeds. Journalist Matthew Yglesias has helpfully made explicit what is usually implied when liberals bring compassion to bear on the question of immigration. Restrictionists' desire to "kick unauthorized migrants out of the United States and curtail the ability of future migrants to come to the United States," he writes, "involves completely discounting the interests of human beings who happen to have been born in Mexico or Morocco or Mali. [There] are perhaps reasons for deciding that people born in Boston or Birmingham count more than people born in Bangladesh or Bolivia, but they're *nationalistic* reasons not egalitarian ones." They're bad reasons, that is, not acceptable ones.[26]

Yglesias allows that there are contestable practical questions about the feasibility of an "open borders regime," which might lead some to disagree with his conviction that such a regime "would substantially increase overall human welfare." But those who raise such objections have a heavy burden to prove their motives are not indecent, since the practicalities will never "resolve the question of whether or not, morally speaking, it makes sense to simply not care about the interests of foreigners," as do, implicitly, the heartless, chauvinistic opponents of open borders.[27]

Thus does immigration solve the problem Mpinga poses for liberalism: his distant suffering is brought within America's borders, the moral and practical realm wherein liberalism operates confidently. Doing so, or at least advocating so, dispels all doubts about liberals' self-identification as the champions of compassion while reaffirming their conviction that cruel indifference to suffering is the exclusive, defining quality of conservatism.

Ideas, like people, often settle down where they're useful. The idea that the United States cannot legitimately discount the interests of people who happen to have been born in Mexico, by frustrating their desire to leave Mexico and come to the United States, appears notably popular among . . . people who happen to have been born in Mexico. That country's per capita GDP was $15,700 in 2012, 69 percent less than that of the United States. (The only other countries adjacent to one another with comparably stark economic disparities are special cases: Hong Kong and China; North and South Korea; and Israel in contrast to all of its neighbors—Egypt, Jordan, Syria, and the Palestinian West Bank—except Lebanon, which is about half as prosperous.) It's not surprising, then, that Mexicans frequently cross the border that their country shares with the United States, a border nearly two thousand miles long. They often do so in violation of American laws, in 2012 accounting for 52 percent of America's 11.7 million "unauthorized migrants," the term used by the Pew Hispanic Center.[28]

A survey taken by the Mexican Migration Project of 1,353 Mexicans living in their native country found that 52 percent believe "Mexicans have a right to be in the U.S." and 66 percent agreed that the "U.S. government has no right to limit immigration." Only 9 percent of those surveyed said they intended to migrate to the United States illegally. (In that nation of 116 million, 9 percent represents more than 10 million people.) Not surprisingly, 82 percent of the people within that subset thought Mexicans have a right to be in the United States, and 86 percent thought the United States has no right to keep them out. The remaining 91 percent of the Mexicans who took the survey said they do not intend to cross the border illegally, but seem disinclined to foreclose the option, or condemn those who would pursue it. Within that larger subset, 49 percent thought Mexicans have a right to be in the United States, and 64 percent believed the American government could not rightfully bar them.[29]

Political scientist Joseph Carens takes a more tempered view of the question than Yglesias or, if the Mexican Migration Project survey is to be believed, most Mexicans. A professor at the University of Toronto, Carens brings his own dual citizenship, Canadian and American, to the subject. His position is that nations have a clear right to keep foreigners out, but only a qualified right to kick them out. The qualification is that however foreigners got into a country, they cease to *be* foreigners after some time spent residing in that new country, and deserve the legal and social status of natives, from whom they have become practically and morally indistinguishable.

> The moral right of states to apprehend and deport irregular migrants erodes with the passage of time. As irregular migrants become more and more settled, their membership in society grows in moral importance, and the fact that they settled without authorization becomes correspondingly less relevant. At some point a threshold is crossed, and irregular migrants acquire a moral claim to have their actual social membership legally recognized.[30]

Inescapably, Carens's framework yields an arbitrary determination of *the* point in the duration of an irregular migrant's stay in a new country when his moral claim to remain there finally trumps its government's right to apprehend and deport him. Carens thinks that "five years of settled residence without any criminal convictions should normally be sufficient to establish anyone as a responsible member of society," but considers it "plausible" that "a year or two is not long enough." How quickly the state's right to apprehend and deport erodes between the start of an irregular migrant's third year in a new country and the end of his fifth year is left unexplained.[31]

A nation that forswears a right to kick out illegal immigrants, however, is going to have a harder time keeping them out in the first place. If we follow Carens by recognizing and respecting the irregular migrant's presence as a fait accompli, we make it a good deal harder to tell prospective migrants they should be regular rather than irregular ones. The disincentives to violate a nation's immigration laws are significantly reduced by the assurance that after five (or fewer) years your transgression will be expunged from the historical record. Meanwhile the disadvantages to obeying those laws, waiting patiently to emigrate until and unless the host country lets you in, remain the same.

We should not be surprised if people adjust their behavior accordingly. Suppose Professor Carens tells his students that their term papers are due on May 1, and that those assignments handed in late will be marked down. Come May 1, half the class pleads for an extension, and Carens obligingly tells them that because he realizes how busy his students are he'll agree to accept late papers whenever they're submitted, and won't impose a penalty after all. We can safely predict that, once it becomes known through the campus grapevine that Carens is one of those instructors who never really enforces any due date, *none* of his students will turn their work in on time. We can also predict that, until this de facto policy becomes universally understood, those students who pull all-nighters because they took his deadlines seriously will feel like idiots for having believed him in the first place.

Carens doesn't see a problem. As long as they have to wait some number of years before the government relinquishes any right to deport them, irregular migrants will be living with a sword hanging over their heads, which is penalty enough. (Students' fears that their late term papers were *going* to be penalized are, by this logic, an adequate equivalent to an actual penalty.) Carens goes on, however, to advocate turning the sword irregular migrants must live under into a butter knife. He is "wary of efforts to criminalize actions that irregular migrants take simply to live ordinary lives," such as "identity theft and the use of false documentation." Enforcing such laws against irregular migrants, unless they're using them for some illegal purpose apart from staying in the country they migrated to irregularly, is "an abuse of the legal process." Prohibit the government from committing such abuses, however, and the irregular migrant's fraught life in the shadows becomes far less shadowy, making it relatively feasible and congenial to stay in the country he entered irregularly while the clock ticks down to the day when the government must abandon all efforts to deport him.[32]

As for the unfairness of his recommendations to regular migrants, Carens says that because countries such as the United States and Canada make almost no provision for unskilled workers to immigrate legally, leniency to irregular migrants does not penalize anyone else. The irregulars are not cutting ahead of those in the queue—there is no queue because there are no regulars. But this assertion sounds like an argument to change our immigration laws rather than to curtail the enforcement of the existing laws. And if we did change them there *would* be a queue, turning the moral problem Carens evades into a tangible difficulty. Furthermore, if the absence of legal pathways for foreigners to reside and work in America justifies curtailing and putting an expiration date on enforcing immigration laws, then Carens is, as a practical matter, closer to the open-borders position of Yglesias, despite stipulating that he doesn't deny "a government's moral and legal right to prevent entry in the first place."[33]

There's another difficulty. While allowing that states have the *right* to control immigration, Carens never acknowledges any reason they would *want* to do so. It remains a purely formal prerogative, in contrast to his detailed, lyrical case for the principle that people "who live and work and raise their families in a society become members, whatever their legal status." Irregular migrants "sink deep roots" as

> connections grow: to spouses and partners, sons and daughters, friends and neighbors and fellow-workers, people we love and people we hate. Experiences accumulate: birthdays and braces, tones of voice and senses of humor, public parks and corner stores,

the shape of the streets and the way the sun shines through the leaves, the smell of flowers and the sounds of local accents, the look of the stars and the taste of the air—all that gives life its purpose and texture.[34]

One of Carens's critics was law professor Carol Swain, that most troublesome of political figures, a black conservative. She does see a reason for America to enact and enforce immigration laws: to protect the economic prospects of the "most vulnerable" Americans, "U.S.-born blacks and Hispanics with high school educations or less" from whom "the unknown millions who are in the country illegally . . . have taken jobs and opportunities to which they were not entitled." Swain cites studies showing that native-born American workers with college degrees have lower unemployment rates than college-educated immigrants, but those without high school degrees have higher unemployment rates than their immigrant counterparts—in the case of native-born blacks, rates more than twice as high. She reverses Carens's moral timetable, suggesting that the illegal immigrants who have been in the United States the longest are the ones *most* deserving of deportation, since their presence is a "form of theft," of limited jobs and public resources, and those who arrived earliest have stolen the most. "I have a dream of one day living in a society where elites apply the compassion offered illegal immigrants to their fellow citizens. . . ."[35]

Hell hath no grievance like a white liberal accused of callousness by a black conservative. The political effect of Swain's argument, Carens asserted, is to divide "disadvantaged groups and [set] them against one another instead of building alliances to promote their common interests." Their common interests are, simply, the liberal domestic agenda: "extending health care, improving education, and expanding economic opportunities for all Americans"—native-born and migrant, regular and irregular. The problem of irregular migrants competing against native-born Americans in the labor market can be solved, Carens says, by making both groups eligible for union membership and minimum wage laws, thereby preventing employers from realizing the benefits of cheaper labor costs when more workers bid down the price needed to hire. And for Swain to echo the "I Have a Dream" speech "is to make a mockery of [Martin Luther] King's commitment to social justice for all. Can anyone doubt where King would stand on [the legal status of irregular migrants], if he were alive today?"[36]

In fact, one can doubt it. In 1991, when Congress was considering legislation to weaken sanctions against employers who hired illegal immigrants, a letter to Senator Orrin Hatch from the Black Leadership Forum, an umbrella group of civil rights organizations, made many of the same points Swain did. It argued that a policy making it easier for illegal immigrants to find and keep jobs would "add to competition for scarce jobs and drive down wages," thereby "undercutting . . . American jobs and living standards." It would, moreover, "inevitably add to our social problems and place an unfair burden on the poor in the cities in which most new immigrants cluster." The letter's lead signatory was Coretta Scott King, the civil rights leader's widow.[37]

The Black Leadership Forum did agree with Carens on the need to achieve social justice by enacting the liberal agenda— make welfare state programs more numerous and generous, while strengthening protections for workers with regulations that increase the minimum wage and favor labor unions. The adequacy of this position is doubtful. Raising the price for something, the way minimum wage laws raise the price for entry-level labor, usually increases the supply of it while reducing the demand. This policy tends, therefore, to decrease the number of jobs paying the minimum wage by giving employers an incentive to substitute capital, often in the form of new technology, for labor that has been made artificially expensive. Furthermore, widening the gap between the wages paid in Mexico and those paid in America would make it harder for Mexicans to get, but better for them to have, a job in America. "Surely raising wages for unskilled work would lure even more immigrants to the United States, just as it has lured them to Western Europe," sociologist Christopher Jencks argued in 2002. "And if employers prefer unskilled immigrants to the unskilled natives who currently apply for $6-an-hour jobs, why would these employers' preferences change when they had to pay $9 an hour?"[38] As an alternative to enforcing immigration laws vigorously rather than perfunctorily, Carens's solution will result in diminished economic opportunities for more native-born Americans, who can console themselves with the thought of the higher wages they might be earning if they weren't unemployed. And the salve for *that* wound, in the words of Mickey Kaus, will certainly turn out to be handling the "distributional and social effects of open borders" with "a bigger web of government income transfers, social provision of benefits, training, and counseling."[39]

According to Carens, we need to enforce the "human, civil, and economic rights to which all irregular migrants are legally and morally entitled."[40] He makes clear that the "all" includes the recently arrived irregular migrants, those not yet in a new country long enough for the government to have renounced its right to deport them. They'll be free to claim their rights without fear of deportation because a "firewall" will separate immigration enforcement from all other government functions. It's not clear whether the rights to which they're morally entitled also include enrollment in the host nation's welfare state programs. If so, the Mpinga dilemma has been addressed, though at this point it would be easier, in terms of both formulating and implementing a solution, to simply allow poor people in Oaxaca and Kinshasa to enroll in Medicaid and Head Start directly, without requiring them to first make long, difficult trips to the United States to collect their benefits. If, on the other hand, we cruelly exclude irregular migrants from our domestic programs, then we'll confine the welfare state to regular migrants and the native-born, who will need more of its help by virtue of competing with larger numbers of irregular migrants for jobs and housing.

ECONOMIC EXPANSION

The policy of inoculating people from economic and social dislocations is consistent with the logic of a poverty researcher's statement to the *New York Times* in 1998: "Idaho has effectively made itself the worst place in the nation to be poor." It had done so, the article makes clear, by taking a hard right turn politically, reducing its "welfare rolls by 77 percent, the steepest cut in the nation." What makes a state a bad place to be poor, then, is a stingy, stigmatizing welfare state instead of a generous, nonjudgmental one.[41]

By implication, the goal—really, *the* goal—of governance is for each state to aspire to be the best place in the nation to be poor, and for each nation to aspire to be the best place in the world. That liberal goal does not necessarily need to be understood in liberal terms, however. For conservatives, a good place to be poor is one where, by virtue of its dynamic economy and proliferating opportunities, those in poverty who are also capable and motivated have excellent prospects to be poor *briefly*. Mpinga Bomboku's family is not destitute because their country's government is insufficiently generous, but because DRC's economy is insufficiently prosperous. Generosity requires wealth to be generous *with*. Even if we agree with Hubert Humphrey that the moral test of government is how well it takes care of the young, old, and needy, prosperity is the practical test we must meet prior to engaging the moral challenge.

Economic growth has always had detractors: both on the Left, of the *Whole Earth Catalog* variety; and on the Right, such as the Southern Agrarians. Among those who view it as fundamentally good, most conservatives are inclined to treat growth as a necessary and virtually sufficient condition for improving human life, while the disposition to regard it a necessary but far from sufficient condition increases with one's political liberalism.

It is important, in any case, to emphasize how necessary that necessary condition really is. Economist Deirdre McCloskey calculates that in "the countries that most enthusiastically embraced capitalism" some two hundred years ago, real, per capita economic growth has increased by 1.5 percent annually. Owing to the miracle of compound interest, this increase has meant a *19-fold increase* in living standards over the past two centuries, which, she contends, is a "change in the human condition" that "ranks with the first domestications of plants and animals and the building of the first towns." McCloskey argues that this enormous economic result had a cause that was cultural rather than economic. Humans did not suddenly become more acquisitive or creative. Rather, "When people treat the marketeers and inventors as having some dignity and liberty, innovation takes hold." The new *respectability* of bourgeois life, the belief that the creativity of capitalism's creative destruction more than offset its destruction, was the decisive attitudinal change that rendered human life in the past two centuries decisively different from what it had been throughout the preceding millennia. In McCloskey's view, "I don't much care how 'capitalism' is defined, so long as it is not defined a priori to mean vice incarnate." The default position for modern thinking, however, characterizes "commercial society at the outset to be bad by any standard higher than successful greed."[42]

An economically dynamic society is likely to be a good place to be poor not only because there will be many opportunities, but because the habits of thought and action conducive to creating those opportunities are also directly beneficial to the aspiring. The time poor people spend being poor is likely to be even briefer by virtue of a bourgeois nation's social capital, the thick network of religious, civic, and informal associations that provide contacts, solace, en-

couragement, and—when necessary—admonitions to those who
are down on their luck. And when economic dynamism and social
capital still leave some people (the disabled, for example) in poverty, a robust economy does the best job of generating the surplus
wealth that will fund charitable and governmental safety nets.

For liberals, by contrast, what makes a place a good place to
be poor is, above all, the strength of both the welfare state and
the social taboo against blaming the victim. In such jurisdictions
it may be possible to be poor briefly, but the main point is to facilitate being poor comfortably, respectably, and indefinitely. Just
before the 2012 election the *New Republic*'s Jonathan Cohn argued
that the "blue states," the eighteen carried by the Democratic presidential nominee in 2000, 2004, and 2008, look "more and more
like Scandinavia." The twenty "red states" carried by the GOP in
those three elections, by contrast, increasingly resemble "a social
Darwinist's paradise." He argues, "By nearly every measure, people
who live in the blue states are healthier, wealthier, and generally
better off than people in the red states." Why? Cohn allows that
causation is difficult to prove, but believes the strong correlation
between government spending and social well-being "is hard to
dismiss." In blue Massachusetts, for example, "health care is available to almost everybody . . . [w]elfare benefits are among the most
generous in the country, and the state spends hundreds of millions
on public housing each year." Red Texas, by contrast, "doesn't even
try to provide the kind of protection for its vulnerable residents
that Massachusetts does. It has more uninsured residents than any
other state in the country; its lawmakers have repeatedly refused
money from the federal government to expand health insurance
for kids. Its welfare program is among the nation's stingiest. . . ."[43]

This stark disparity would explain why civilized Massachusetts
is growing so much more rapidly than barbaric Texas . . . if that
were the case. In fact, the population of Massachusetts was 8.8
percent larger in 2010 than it had been in 1990, meaning it grew

at one-third the rate of the other forty-nine states, while the Texas population increased by 48 percent, more than twice as fast as the rest of America. More generally, the blue states' total population increased by 15.9 percent between 1990 and 2010, while the red states grew 32.9 percent.[44]

The moral of the story appears to be that the blue states are good places to have money, partly as a result of a regulatory environment that privileges established enterprises against newcomers, and land-use policies that drive up the cost of housing in order to protect those who can afford to live there from problems like sprawl and congestion.[45] They're also relatively good places not to have money, for all the reasons Cohn applauds. It's just that blue states are not such good places to *make* money, which is why the red states grow so much more rapidly. It's no surprise, then, that a *Chief Executive* magazine survey of five hundred business leaders found that the best states for business—in terms of taxes and regulations, and also public education and health, quality of life, and housing affordability—were a mix of red and purple ones, while the worst were solid blue. And, predictably, the best states for business accounted for a larger share of the national population in 2010 than in 1990, while the worst accounted for a smaller share. In lowest-ranked California, the magazine points out, the average lead time necessary to open a restaurant is two years, compared with the eight weeks or fewer that are customary in top-ranked Texas. Taking note of the relative opportunities and impediments, the company that owns the Carl's Jr. chain plans to open three hundred restaurants in Texas and zero in California.[46]

Cohn has a simple solution for this predicament, one that has nothing to do with getting blue states to reconsider tax and regulatory policies inconducive to economic growth. Quite the opposite—if Americans are voting with their feet against the blue-state model, nationalizing that model will render all such relocations pointless. The problem, Cohn believes, is that American federalism has left us with fifty safety nets, which is forty-nine too many. Giving "states a lot more control over the size and shape of the social welfare state" would mean giving them "the liberty to let a whole class of citizens suffer." That must not happen. "This country has room for different approaches to policy," Cohn writes. "It doesn't have room for different standards of human decency." There should be room for just one standard, one that closely resembles the Massachusetts standard while repudiating the appalling one favored in Texas.[47]

Cohn's call for a bluer, more Scandinavian America comes at a time when some in northern Europe are voicing fears that their social policies have become a little too Scandinavian. When a Danish legislator challenged a skeptic of the hypergenerous welfare state to see for himself how hard it was, still, to live on what Denmark provided the poor, the answer turned out to be . . . not very hard at all. He discovered "Carina," a thirty-six-year-old single mother who had been on welfare continuously since she was sixteen. Her total benefits package was worth $2,700 a month, more than the amount many Danes who work full-time live on. No Scandinavian country is going to resemble Texas anytime soon, but the *New York Times* reported in 2013 that "Denmark has been at work overhauling entitlements, trying to prod Danes into working more or longer or both."[48]

"Carina" had the judgment to use a pseudonym and, eventually, stop talking to the press altogether, neither of which can be said of Susan Moore, whose biography is quite similar. Moore was declared "Britain's Laziest Woman" by the *Sun* in 2004, when it was discovered that she hadn't held any kind of job since dropping out of college at age eighteen in 1988. Susan shared a home with her divorced mother, for which they were receiving a £45 weekly housing allowance. Both also received a "Jobseeker's Allowance," worth £40 a week in Susan's case, though she hadn't sought a job in sixteen years, and her mother had not done so since Susan was born in 1969. Ms. Moore turned down a job that would have involved answering phones on the weekend since "I shop on a Saturday, and on Sunday I sit at home and relax a bit." The British welfare state, though giving out assistance with fewer strings attached than even the bluest parts of America, is less generous than Denmark's. As a result, Moore received "just enough to enable her to avoid making anything of her life," according to columnist Mark Steyn, "enough to let her sit around all week 'listening to CDs and watching videos.'"

> "I just haven't been given a chance," says Susan. But when the space on your CV for the period from adolescence to early middle-age is one big blank, no one's ever going to give you a chance. It's hard to think of anything capitalism red in tooth and claw could have done to Susan Moore that would have left her worse off than the great sapping nullity in which Her Majesty's Government has maintained her for her entire adult life.[49]

Several lessons can be drawn from the stories of Betsy Wilson, Mpinga Bomboku, "Carina," and Susan Moore. First, as conservatives are always insisting, those keen to divide wealth cannot hurtle along disdaining the people and processes that multiply it. Few Danish experts, the *New York Times* reports, believe Denmark can afford to maintain its full menu of welfare state benefits, which includes "free" maid service for the elderly who need it, regardless of their income. They see, instead, the necessity of "trying to wean more people—the young and the old—off government benefits." Among Danes between the ages of 15 and 64, 27 percent are not in the workforce, and many of the rest "work short hours and all enjoy perks like long vacations and lengthy paid maternity leaves, not to speak of a de facto minimum wage approaching $20 an hour." Denmark's minister of social affairs and integration told the paper, "In the past, people never asked for help unless they needed it." Today, however, "They think of these benefits as their rights. The rights have just expanded and expanded." What people become accustomed to they eventually believe they are entitled to. But no national economy is dynamic enough to pay for a mass entitlement to prolong college into your mid-thirties and then commence retirement by your mid-fifties. Certainly Denmark is not. Its per capita GDP of $38,300 is three-fourths the size of America's.[50]

Conservatives, worried about the macroeconomic consequences of the taxes, borrowing, and regulations that make a welfare state like Denmark's possible, often invoke the French author Frédéric Bastiat. "There is only one difference between a bad economist and a good one," he wrote in 1850. The "bad economist confines himself to the *visible* effect; the good economist takes into account both the effect that can be seen and those effects that must be *foreseen*." The import of this simple distinction is "tremendous" because "the bad economist pursues a small present good that will be followed by a great evil to come, while the good economist pursues a great good to come, at the risk of a small present evil."[51]

MORAL CONTRACTION

Second, liberals betray neither compassion nor regret for enacting policies that enable some citizens to lead lives amounting to great sapping nullities. This outcome is not so much unforeseen as dismissed. Liberals resist the conclusion that an adulthood squandered listening to CDs and watching videos in public housing is a suffering situation, since nothing in that tableau distresses the liberal onlooker the way evicting Susan Moore and demanding that she get a job would. And if liberals find it difficult to commiserate with Ms. Moore they find it impossible to condemn her, as that would be moralistic and hurtful.

The word "judgmental," which adroitly passes judgment against those who pass judgment, has grown up with modern liberalism, having been used for the first time in 1909, according to the *OED*. Liberals, sure that they're right to condemn those who are too sure that they're right, are defiantly nonjudgmental of lifestyle choices, while being vehemently judgmental of lifestyle scolds. "Lifestyle," first used in 1915, is only slightly newer than "judgmental" and has the same topspin against the idea that some ways of life are better and others are worse.

But people convinced there is no reason they should ever be ashamed are left with no basis on which they can ever be proud. Social scientist Charles Murray contends that happiness, which the Declaration of Independence says men have an inalienable right to pursue, and which James Madison in Federalist No. 62 called *the* object of government, was understood by America's Founders "in its Aristotelian sense of lasting and justified satisfaction with life as a whole." A "life well-lived" is usable shorthand for this concept, and it takes fierce commitment to the principle of being nonjudgmental about lifestyles to insist we have neither the right nor the basis to declare that "Carina" and Susan Moore are far along in the process of fashioning lives badly lived. Murray argues that a life may be well lived by some who are guided by "one of the world's great religions" or others who take seriously "one of the world's great secular philosophies." It cannot, however, be lived by those who believe that because humans "are a collection of chemicals that activate and, after a period of time, deactivate," the highest "purpose of life is to while away the intervening time as pleasantly as possible."[52]

Kindness covers all Barack Obama's political beliefs. But according to C. S. Lewis, kindness is "the desire to see others than the self happy; not happy in this way or that, but just happy." Secular liberals' project may be understood as an effort to order the world as God would if (a) He existed and (b) weren't such a Grouch.

What would really satisfy us would be a God who said of anything we happened to like doing, "What does it matter so long
as they are contented?" We want, in fact, not so much a Father in
Heaven as a grandfather in heaven—a senile benevolence who,
as they say, "liked to see young people enjoying themselves," and
whose plan for the universe was simply that it might be truly said
at the end of each day, "a good time was had by all."[53]

A serious problem with kindness (or compassion, or empathy)
is that when severed from any estimable, challenging conception of
a life well lived it leads directly, according to Lewis, to "a certain
fundamental indifference to its object, and even something like
contempt for it."

> Kindness consents very readily to the removal of its object—we
> have all met kindly people whose kindness to animals is con-
> stantly leading them to kill animals lest they should suffer.
> Kindness, merely as such, cares not whether its object becomes
> good or bad, provided only that it escapes suffering. As Scripture
> [Hebrews XII, 8] points out, it is bastards who are spoiled: the
> legitimate sons, who are to carry on the family tradition, are
> punished. It is for people whom we care nothing about that we
> demand happiness on any terms: with our friends, our lovers,
> our children, we are exacting and would rather see them suffer
> much than be happy in contemptible and estranging modes.[54]

Determining whether a collection of chemicals is passing the
time pleasantly requires little acuity and no censoriousness, which
makes any cause of unpleasant time-passing an appropriate object
of compassionate remediation. Determining whether a human
being is engaged in a life well lived is harder, and inescapably
entails being judgmental. Liberals feel called upon to simultaneously obey two imperatives. On the one hand, they must feel bad

for, and then enact government programs to assist, the afflicted. On the other, they must not entertain certain obvious questions about the lifestyles of the afflicted, including: (a) whether the afflicted suffer from afflictions caused or aggravated by their own choices and habits; and (b) whether the lives they lead after liberal government programs have removed their afflictions amount to lives well lived. The project adhering to both imperatives requires welfare state policies that, by removing causes of suffering, enable those who prefer the great-sapping-nullity lifestyle to pursue it without feeling inferior to, or judged by, those who pursue any other lifestyle.

Taking Care of Our Own

Third, to return to Betsy and Mpinga, the question of what compassion demands of us is inseparable from the question of how widely we draw the circle before it starts to demand less and, ultimately, nothing. The primitive tribal sentiments at the heart of patriotism, which liberals disdain, are extremely useful for fostering the spirit of caring and sharing, which liberals exalt. American liberals gaze longingly at Scandinavia. "The Danish model of government is close to a religion here, and it has produced a population that regularly claims to be among the happiest in the world," the *Times* reports from Copenhagen. But Denmark is a nation of 5.5 million people, fewer than live in Wisconsin. That small population is ethnically and religiously homogeneous, defined by a distinct national character forged over long centuries.[55]

Neighboring Sweden, another model for American liberals, is only somewhat larger—its population of 9.1 million is smaller than North Carolina's or Los Angeles County's—but comparably lacking in diversity. As a result, its welfare state is "founded on a level of cultural homogeneity and an inheritance of social capital that simply isn't available in a polyglot republic-cum-empire like our own," according to Ross Douthat. "Sweden has . . . no real linguistic or religious diversity, no experience of chattel slavery or mass immigration . . . and a culture of Lutheran thrift and prudence that endures even though Lutheranism itself is on life support."[56]

The Bruce Springsteen song "We Take Care of Our Own" unintentionally illustrates the dilemma. It attempts to make patriotism safe for compassion by characterizing social justice as the patriot's central concern and highest expression. "Wherever this flag's flown," says the chorus, "We take care of our own." The song challenges the listener about a decline of fellow-feeling:

> *I've been stumbling on good hearts turned to stone;*
> *The road of good intentions has gone dry as bone.*

"We Take Care of Our Own," released on Springsteen's 2012 album, *Wrecking Ball*, became a quasi-official anthem of the Obama reelection campaign. It was played at rallies, including after the president's acceptance speech at the Democratic convention. A year after his victory, President Obama was still citing the song. In a statement issued on the one-year anniversary of Hurricane Sandy, Obama said of the ongoing recovery efforts, "That's who we are as Americans—we take care of our own. We leave nobody behind."[57]

To declare that we take care of our own does not rule out the possibility we take care of others, too. But it's a clear, vigorous—and in some contexts, truculent—assertion that we take care of our own *first*, and help others, if at all, only after having made certain we've done all we can at home.

It would appear, however, that relying on the principle of taking care of our own creates problems for liberalism more severe than those it solves. For one thing, it raises uncomfortable questions about resolutely taking care of the business of taking care of our own, as opposed to advertising the depth and refinement of our empathy by appropriating ever more money to take-care programs that are badly conceived, implemented, and administered. It raises, as well, the question of whether it's smart or seemly to chastise Americans for failing to take care of our own at the same time liberals defend enormous middle-class entitlement programs, such as Social Security and Medicare, that require government to spend huge sums to take care of people capable of taking care of themselves.

Worst of all, in the context of our discussion of Betsy and Mpinga, is the question of whether liberals are entirely comfortable appealing to an intensified tribalism in their closing argument. In 2012 the federal government spent 14.3 percent of GDP on domestic welfare state programs, 100 times more than the 0.14 percent of GDP it spent on international humanitarian aid. The voters' preference for taking care of our own, and corresponding aversion to taking care of those not our own, looks pretty robust already.

I point this out because if taking care of our own is to be a central component of how liberals justify themselves, the question of how we determine who qualifies as "our own" becomes pivotal. According to Tocqueville, patriots "love their country as they love the mansion of their fathers."[58] This makes sense when we recall that "patriot" derives from the Greek word meaning "of the father," and is related to such English words as "patriarch" and "paternity." Liberals' grave misgivings about patriotism, however, mean they are usually the last people, not the first, to contend that the causes of progress and social justice will be served by a heavier reliance on what historian Jerry Muller calls "ethnonationalism." He writes, "When French textbooks began with 'Our ancestors the Gauls' or when Churchill spoke to wartime audiences of 'this island race,' they appealed to ethnonationalist sensibilities as a source of mutual trust and sacrifice."[59]

The persistence and even intensification of these feelings remains a potent geopolitical fact. After eighty-one years as a distinct nation carved out of the collapsed Austro-Hungarian Empire in 1918—decades spent being independent, then dominated by Nazi Germany and Soviet Russia—Czechoslovakia took only three years after its sovereignty was restored by the end of Soviet domination in 1989 to conclude it was two peoples, not one, each of which deserved its own nation. Not all divorces are so amicable. Belgium has been an independent nation since 1830, but ethnonationalistic antagonism between a Flemish majority, most of whom speak Dutch, and large francophone Walloon minority perpetually threatens to split the country into two even smaller ones. The Basques, Kurds, and Quebecois have never inhabited their own sovereign nations, but their separatist movements have been politically determined and sometimes violent.

Ethnonationalism figures differently, but not trivially, in America's political equations. This has been true from the start. According to the Declaration of Independence, by 1776 it had become "necessary for one people to dissolve the political bands which have connected them with another." The phrase plants an axiom, treating as a settled fact what was, in reality, a contested question: Were the Americans indeed one people and the British another in 1776, or did they *all* remain one people, as had been widely and uncontroversially believed on both sides of the Atlantic for more than a century? The Declaration argues as if the existence of an American "us" distinct from a British "them" were a self-evident truth in its own right. Historians who study the colonial era have, in fact, found a good deal of evidence pointing to the emergence of a shared, important American identity. According to political scientist Samuel Huntington, "Before 1740 the term 'America' described a territory not a society. Beginning then, however, the colonists and others began to speak of Americans collectively." He says that their "collective experiences" prior to the Revolutionary War created "a common consciousness" among these Americans.[60]

The sense that patriotism was inherently ethnonationalistic, thereby requiring a new nation to fortify the shared identity that set its people apart from all others, continued in the Founding era. In Federalist No. 2, John Jay is at pains to describe American society in terms that make its national unity appear indisputable:

> Providence has been pleased to give this one [geographically] connected country to one united people—a people descended from the same ancestors, speaking the same language, professing the same religion, attached to the same principles of government, very similar in their manners and customs, and who, by their joint counsels, arms, and efforts, fighting side by side throughout a long and bloody war, have nobly established general liberty and independence.[61]

American ethnonationalism ceded ground throughout the nineteenth century as nativist advocates of strict controls on immigration won few political victories and suffered many defeats. But Americans remained committed to the idea of a nation that, even though not descended from the same ancestors, did speak the same language, and did share manners, customs, and religions that, if not identical, were at least similar and compatible. In most countries, ethnonationalism conferred, automatically and pervasively, the benefits of cultural nationalism. In increasingly plural America, cultural nationalism was made to perform this work as part of a conscious project, given our weakened ethnonationalism's capacity to automatically confer cultural unity. Pluralism was a fact, but that fact militated against, not in favor of, turning pluralism into an ideology. According to historian John Fonte, "The assimilation of the Ellis Island generation succeeded only because Progressive politicians including Theodore Roosevelt and Woodrow Wilson insisted on 'Americanization' and crushed the proto-multicultural activists. . . ."[62]

In the twenty-first century, facts on the ground and ideas in the air dilute, if they do not effectively preclude, the Americanization of a hundred years ago. The Ellis Island immigrants of that era, most of whom arrived from eastern or southern Europe, had all made a long trip to America. Shuttling between their new and old countries was impossible, returning home after achieving success was not the point, and returning home after failure would have been a disgrace. The immigrants had made a big commitment to America the minute they set foot here. Because they arrived from a large number of countries, each speaking a different language, assimilation was a practical imperative. The number of immigrants from any one country, that is, was small enough to discourage life and work within a homogeneous, unassimilated enclave. Immigrants from Country A who wanted to take advantage of opportunities in workplaces employing both native-born Americans and immigrants from countries B, C, and D, or to find cheaper and better housing than what was available in neighborhoods dominated by emigrants from the same country, had strong incentives to learn English and make sure their children did.

It's different today. Most immigrants are from Mexico and other Latin American countries. It's easier than it was for the Ellis Island immigrants to get by without learning English, especially for those who work in industries dominated by other Spanish-speaking immigrants, and who reside in Spanish-speaking enclaves. "Roughly 10 percent of the American population now speaks Spanish at home," Christopher Jencks reported in 2001. "These households are concentrated in and around a few cities. . . ."[63]

Because of geographic proximity and lower travel costs, today's immigrants are likely to have a less attenuated relationship with their native land, and a more qualified one with their adopted country, than immigrants did a century ago. According to Jencks:

> Many Mexicans . . . see themselves as sojourners who will return home once they have made some money. The typical Mexican male earns about half what a non-Latino white earns, so if he compares himself to other Americans he is likely to feel like a failure. But if he compares himself to the Mexicans with whom he grew up, he is likely to feel quite successful. So he clings to his Mexican identity, sends money back to his parents, goes home for holidays with gifts that his relatives could not otherwise afford, tries to buy property in Mexico for his retirement, and retains his Mexican citizenship.[64]

A serious difficulty for liberalism, then, is that there appears to be a strong, reliably negative correlation between humans' "take care" impulses and their "our own" ones. Very much to his consternation, sociologist Robert Putnam (of *Bowling Alone* fame) determined in 2006 that diversity ravages the fellow-feeling that undergirds cohesive societies and generous welfare states. In the "presence of diversity," he told the *Financial Times*, "we hunker down. We act like turtles. The effect of diversity is worse than had been imagined. And it's not just that we don't trust people who are not like us. In diverse communities, we don't trust people who do look like us."[65] One analysis of neighborhoods did a large-scale comparison between measures of homogeneity and measures of social cohesion. According to social scientist Richard Florida, "the same basic answer kept coming back: The more diverse or integrated a neighborhood is, the less socially cohesive it becomes, while the more homogenous or segregated it is, the more socially cohesive."[66]

Putnam's solution to this problem is deeply unpersuasive.

"What we shouldn't do is to say that they [immigrants] should be more like us," he told a reporter. "We should construct a new us."[67] The Ellis Island paradigm of assimilation was, by that standard, exactly wrong. The point should have been not to Americanize immigrants but to immigrant-ize America. The problem of taking care of our own, already severe, is sure to be compounded by the principle that those who choose to join our society, whom we have a tenuous right to keep out in the first place, are entitled not only to be taken care of, but to have our society's contours altered until they feel as at home here as they did in the countries they left. To hope that the political will to take care of our own will survive a proscription against telling those who want to become our own that they should be more like us cannot be squared with any conception or experience of social cohesion.

There's a final problem connected to immigration. The enterprise of taking care of our own will not be confined to taking care of our own more than we take care of others. It can also entail immigration policies that take care of our own at the expense of others. David Goodhart points out that the nation of Malawi, with a per capita GDP of $900,

> has lost more than half of its nursing staff to emigration over recent years, leaving just 336 nurses to serve a population of 12 million. Rates of perinatal mortality doubled from 1992 to 2000, a rise that is in part attributed to falling standards of medical care. Excluding Nigeria and South Africa, the average country in sub-Saharan Africa had 6.2 doctors per 100,000 of population in 2004. This compares with 166 in the [United Kingdom], yet about 31% of doctors practising in the UK come from overseas, many from developing countries.[68]

We can be sure that when the Bombokus learn that the one clinic where they could take Mpinga in emergencies has closed down, because its staff has emigrated to the Global North to care for children like Betsy Wilson, they'll be keen to learn more about the politics of kindness.

Chapter 3

HOW LIBERAL COMPASSION'S PROBLEMS ARE NOT RESOLVED EVEN WHEN WE RESTRICT CONSIDERATION OF IT TO DOMESTIC POLICY

So, liberals have boundary issues. They want us to take care of our own without getting all harsh and restrictive about disqualifying anyone from being one of our own. While these issues, which have no obvious or imminent resolution, put a question mark after liberal compassion, they do not draw a line through it. Given the trouble posed by international issues, it's no surprise the liberal disposition includes a strong preference to alleviate intranational suffering.

Hard cases make bad law, say the legal scholars. Mpinga Bomboku presents liberals with a hard case, and they have no clear path to make good policy from it. This chapter will look at the other end, easy cases. I'll examine how liberal compassion takes care of our own when we remove questions about who constitutes our own from the equation.

HELPLESS

When we set aside boundary issues, and consider only those people clearly our own, the remaining questions concern whom to feel sorry for, why to feel sorry for them, and how to act on our compassionate feelings. As Hubert Humphrey's formulation about the supreme moral importance of helping children, the aged, and those in the shadows of life suggests, liberals have long believed that the way to put their cause's best foot forward is to put their clients' worst foot forward. Emphasizing the helplessness of those whom liberals want to help has been a staple of liberal thinking and discourse since the New Deal. "I'm getting sick and tired of all these people on the [Works Progress Administration] and local relief roles being called chiselers and cheats," Harry Hopkins, one of FDR's closest advisors, said in 1936. "These people are just like the rest of us. They don't drink any more than us, they don't lie any more, they're no lazier than the rest of us. . . . I have gone all over the moral hurdles that people are poor because they are bad. I don't believe it."[1]

President Obama sounded the same theme in his second inaugural address: "We recognize that no matter how responsibly we live our lives, any one of us at any time may face a job loss or a sudden illness or a home swept away in a terrible storm." From that premise he proceeded directly to the conclusion, "The commitments we make to each other through Medicare and Medicaid and Social Security, these things do not sap our initiative, they strengthen us."[2]

The poor are "just like the rest of us," only less fortunate—Rawlsianism in a nutshell. Hopkins and Obama were each speaking a few years after the onset of a severe economic contraction, so one could reasonably assume that many of their listeners, even those who kept their jobs or homes, had known people who suffered such losses, and had experienced the dread of downward mobility. The poor seem less different from the rest of us in hard times than in other times.

Liberals *always* want America to be more compassionate than it is, however, not just during economic downturns. It is no coincidence, then, that liberals who go to great lengths to express their compassion are especially apt to stress their empathy for children. Kids are equally cute during booms and busts. Children are also unqualifiedly not responsible for whatever suffering they endure. Their sufferings are, instead, entirely the result of other people's mistakes, neglect, improvidence, or sheer bad luck. All the other sufferers in Humphrey's roster of the afflicted may, at least in theory, present more complicated cases. Some of the aged might have made better provision for themselves when they were young, for example, just as some of the sick might have taken better care of themselves when they were healthy.

Children, as a class of sufferers, don't raise such problems, so they are often front and center when liberals make their case—sometimes literally. In January 2007, as Representative Nancy Pelosi waited on the floor of the House of Representatives while the newly elected Democratic majority voted to make her Speaker, she was surrounded by a group of children assembled for the occasion. Pelosi held an infant in her arms as the votes were cast and counted, then concluded her first speech as Speaker with the words, "For these children, our children, and for all of America's children, the House will come to order."[3] President Bill Clinton had stood at the same podium to give his 1996 State of the Union address, and did not physically drag children with him to make his arguments, but went to unusual lengths to drag them into the text of his speech. "For the first time since the dawn of the nuclear age," he informed a bemused nation, "there is not a single Russian missile pointed at America's children."[4]

Such mawkish excess challenges conservatives to decide: (a) whether their liberal friends are mostly cynical or mostly sappy;

and (b) which is worse. It's not really necessary to choose, though. People can be moralistic *and* cynical, really believing what they believe, while convinced that certain ways of presenting their ideas are especially resonant. The liberal activist Marian Wright Edelman told an interviewer that she founded the Children's Defense Fund because in 1973 America "was tired of the concerns of the sixties. When you talked about poor people or black people, you faced a shrinking audience." However, "I got the idea that children might be a very effective way to broaden the base for change."[5]

Natural disasters work, too, occasioning President Obama's allusion to a "terrible storm," three months after Hurricane Sandy devastated the Atlantic Coast. Columnist Matt Miller used a subsequent disaster, Typhoon Haiyan in the Philippines, to say if "you feel it's urgent to help the victims" of that storm, "then deep in your heart you also support Obamacare," and a bigger welfare state in general. The connection? "When human beings are left vulnerable and desperate by events beyond their control, we want to help. Empathy for human frailty and powerlessness in such a tragedy evokes compassion. We say such victims 'deserve' help because they are suffering through no fault of their own."[6]

FAMILIES, VILLAGES, AND SCALE

Liberals believe the thing to do for helpless people is to help them. The way they impart this view to a democracy of some 300 million people is to insist that the emotional responses and moral duties that would come naturally to the most intimate human associations are, for all practical purposes, the ones that apply in the same way within the most extensive ones. Mario Cuomo, as we have seen, said Democrats believe in a "single fundamental idea," that of "family, mutuality, the sharing of benefits and burdens for the good of all, feeling one another's pain, sharing one another's blessings. . . ."

Cuomo's idea has a long tenure in the rhetoric of social reform. In *What Eight Million Women Want*, published in 1910, the suffragist Rheta Childe Dorr argued, "Woman's place is in the home. . . . But Home is not contained within the four walls of an individual home. Home is the community. The city full of people is the Family. The public school is the real Nursery." If the reformers' goals are achieved, then

> [t]he city will be like a great, well-ordered, comfortable, sanitary household. Everything will be as clean as in a good home. Every one, as in a family, will have enough to eat, clothes to wear, and a good bed to sleep on. There will be no slums, no sweat shops, no sad women and children toiling in tenement rooms.[7]

According to Hillary Clinton's 1996 book, *It Takes a Village*, "Parents bear the first and primary responsibility for their sons and daughters," but children "exist in the world as well as in the family," and "will thrive only if their families thrive and if the whole society cares enough to provide for them." The African proverb about what's required to raise a child, which gave her book its title, remains applicable in modern America, even though a village "can no longer be defined as a place on a map, or a list of people or organizations." What matters is that the village's "essence remains the same: it is the network of values and relationships that support and affect our lives."[8]

It's not clear how far liberals are prepared to take the conceit of America as one very big family or village. Some begrudge Clinton's stipulation about parents' primary role. Marian Wright Edelman praised the way her parents had raised her to honor "the life-giving values of faith, integrity, and service," and claimed that in her vocation as a political activist she was doing "exactly what my parents did—just on a different scale." Indeed, if America is going to be serious about the welfare of children, as such, then we need to overcome the inclination to "distinguish between our own and other people's children."[9]

Similarly, in a 2013 announcement promoting her cable network, MSNBC host Melissa Harris-Perry said:

> We have never invested as much in public education as we should have because we've always had kind of a private notion of children. Your kid is yours and totally your responsibility. We haven't had a very collective notion of "These are our children." So part of it is we have to break through our kind of private idea that kids belong to their parents or kids belong to their families and recognize that kids belong to whole communities. Once it's everyone's responsibility and not just the household's, then we start making better investments.[10]

When some conservative writers derided Harris-Perry's message, she pushed back against her "hateful" and "vitriolic" critics. "I have no designs on taking your children," she wrote on the channel's website. Rather, "my message in that ad was a call to see ourselves as connected to a larger whole." As such, it was just common sense and common decency, not part of a sinister campaign to raise children collectively. Harris-Perry sees her call as part of the encompassing sense of responsibility that scales up from volunteers who serve as crossing guards even if they don't have children in the schools they're protecting, to childless homeowners who ungrudgingly pay the property taxes that support public education, to parents who become gun control activists in cities that have suffered armed violence against children.[11]

Even as a rhetorical trope, however, the idea of the nation as one big family, or village, is unpersuasive and unsettling. Clinton's description of the modern village as the "network of values and relationships that support and affect our lives" doesn't exclude anything, and a "category" that encompasses everything doesn't really designate anything. Similarly, adults who truly succeeded in overcoming the inclination to distinguish between their own and other people's children would be monstrous, not virtuous. Normal, decent people array their affections and obligations in concentric circles. We take care of our own, but do not regard all people as equally and identically our own, so we do not care for all in the same way or to the same extent.

There are things to be said in favor of heeding then-senator Obama's admonition to broaden the ambit of our concern. His call, however, to "empathize with the plight of others, whether they are close friends or distant strangers," implies we should empathize with distant strangers in ways increasingly similar to, and ultimately indistinguishable from, the ways we empathize with close friends. Such advice, taken seriously, would do more to make us bad friends than good strangers.

Broadening the ambit of our concern would be more plausible, promising, and admirable if its advocates respected the existing ambits of our concern. The point should not be to regret or fight against our particularist inclinations, nor to somehow replicate our feelings for those who are closest to us when arranging our feelings and conduct toward those who are distant and anonymous. Whatever prospects there are for expanding empathy rest on first honoring the operation of our compassionate impulses in their natural ambits. As the late political theorist Jean Bethke Elshtain argued, we "cannot possibly blur all the lines and generate a generic, all-purpose 'love' for all children everywhere. Indeed, we cannot even recognize our more diffuse and less direct responsibilities to 'children' unless we understand what it means to be responsible to the particular children who have been entrusted to our care."[12]

DEPENDENCE AND SELF-RELIANCE

There's a second dangerous oversimplification in ideas like Cuomo's and Clinton's. It's true that nations are not big families or villages, but it's also true that even families and villages have internal relationships far more varied and subtle than simply sharing benefits and burdens by feeling one another's pain. Even the simplest human associations embrace complex, often contentious, arrangements about the internal allocation of authority, functions, status, rights, and duties. If the personal is political, as feminists contend, it's safe to conclude the political is really political. Waving the word "mutuality" at obstinate psychological and sociological realities does not banish them from either the smallest or largest human groupings.

The politics of kindness, taken seriously, seeks to subordinate all these other considerations to the compassionate desire to take care of our own. It reduces all relationships in a nation to the dichotomy posited to govern families and villages: the subjects who experience feelings of compassion and the objects whose sufferings give rise to those feelings. The empathizers and the empathizees, in other words, who become the helpers and the helpless. To assess the feasibility and desirability of the politics of kindness, however, we need to keep other kinds of relationships in mind. The helpless are not just helpless, and the helpers not just helpful. There are, instead, complex circumstances and relationships within each group, and also between them.

Helplessness, for example, is not binary but scaled, not uniform but diverse. The helpless include some who could have done things in advance to prevent or mitigate their suffering, such as buying insurance or making more prudent, less risky choices. Even natural disasters raise questions of "moral hazard." If people choose to live on floodplains or fault lines, compassionately rebuilding their homes and neighborhoods with disaster relief funds might encourage them to stay in such places rather than relocate to regions that would be safer for them and cheaper for us. According to William Galston, a former Clinton administration official now at the Brookings Institution, only 8 percent of Americans who: (a) finish high school; (b) marry before having a child; and (c) postpone marriage until after the age of twenty wind up impoverished. By contrast, of those who fail those life assignments, 79 percent are poor.[13]

Such achievements are not always easy, but neither are they heroic. Compassion that responds to suffering as such, however, without considering how the sufferer's decisions or habits might have inaugurated, perpetuated, or aggravated his suffering harbors the potential for great harm. Charles Blow demolished a straw man when he ascribed to conservatives the belief that "Whatever your lesser lot in life, it's completely within your means to correct." That "completely" misrepresents both his political targets and the sociological reality. Each of us will live a life that turns out a particular way. That outcome will be the result of some things we can control, such as the choices we make and habits we cultivate, and some things we cannot control: how we fare in the genetic lottery of cognition, health, and attractiveness; the time and place we're born; the usefulness of the cultural starter kit we get from the family, ethnic group, and religion in which we're raised; and so on. It's impossible to make a tidy, confident distinction between what's in our control and what's beyond it.

But it certainly *seems*, given the epistemological impossibility of definitively apportioning causality between pluck and luck, better advice to emphasize the former than the latter. That is, individuals who dwell on or even exaggerate their ability to overcome, through discipline and determination, the obstacles in front of them are more likely to fashion lives well lived than those who dwell on or exaggerate the height of the mountains standing between them and their goals. Liberals work constantly to make us aware of the dangers of blaming people for things beyond their control. They're equally determined, though, to deny the opposite danger: giving people reasons and incentives to do less than they might to live successfully and admirably.

EMPATHY AFTER DALLAS

The admonition against blaming the victim is, on its own terms, re-
dundant. Victims are, by definition, not to blame for their plights.
The hard and important question is not whether to blame victims,
but to figure out whether and in what sense any particular sufferer
is a victim.

As I suggested in Chapter One, liberals' understanding of the
victimhood of victims was reshaped in the aftermath of President
Kennedy's assassination in 1963. Compassion had been an important element of liberalism since the New Deal, but one constrained
by other political considerations during the middle of the twentieth century. Journalist Joe Klein argues that the Roosevelt marriage was a microcosm of these political tensions. In 1941, as it
became increasingly doubtful America could avoid war with Germany, which had used aerial bombing against civilian population
centers in Europe, the president thought the Office of Civil Defense should attend to . . . civil defense: fire departments, air-raid
shelters, evacuation plans. The First Lady, Eleanor Roosevelt, who
spent four embarrassing months as the agency's assistant director,
thought morale boosting and social justice were equally important
to civil defense, and wanted to use some of the allocated funds for
public housing and day-care centers. When Congress rebuked her
by explicitly banning civil defense funds for "instruction in physi-
cal fitness by dancers," which was a pet project designed to impart
rhythmic training in order to keep children relaxed in air-raid
shelters, she resigned her position. Even a sympathetic biographer
called Mrs. Roosevelt's ideas about defense "absurdly broad" and
"naïve."[14]

Through the end of her life in 1962, the Eleanor tendency was
restrained by other facets of liberalism. Midcentury liberalism was,
as conservative author John O'Sullivan has argued, "meliorist,
pragmatic, patriotic, and problem-solving."[15] November 22, 1963,

marks the breaching of the walls that had confined and tempered liberal compassion.

It's not just that Kennedy's assassination was a terrible and shocking tragedy, but that liberals decided instantly and emphatically to make it a meaningful rather than a senseless tragedy. The facts, especially those about Lee Harvey Oswald's communist sympathies, were not allowed to get in the way of a good martyrdom. JFK died for civil rights, a cause to which he had been decidedly cool throughout his political career, and as a victim of right-wing extremism. James Reston of the *New York Times* wrote the day after the shooting that the president was a "victim of a violent streak he sought to curb." His death meant that "something in the nation itself, some strain of madness and violence, had destroyed the highest symbol of law and order." Chief Justice Earl Warren declared Kennedy had "suffered martyrdom as a result of the hatred and bitterness that has been injected into the life of our nation by bigots." Democratic Senate majority leader Mike Mansfield said that Kennedy had given his life so "there would be no room for the bigotry, the hatred, prejudice and the arrogance which converged in that moment of horror to strike him down."[16]

Fifty years have not sufficed to get liberals to abandon sophistries about right-wingers' guilt for Kennedy's death. In 2013 the *New Yorker*'s George Packer conceded that Oswald's avowed Marxism "might seem to absolve [Dallas's] right wing of any responsibility" for the assassination—but not really, of course. In fact, villains sent over by liberal central casting were to blame. Through a process of psychological osmosis, the "potent brew of right-wing passions . . . suffused many people in Dallas with the spirit of dissension and incipient violence during the early sixties. . . ." The fact that "Dallas was the last large American city to desegregate its schools" augments, somehow, its culpability in Kennedy's murder. In this context, according to Packer, Oswald was merely "a malleable, unstable figure breathing the city's extraordinarily feverish air."[17]

Liberals had gone into the 1960s declaring that America was in such great shape—thanks to liberalism itself, they boasted, which had secured prosperity, contained communism, and promoted racial harmony—that bold new improvements were attainable. After the inflection point of Dallas, it came out of the 1960s insisting that America was in such terrible shape that enacting, generously funding, and successfully implementing a maximally transformative liberal policy agenda was imperative if the country was to avert an imminent and deserved collapse.

Two of the most influential books on political economy published during America's extraordinary economic boom in the quarter century after World War II—John Kenneth Galbraith's *The Affluent Society* (1958) and Michael Harrington's *The Other America* (1962)—provided liberals a frame to appeal to voters' compassion in the same way charities appeal to donors' compassion. America was an affluent society where most people enjoyed greater wealth, better prospects, and more economic security than they had before. They were, indeed, better off than any people in any nation had ever been before. Not only were the terrible memories of the Great Depression receding, but politicians and commentators spoke expansively about how the acquisition of Keynesian tools for macroeconomic management ensured no such depression would ever happen again. Instead, affluent America could look forward confidently, almost complacently, to getting more and more affluent.

There were, however, stubborn "pockets of poverty" in the other America—urban slums, the hollows of Appalachia, and Indian reservations—not yet prospering from the rising tide that had lifted so many boats. The scandal of poverty in the midst of plenty conduced to an obvious solution: government programs would use an affluent society's affluence, redirecting a portion so small the prosperous majority would scarcely miss or even notice it, to lift the impoverished denizens of the other America into a nation rendered more unified and decent. "Today, for the first time in our history,"

President Johnson said in his 1964 message to Congress calling for a War on Poverty, "we have the power to strike away the barriers to full participation in our society. Having the power, we have the duty."[18]

Four years to the day after LBJ sent that message, Senator Robert Kennedy of New York declared his presidential candidacy, challenging Johnson for the 1968 Democratic nomination. He made clear during his brief, doomed campaign that one of the worst things about the war in Vietnam was that it deprived the War on Poverty of both fiscal resources and moral urgency. In his biography of RFK, Arthur Schlesinger notes approvingly that Kennedy decried the "madness" he encountered at a college campus in 1967 when a majority of the students in an audience favored more rather than less bombing in Vietnam. "Don't you understand that what we are doing to the Vietnamese is not very different than what Hitler did to the Jews?" Kennedy said.[19]

So brief and modest were the sacrifices required to eliminate poverty, as characterized by Johnson, that they barely qualified as burdens: "Our history has proved that each time we broaden the base of abundance, giving more people the chance to produce and consume, we create new industry, higher production, increased earnings and better income for all." Kennedy, by contrast, offered himself as a Savonarola who would summon affluent Americans to redeem themselves by renouncing their smug, callous self-indulgence. Campaigning in his first primary contest after entering the race, Kennedy found himself in a tense confrontation at the Indiana University medical school. A questioner in the audience for his speech asked, "Where are you going to get all the money for the federally subsidized programs you're talking about?" Kennedy looked at the "incipient M.D.'s about to enter lucrative careers," as Schlesinger described them, and said, "From you." He went on to tell the students:

Let me say something about the tone of these questions. . . .
You are the privileged ones here. It's easy to sit back and say it's
the fault of the federal government, but it's our responsibility
too. It's our society, not just our government, that spends twice
as much on pets as on the poverty program. It's the poor who
carry the major burden in Vietnam. You sit here as white medical students, while black people carry the burden of fighting in
Vietnam.

Leaving that campaign appearance, "shaking his head incredu-
lously," according to Schlesinger, Kennedy said to a reporter, "They
were so comfortable, so comfortable. Didn't you think they were
comfortable?" Three days later, at Valparaiso University, Kennedy
challenged students again: "You tell me something now. How many
of you spend time over the summer, or on vacations, working in a
black ghetto, or in Eastern Kentucky, or on an Indian reservation."
(Of Kennedy's undergraduate years, Schlesinger notes briefly, "His
Harvard life was the football field, the training table, the Varsity
Club.")[20]

This new outlook was, in both senses of the term, radically different from the way liberalism had presented itself from the New
Deal through the early 1960s. In that older conception, the purpose of the liberal enterprise was to enable America to fulfill its
historic and global potential. In characterizing that mission, liberal
politicians and intellectuals appealed to the national pride of citizens who regarded America as fundamentally and even singularly
decent. By the late 1960s, however, liberals declared, often stri-
dently, that America now stood revealed as a nation fundamentally
and even singularly depraved.

Nicholas Lemann wrote in 1998 that every president from
Truman to Carter "felt a twinge of terror" at the possibility of receiving Arthur Schlesinger's disapproval, since he so powerfully
shaped and expressed "the good opinion of the centrist-liberal es-

tablishment."[21] In 1968 Schlesinger gave a commencement address in which he called Americans "the most frightening people on this planet . . . because the atrocities we commit trouble so little our official self-righteousness, our invincible conviction of our moral infallibility." "It is almost as if a primal curse has been fixed on our nation," he said, "perhaps when we first began the practice of killing and enslaving those whom we deemed our inferiors because their skin was another color." As a result, "we can no longer regard hatred and violence as accidents, as nightmares, which will pass away when we awake. We must see them as organic in our national past. . . ." Schlesinger informed the graduates and their proud parents that Americans could begin to atone for their wickedness only by recognizing "that the evil is in us, that it springs from some dark, intolerable tension in our history and our institutions."[22]

The speech was, admittedly, given under great duress. Robert Kennedy, Schlesinger's friend, had been shot the night before in Los Angeles, hours after winning California's Democratic presidential primary, and lay mortally wounded in a hospital as Schlesinger stepped to the podium. But the fact that Schlesinger turned the speech into a magazine article later that year, then included it in a collection of his writings published in 1969, *The Crisis of Confidence*, suggests he did not regard the circumstances of its delivery as particularly extenuating. (Schlesinger had published a collection in 1962 titled *The Politics of Hope*.) Nor did the fact that Sirhan Sirhan's politics had no more to do with American race relations than did Lee Harvey Oswald's with right-wing Texans affect Schlesinger's interpretation of the tragedy's meaning.

The jeremiad, in any case, had become liberalism's preferred mode of expression by 1968. And with the change in tone had come a change in substance, altering how liberals characterized the victimhood of America's victims. The defining feature of America's empathizees, as interpreted by its most committed empathizers, was no longer that they were the victims of happenstance, such as a natural disaster. They were not even, as Eleanor Roosevelt liberals would have thought, victims of social conditions that a good society was earnestly striving to reform, ones it had not yet but would presently improve. Rather, America's victims were victims *of* America, of the crimes and depredations that were its defining characteristics, and with which a smug, deluded nation had never begun to reckon until disenthralled liberals and New Leftists insisted on this searing honesty. Under these radically reinterpreted circumstances, the helpers had no moral leverage to exert against the helpless. It was, instead, the victims who possessed all the moral leverage against the victimizers: only massively intensified empathy could begin to atone for and repay the debt owed by the "privileged ones" to the underprivileged ones. The moral logic of compassion gave way to the moral fervor of guilt and redemption.

THE WHITE MAN'S BURDEN OF PROOF

Liberal guilt was, above all, white liberal guilt because, as the remarks by Robert Kennedy and Arthur Schlesinger indicate, whites' treatment of blacks came to be considered America's original sin. The moral power of this argument was quickly discerned by feminists, Hispanics, American Indians, homosexuals, and the physically disabled, whose movements rested on arguments that their constituents suffered from oppression fundamentally similar to white racism.

The passionate commitment to this idea makes its difficult to recall there was an earlier epoch, now highly embarrassing, when the liberal conscience was not particularly troubled by racial disparities and injustices. The progressives of a century ago, influenced by Darwin, were strongly inclined to ascribe disparities among racial and ethnic groups to innate differences. One of the most important progressive intellectuals, Richard T. Ely, founder of the American

Economic Association, wrote in 1898 that blacks are "for the most part grown-up children, and should be treated as such." Regarding, more generally, classes of people he considered inferior, Ely wrote in 1922, "We must give to the most hopeless classes left behind in our social progress custodial care with the highest possible development and with segregation of the sexes and confinement to prevent reproduction."[23]

American whites who sincerely believed they had blacks' best interests at heart did not have to traffic in eugenics to take positions that astound today. The feminist and social reformer Charlotte Perkins Gilman, for example, wrote "A Suggestion on the Negro Problem" for the *American Journal of Sociology* in 1904. It asks, "What can we do to promote the development of the backward race so that it may become an advantageous element in the community?" The urgency of that problem derives from "the unavoidable presence of a large body of aliens, of a race widely dissimilar and in many respects inferior, whose present status is to us a social injury. If we had left them alone in their own country this dissimilarity and inferiority would be, so to speak, none of our business." But we didn't, and so must make the best of the situation created by slavery, the subsequent decision that slavery was morally and practically untenable, followed by the "consummate mishandling" of the integration of freed slaves and their descendants into American society.

Fortunately, there are reasons to be encouraged. "The African race, with the advantage of contact with our more advanced stage of evolution, has made more progress in a few generations than any other race has ever done in the same time, except the Japanese." To accelerate this progress, Gilman proposes to "carefully organize in every county and township an enlisted body of all negroes below a certain grade of citizenship," so that "the whole body of negroes who do not progress, who are not self-supporting, who are degenerating into an increasing percentage of social burdens or actual criminals should be taken hold of by the state." The men, women, and children enlisted in this "new army" will take pride in "its uniforms, its decorations, its titles, its careful system of grading, its music and banners and impressive ceremonies."

The "army's" goal would be to render itself unnecessary, but only, it seems, after first being rendered mandatory: "As fast as any individuals proved themselves capable of working on their own initiative they would be graduated with honor. This institution should be compulsory at the bottom, perfectly free at the top." Ultimately, "Every negro graduated would be better fitted to take his place in the community," while "[e]very negro unable to graduate would remain under wise supervision. . . ." Blacks, in short, would be treated as wards of the state as they served a kind of apprentice citizenship. While awaiting clearance for full participation in the nation's civic and economic life, they would be given "proper food, suitable hours of work, rest, and amusement; without the strain of personal initiative and responsibility to which so many have proved unequal. . . ."[24]

Gilman's rationale is that of the colonialist: the more civilized have a duty to uplift the less civilized, and therefore a right to protect them from the consequences of their barbarism. Arguments like hers and Ely's show the perils of recommending compassionate policies on the basis of sufferers' helplessness. In particular, empathizers who generalize from children's needs and limitations can wind up infantilizing empathizees. The helpless, by virtue *of* their helplessness, don't know how to get *beyond* their helplessness. The helpers do, though, and through solicitous feelings and actions will spare the helpless "the strain of personal initiative and responsibility."

Such sentiments have not disqualified Gilman from becoming a hero to modern feminists—in 1994 she was inducted into the National Women's Hall of Fame, located in Seneca Falls, New York. Gilman expressed the consensus of her time and peers, as did liberals in subsequent decades who betrayed no evidence of thinking that racial justice required anything more from whites than the social reformer's noblesse oblige and "wise supervision." According to historian David Kennedy, President Franklin Roosevelt did "precious little . . . to improve the lot of black Americans," preferring to spend political capital on establishing the New Deal, and then on winning World War II.[25]

Civil rights gained new salience after the war, prompting Strom Thurmond's "Dixiecrats" to walk out of the 1948 Democratic convention. But the Democratic presidential nominee in 1952 and 1956, Adlai Stevenson, was decidedly lukewarm about the issue, not just as a matter of political calculation but out of personal preference. He selected an Alabama segregationist, John Sparkman, to be his running mate in 1952, and gave a speech that denounced "the reckless assertions that the South is a prison, in which half the people are prisoners and the other half are wardens." In private communications, write historians Abigail and Stephan Thernstrom, "Stevenson worried about the 'extremism' of 'Negro leaders' and fumed about 'NAACP stubbornness.'"[26] What's striking is that such attitudes did nothing to prevent Stevenson from being the liberal hero of the same decade that also saw *Brown v. Board of Education* and the Montgomery bus boycott. Instead, "He became the favorite of, and drew into Democratic volunteer efforts, cadres of youngish, highly educated professionals and intellectuals," in the words of Michael Barone.[27]

A dispassionate approach marked liberal thinking about race into the early 1960s, when the "tough, pragmatic tendency" inside the Democratic Party held sway against a more urgent concern with social justice. Nicholas Lemann notes that Senator John Kennedy, anticipating a presidential campaign, "voted with his Southern colleagues to put an amendment into the Civil Rights Act of 1957 that guaranteed jury trials (that is, certain acquittal) to people accused of violating blacks' voting rights." As for the growing number of blacks who had left the South for northern cities, the 1960 Kennedy campaign treated them as just one more ethnic voting bloc, "not people with special problems and a unique moral claim on the government's help."[28]

President Kennedy continued to engage the civil rights issue warily during his brief presidency. When he gave a televised address on the subject in June 1963, he appealed to racially neutral criteria of justice. "The heart of the question is whether all Americans are to be afforded equal rights and equal opportunities, whether we are going to treat our fellow Americans as we want to be treated." JFK explicitly stipulated the importance of reciprocity. "We have a right to expect that the Negro community will be responsible, will uphold the law, but they have a right to expect that the law will be fair, that the Constitution will be color blind. . . ."[29] Within three years, Vice President Hubert Humphrey would say of the slums and riots, "If I lived in such conditions, I could lead a mighty good revolt myself."[30]

Others went farther. When whites' sins of commission and omission were reckoned to be so horrific as to preclude atonement, so damaging as to dwarf any possible reconciliation, liberal compassion turned into liberal guilt, and then into self-contempt. In 1967 the literary critic Susan Sontag wrote, "Mozart, Pascal, Boolean algebra, Shakespeare, parliamentary government, baroque churches, Newton, the emancipation of women, Kant, Balanchine ballets, *et al.* don't redeem what this particular civilization has wrought upon the world." Taking that era's condemnation of America's policies in Vietnam jungles and inner-city slums to its logical conclusion, she argued:

> The white race is the cancer of human history; it is the white race and it alone—its ideologies and inventions—which eradicates autonomous civilizations wherever it spreads, which has upset the ecological balance of the planet, which now threatens the

very existence of life itself. What the Mongol hordes threaten is far less frightening than the damage that Western "Faustian" man, with his idealism, his magnificent art, his sense of intellectual adventure, his world-devouring energies for conquest, has already done, and further threatens to do.[31]

Sontag would later qualify this remark by saying she had been unfair . . . to cancer patients. Her accusation offered no path to salvation, either through faith or good works. "This is a doomed country," she wrote. "I only pray that when America founders, it doesn't drag the rest of the planet down, too."[32]

Sontag's formulation was more strident than the one put forward by the National Advisory Commission on Civil Disorders (the "Kerner Commission") in 1968, but shared a similar political orientation. "Segregation and poverty have created in the racial ghetto a destructive environment totally unknown to most white Americans," the report stated. "What white Americans have never fully understood but what the Negro can never forget—is that white society is deeply implicated in the ghetto. White institutions created it, white institutions maintain it, and white society condones it." Upon examining race riots in the summers of 1965, '66, and '67, the commission stated that without "a commitment to national action—compassionate, massive and sustained," requiring "unprecedented levels of funding and performance" for programs that "produce quick and visible progress" in black inner-city neighborhoods, the riots would continue and intensify. One did not need to read between the lines very intently to gather that the failure to commit to the agenda of massive compassion would render future riots not only impossible to prevent, but impossible to deplore.

The Kerner Commission report proved to be highly questionable, both as a sociological analysis and as a political manifesto. Its reduction of American race relations to the proposition that white racism causes black riots disregarded abundant evidence that would, at least, complicate this narrative. The commission ignored some obvious questions: "why liberal Detroit blew up while Birmingham and other southern cities—where conditions for blacks were infinitely worse—did not," as Stephan Thernstrom asked on the report's thirtieth anniversary. "Likewise, if the problem was white racism, why didn't the riots occur in the 1930s, when prevailing white racial attitudes were far more barbaric than they were in the 1960s?"[33]

The Kerner Commission made the same political calculation as Robert Kennedy, who started his presidential campaign less than three weeks after the report on the rioting was released. Both hoped that white fear and guilt would compound the political force of compassion, a calculation that presupposed the moral credits blacks had amassed through centuries of slavery and discrimination were inexhaustible. This assessment was less implausible during the most heroic days of the civil rights era than it had become by 1968, following the rise of the Black Power movement and the long, hot summers the Kerner Commission examined. As it turned out, the political challenge of convincing whites they had an enormous, unqualified obligation to help blacks became harder, not easier, after television news coverage of riots in Los Angeles, Newark, Detroit, and other cities showed blacks helping themselves—to groceries, furniture, and television sets carried away from looted stores.

MINIMIZERS AND MAXIMIZERS

It seems, then, that getting compassion right—determining and then discharging empathizers' moral and political obligations to empathizees—is necessarily bound up with assessments about empathizees' capacity and duty to help themselves. We can express the moral equation this way: if X is the amount of goods/services/opportunities/purchasing power we think people need and deserve;

and Y is the amount we think they can and should be able to secure through their own efforts; then X - Y = Z, the amount a decent, compassionate society is obligated to provide for them, assuming it has the practical capacity to meet that obligation. The question of how much and what exactly X comprises will be contested, of course. Even those who agree with Adam Smith about the necessity of possessing no less than would be shameful for the lowest rank of people in a particular time and place, may disagree about what exactly that means. In one sense, then, the absolute value of Y and Z will always fluctuate with the prevailing ideas about X. For any given X, however, Y and Z will always be in a perfect zero-sum relation: The more we think people can and should do for themselves, the less we think we ought to do for them. Conversely, the less we expect people to do on their own, the more we think should be done for them.

To argue for a larger Z, more government support for the poor, which liberals have done every day since the start of the New Deal, necessarily commits them to the proposition that it's unrealistic and unfair to expect too much Y, individuals' efforts to alleviate their own suffering. To the campaign ongoing since the 1930s to insist on the helplessness of sufferers, liberals in the 1960s added the contention that large classes of sufferers could not be justly expected to help themselves. The understanding before Dallas was that it was unfair, because unrealistic, to expect the poor to do very much to overcome their poverty. Compassion dictated a generous welfare state because the poor lacked the practical capacity to help themselves. The understanding after Dallas was that compassion dictated a *really* generous welfare state because Americans who weren't poor lacked the moral capacity to tell the poor to help themselves, since the poor *were* poor as a result of what had been done to them, rather than because of anything they had failed to do for themselves. Marian Wright Edelman's strategic decision in 1973 to make children rather than blacks the face of victimhood argues that these different imperatives can be emphasized or deemphasized as political circumstances dictate.

In either case, though, empathizers relate to empathizees in terms of how little the former can expect of the latter. There are good reasons to doubt that this is a healthy relationship, or to the benefit of either party. If the poor are not to be blamed for their poverty, then the dispositions and habits that have done the most throughout human history to lift people *from* poverty end up discarded and scorned. This amounts to a compassionate formula to keep the objects of our compassion permanently dependent and aggrieved.

To regard the perpetuation of dependency as a problem presupposes the ultimate goal of the politics of kindness is for as many of the poor as possible to become *formerly* poor, and do so through their own efforts rather than be propped up indefinitely like Britain's Susan Moore. This may not be a safe assumption, as one of compassion's risks is politicized codependence. "The aim of liberal government should be not to increase the incidence of compassion but to reduce the opportunity for it," Mickey Kaus found it necessary to remind *New Republic* readers. "Compassion isn't politics. . . . Charity is a noble impulse. But it is not the relation of free, equal citizens."[34]

Empathizers who get to feel like good people because of their empathy, however, may prefer to regard empathizees' sufferings as chronic conditions to be managed rather than transitory ones to be solved. "Pity is about how deeply I can feel," Elshtain argued. "And in order to feel this way, to experience the rush of my own pious reaction, I need victims the way an addict needs drugs."[35]

Assessing Bill Clinton's presidency as it was ending, economist Glenn Loury (a onetime Reagan conservative who moved to the left of Third Way Democrats during the 1990s) lamented that because of the 1996 welfare law, "the conservative distinction between 'deserving' and 'undeserving' poor people has now been written into national policy—and by a Democratic Administration." Under Clinton,

> [t]he Democrats' mantra became "If you work hard and play by the rules, you shouldn't be poor." But where does that leave the great number of people who are unable (or unwilling) to "work hard and play by the rules"? By implication, they (and their children) deserve to be poor.[36]

According to Loury, the difference between being poor because you're unable to work and being poor because you're unwilling to work is, literally, parenthetical. Such thinking is Rawlsian in the sense it places *every* quality that can affect the trajectory of our lives behind the veil of ignorance. No one deserves to be ugly or beautiful, sick or healthy, stupid or smart. Even qualities we believe integral to moral character—such as industry, honesty, and judiciousness—do not reveal who we are but depend on such contingencies of social circumstance as how we were raised and socialized. Those who had the unmerited good fortune to grow up in stable, loving families, attend good schools, and belong to nurturing communities have the inside track to the acquisition of habits and dispositions that will serve them well throughout their lives, not least by eliciting the admiration of others. Conversely, no one deserves to grow up in a dysfunctional or abusive family, attend crappy schools, and be raised on mean streets. The shortcomings we discern in the products of those environments reflect forces that have worked on them from the outside in, rather than facets of character that manifest themselves from the inside out.

But exempting the poor from otherwise widely applicable standards of conduct, like sparing them the strain of personal initiative and responsibility, calls into question how there can be moral agents in the pews capable of being inspired or abashed by liberals' sermons. Being diligent and sober isn't to A's credit, just a reflection of the good hand he happens to have been dealt. Similarly, B can't be blamed for being a lazy drunk, because those qualities reflect the bad hand *he* was dealt. It would seem to follow that whether any of us is empathetic or stone-hearted regarding others' travails is simply the result of accidents of our natural endowment and the contingencies of our social circumstances. Some people, by virtue of disposition and upbringing, lie awake at night, distraught, as their thoughts turn to hungry children in distant countries. Other people, also as a result of forces having no relation to their moral worth, sleep peacefully despite knowing of acute suffering in their own city.

But the whole point of liberalism is that people *are* capable of being swayed—by reason, evidence, and an inexhaustible stockpile of sad stories—to vote for liberal measures and politicians. Liberalism seeks to give government the "vibrant personal character that is the very embodiment of human charity." This principle was put forward not in an arid philosophical treatise, but in a politician's campaign speech—specifically, Franklin Roosevelt's acceptance speech at the 1936 Democratic convention.[37]

Liberals are wasting their time and everyone else's if people are incapable of being moved, persuaded, and galvanized by admonitions to be more compassionate. And liberalism is vindictive, not righteous, if it stigmatizes people for insensitivity that results from their accidents of natural endowment and contingencies of social circumstance. Being "appalled" by Mitt Romney's "inability to empathize with people who are less advantaged than he is," as was one journalist who denounced the Republican presidential nominee, makes no sense if Romney's empathetic shortcomings manifest genetic or biographical causes over which he had no control.[38]

Liberalism presupposes, then, that people are capable of responding to compassionate appeals, and can be justly blamed and criticized if they fail to heed them. One kind of exhortation is worth making, then, and a corresponding moral shortcoming worth deploring. But if one, why not others? If it is possible to induce and expect people to be more compassionate in order to alleviate the suffering of others, it should also be possible to induce and expect people to be more disciplined, responsible, and provident to prevent and alleviate their own suffering.

THE BURDEN OF NOT BEING JUDGED

The question of self-reliance affects the relationship between empathizers and empathizees in a further way. If compassion rules out expecting much from those who suffer, then the moral and political leverage that empathizees wield against those who feel sorry for them will come to depend on their own incapacity. This correlation of moral forces operates with particular strength when empathizers and empathizees unite in the belief that the historic grievances of those who suffer preclude anyone else from calling on them to be self-reliant. The basic choice open to blacks after the landmark legislation and court decisions of the civil rights era, according to the Hoover Institution's Shelby Steele, was between advancing "through education, skill development, and entrepreneurialism," or "pressuring the society that had wronged us into taking the lion's share of the responsibility for resurrecting us." The second course became all but inevitable when the post–civil rights narrative of white guilt and black victimhood decreed "that no black problem—whether high crime rates, poor academic performance, or high illegitimacy rates—could be defined as largely a black responsibility, because it was an injustice to make victims responsible for their own problems."[39]

And with that choice came the imperative not to let whites off the hook, not to do or say anything that would encourage whites to believe that black problems were black responsibilities, not white ones. In 2013, after George Zimmerman's acquittal in the killing of Trayvon Martin, for example, the question of race and crime was debated vehemently. One writer, John McWhorter, a black professor of literature at Columbia, took to *Time* magazine's website to rebut those who "pretend that the association of young black men with violence comes out of thin air."[40] The evidence is, indeed, unambiguous. "Homicide Trends in the United States, 1980–2008," issued by the U.S. Department of Justice's Bureau of Justice Statistics, shows clearly that Murder Inc. is not an equal opportunity employer. It discriminates against the aged: people under the age of 35 committed 76.5 percent of all murders in that twenty-nine-year span, though they accounted for 47.3 percent of the national population in the 2010 census. It discriminates against women: males accounted for 89.5 percent of all "homicide offenders" between 1980 and 2008, but were 49.2 percent of the population in 2010. And it discriminates against whites: blacks accounted for 52.5 percent of homicide offenders despite being 12.6 percent of the population in 2010. In particular, the report found that white males between the ages of 14 and 24 accounted for 6 percent of the national population in 2008 but 16 percent of the population of homicide offenders. They were, then, 2.67 times as likely to commit a murder as they would be if homicide offenders were drawn randomly from the overall population. Young black males that year accounted for 1 percent of the national population but 27 percent of all homicide offenders, making them 27 times more likely to commit a homicide than a random selection would predict, or 10.1 times more likely than their white peers.[41]

One website comment on McWhorter's article allowed that its thesis—"the black community has failed to confront fully the behavioral problems within its own ranks, including violence perpetrated by young males"—is "a valid one," since "individuals and groups should address their own shortcomings before rushing to condemn the failings of others." The problem was not with the argument but with the effect it would have. "*Time* readers are mainly white," and are likely to react to the article "by thinking, 'McWhorter confirms what I've always thought—it's all their fault. They have to change. I don't have to.'"[42]

Any political cause that has arrived at the determination that the truth will set you back needs to consider its predicament carefully. The logic of compassion and victimhood transforms weakness into strength, as sufferers' greatest power becomes their capacity to rebuke and intimidate those held to have immiserated and then neglected them. Because self-discipline and self-reliance, along with candor about the power of these qualities to alleviate suffering, undercut this message, they amount to disloyalty within the afflicted group. The sort of loyalty that viewpoint compels, however, makes empathizees that much more dependent on empathizers' compassion and guilt, that much less likely to take the steps to advance and flourish regardless of how sorry other people feel for them.

Southfield, Michigan, is a suburb north of Detroit, separated from the city by Eight Mile Road (the one made famous in 2002 by the Eminem movie, *8 Mile*). After the housing market crash of 2008, black Detroit residents began moving to Southfield, not only to take advantage of its reduced housing costs, but to get away from the deteriorating city's quality of life. "The kids are running around without any control," one worker in an auto factory told Corey Williams of the Associated Press about his reasons for leaving Detroit. "They walk down the middle of the street and block traffic. There was gunfire at night. It was a common thing to hear gunfire."[43]

Many residents who had been established in Southfield for years were less than welcoming. Part of their reaction was simple economics. Newcomers were buying houses at prices steeply discounted from ones that had prevailed a few years earlier. Foreclosed homes that could not be sold were rented, and sometimes subdivided, increasing the proportion of Southfield residents with a renter's tenuous investment in, and attachment to, the community. It's "not my fault you paid $250,000 and I paid a buck," said a man who moved from Detroit in 2008 when he bought a foreclosed house for $109,000, one that had previously sold for $220,000.

But property values are not easily disentangled from civic values. A printer who moved to Southfield in 1988 said, "The reason suburbs are the way they are is because a certain element can't afford to live in your community. If you have $300,000, $400,000, $500,000 homes you're relatively secure in the fact that (the homeowners) are people who can afford it." Some of his long-established neighbors were less circumspect in complaining about that certain element. "During the summer months, I sat in the garage and at 3 o'clock in the morning you see them walking up and the down the streets on their cell phones talking," a retired autoworker said. "They pull up (in cars) in the middle of the street, and they'll hold a conversation. You can't get in your driveway. You blow the horn and they look back at you and keep on talking. That's all Detroit." Regarding the new arrivals, Southfield's police chief Joseph Thomas said sternly, "They still think it's okay to play basketball at three o'clock in the morning; it's okay to play football in the streets when there's a car coming; it's okay to walk down the streets three abreast. That's unacceptable in this city."

But for one detail, Southfield's problems would fit right into a 1970s after-school special about uptight, bigoted white suburbanites disdaining and thwarting blacks who were merely seeking a better quality of life. That one detail, however, is important: the police chief and long-established Southfield residents Williams interviewed were black themselves. Southfield's population was 54 percent black and 39 percent white in 2000, according to the Census Bureau, shifting to 70 percent black and 25 percent white by 2010. "It's not a black-white thing," Chief Thomas said of his city's tensions in the 2011 article. "This is a black-black thing. My six-figure blacks are very concerned about multiple-family, economically depressed people moving into rental homes and apartments, bringing in their bad behaviors." Two of the black residents interviewed in the story, who had left Detroit years ago to get away from its bad behaviors, tell Williams they're considering leaving Southfield before the behaviors *there* get any worse, even if relocating means selling their homes at a loss.

The long-established black residents of Southfield who disapprove of the conduct of the blacks recently arrived from Detroit cannot be guilty of racism. But they must, for the sake of liberal coherence, be guilty of something. If *they* warily denigrate the bad behaviors of the "element" moving from the inner city, and speak candidly about being so determined to move away from this element that they're prepared to wipe out all their home equity as grimly motivated sellers, it becomes harder to accuse whites of racism for the same opinions and actions.

If not racism, then the transgression must be "classism within the black community," according to Sheryll Cashin, a Georgetown law professor quoted in the news article. Poor blacks "have developed their own culture, one that is very different from mainstream America," she says, and middle-class blacks are as obligated as middle-class whites to get past their objections to that culture. Indeed, the imperative of racial solidarity leaves them more obligated. "To the higher income black people, if you don't want to love and help your lower-income black brethren, why would you expect white people to?" Cashin asks. "You can try to flee or you can be part of the solution."

Her position is like Robert Putnam's: mainstream America's obligation is to form a new us, one that repudiates the qualities that made it mainstream, in order not to discomfit those who want to join the mainstream while continuing to think and live in opposition to its norms. And her position is like McWhorter's commenter in assuming that, after the civil rights era, the ultimate prize on which blacks should keep their eyes is white solicitude. Any black words or deeds that might be construed to mean whites'

guilt has been expiated, whites' obligations discharged, are betray-
als. Victimhood means that the victimized group's socioeconomic
status depends heavily on two big variables: how badly they've been
treated by mainstream America, and how strenuously mainstream
America tries to make amends.

The inadequacy of this equation was conveyed, inadvertently,
by the *Atlantic*'s Ta-Nehisi Coates in a 2013 blog post, "A Rising
Tide Lifts Mostly Yachts." Using a chart based on Census Bureau
data, it showed how little median household incomes disparities
had changed among America's racial groups over the preceding
forty years. Specifically, it showed that in 2012 the median household income for blacks was 41.6 percent lower than that for non-
Hispanic whites, and Hispanics' median household income was
31.6 percent lower. It also showed, however, though the accompa-
nying article did not discuss it, that Asians had a median household
income 20.4 percent larger than non-Hispanic whites. If discrimination were determinative, one might expect (after stipulating that
Asians have suffered less severe discrimination) that Asians would
be doing better than blacks and Hispanics. One would not expect,
however, they would be doing better than the majority group that
had discriminated against them.[44]

The frequency with which groups, throughout history and
around the world, have flourished despite having been oppressed,
often quite brutally, reinforces the notion that it's better to err on
the side of overestimating our ability to shape our destinies than
to err on the side of overestimating the power of the forces stacked
against us. If discrimination explained most of what we need to
know about disparities among various groups, it should be quite
unusual to find such victimized groups possessing a dispropor-
tionately large amount of life's good things and a disproportion-
ately small amount of the bad ones. In fact, as Hoover Institution
economist Thomas Sowell points out, people of Chinese ancestry
have been and continue to be targets of discrimination throughout

Southeast Asia. Yet in Malaysia, Indonesia, Vietnam, Thailand, and the Philippines, "the Chinese minority—about 5 percent of the population of southeast Asia—owns a majority of the nation's total investments in key industries. By the middle of the twentieth century, the Chinese owned 75 percent of the rice mills in the Philippines, and between 80 and 90 percent of the rice mills in Thailand." Looking at America, Sowell notes, "Japanese immigrants to the United States also encountered persistent and escalating discrimination, culminating in their mass internment during World War II, but by 1959 they had about equaled the income of whites and by 1969 Japanese American families were earning nearly one-third higher incomes than the average American family."[45]

There are *no* clear counterexamples: groups that have acquired significant, durable social and economic advantages by feeling sorry for themselves, or by inducing other, more powerful groups to feel sorry for and guilty about them. What such groups secure, instead, is the "advantage" of being dependent on the kindness of strangers, an advantage that debilitates individuals struggling to build lives and communities on sturdier foundations. The implicit moral baseline against which liberals condemn white American racism against minority groups is, like Plato's Republic, a city in speech. In that hypothetical nation, people of different races, creeds, and ethnicities have a long history of harmonious, mutually respectful relations. Every subset of the population—from the corporate boardroom to the faculty lounge, unemployment line, or prison yard—is a demographic miniature of the entire society.

No such society has ever existed, and the wisdom of treating that baseline as a yardstick or goal is highly doubtful. The most profound causes of differences among ethnic or racial groups are not, Sowell argues, social injustices but *cosmic* injustices. It isn't fair, if the term even applies sensibly, that sub-Saharan Africa, surrounded by vast oceans and a desert as big as the continental United States, has few natural harbors or navigable rivers. Its inhabitants, as a result, had limited contact with people from other continents, as well as with one another, and therefore limited access to civilizational advances. (With only a tenth of the world's population Africa has a third of the world's languages.) To take another consequential but amoral happenstance, Europe and Asia had horses and oxen. Until Europeans brought them in the sixteenth century, North and South America did not, a basic difference that profoundly affected agriculture, commerce, warfare, prosperity, and the cultural advances prosperity makes possible. Being conquered by Rome was no picnic, but the parts of Europe that were incorporated into the Roman Empire acquired an alphabet and a written language centuries before the parts that weren't, giving them an enormous head start compared to the peoples whose ancestors had never encountered the Roman legions. None of the resulting advantages and disadvantages from any of these historical or geographical circumstances are "fair," but any project to scrub the world clean of all such cosmic injustices falls on a spectrum between the quixotic and the apocalyptic.[46]

SELFISH SELF-RELIANCE

Compassion's imperatives, as understood by liberals, militate against self-reliance. So far, I've discussed how this prohibition affects relations between empathizers and empathizees, or within the ranks of empathizees. It also, however, complicates life within the subset of the population who see their role as empathizing rather than being empathized with.

After 2012's Hurricane Sandy, *New York Times* columnist Nicholas Kristof deplored the growing number of homeowners who acquired and used standby generators to provide electricity when the power grid failed. Better, he said, that Americans, especially wealthy ones, pay higher taxes that could be used to make electrical service more reliable (as well as cleaner, to mitigate the global warming that allegedly caused Sandy) than to spend some of their less encumbered after-tax incomes on generators that benefit only a single household. The same antisocial self-reliance, he complains, leads Americans who can afford it to move to gated communities rather than support the taxes needed for good policing, enroll their children in private schools rather than pay for good public ones, and buy their own books and magazines (and *Times* subscriptions?) rather than support public libraries. Again and again, he complains, "we see the decline of public services accompanied by the rise of private workarounds for the wealthy."[47]

Kristof is blasé about selfishness compared to *Slate*'s Allison Benedikt, who admonished her readers in 2013, "You are a bad person if you send your children to private school. Not bad like *murderer* bad—but bad like *ruining-one-of-our-nation's-most-essential-institutions-in-order-to-get-what's-best-for-your-kid* bad. So, pretty bad." Benedikt doesn't go as far as Marian Wright Edelman or Melissa Harris-Perry in urging us to jettison the distinction between our own children and other people's. It's OK to care for your own kids, that is, but empathy demands recognition of the certain fact that other parents care for theirs. The only decent way to act on this knowledge is to channel your concern for your own child into collective actions that will help all children, forswearing individual solutions that will benefit your child while facilitating neglect for other people's. "Everyone needs to be invested in our public schools in order for them to get better," Benedikt states. "Whatever you think your children need—deserve—from their school experience, assume that the parents at the nearby public housing complex want the same. . . . Send your kids to school with their kids."[48]

"We need a moral adjustment," Benedikt believes, "not a legislative one," so she opposes outlawing private schools. This makes her a diffident opponent of private schools compared to her *Slate* colleague Matthew Yglesias, who not only agrees that sending children to such schools is shameful, but believes continuing their tax-exempt status is "outrageous."[49] In stopping short of advocating the abolition of any alternative to public education both Benedikt and Yglesias are squishes compared to John Cook (who happens to be Benedikt's husband), a proponent of "forcibly transferring ownership of all existing private schools to the school district in which they reside." Though his prescription is the most radical, Cook's diagnosis is the same: "Wealthy people tend to lobby effectively for their interests, and if their interests were to include adequate public funding for the schools their children attend, and libraries, and air-conditioning, those goals could likely be achieved without having to resort to unpleasant things like teachers' strikes." Cook has not, thus far, extended this logic to conscripting millionaires to live in public housing projects. "Radical inequality" may be "OK for adults," he allows, but "when it comes to children, it's perverse to dole out educations based on arbitrary circumstances completely beyond their control.[50]

Thus does twenty-first-century liberalism reconcile, in a manner very different from eighteenth-century liberalism, private interests and the public welfare. The old civic architecture arranged for ambition to counteract ambition, thereby supplying the defect of better motives. The new civic architecture fuses ambitions. The defect of better motives is to be overcome by condemning or prohibiting practices through which people seek to advance the interests of their own families, unless those actions are of a sort that advances the interests of all families similarly situated.

Even when parents try to do what Kristof and Benedikt consider the right thing, however, this regrettable penchant to care especially for one's own children keeps posing problems. New York City's Public School 163, on Manhattan's Upper West Side, offers both General Education and Gifted and Talented programs to its students, pre-kindergarten through the fifth grade. Of the 652 students enrolled in 2013, according to the *New York Times*, some 63 percent are black and Hispanic, 27 percent are white, and 6 percent are Asian. Of the 205 children in gifted classes, however, 47 percent are white, 15 percent are Asian, and 32 percent are black and Hispanic. By contrast, only 18 percent of the 447 students in the school's other classes are white.[51]

Those Upper West Side parents with fond memories of Lester Maddox may be untroubled by such disparities, but they're a source of distress to others. One P.S. 163 teacher told the *Times* that "there's no way I'd put my kid in a general-education class here, no way, because it's right next to the project and all the kids in general education come from the projects." In her experience, "many of the children in her general education classes were at grade level or below and did not get the same support from their parents that the children in the gifted classes got. 'They're tougher kids,' she said of the general education students in the school."

According to the *Times*, "several parents and teachers wondered whether white parents would stay if not for the gifted classes." One parent, who "requested anonymity for fear of reprisals," said, "I don't see any white families coming to register their children for general education. They come straight to gifted and talented." Another parent, who also "did not want to be identified for fear of animosity from other parents," explained the selection of P.S. 163 and its advanced program:

> I guess it is a question of, "How much diversity do you feel comfortable with?" Do I want him to be the only white kid in an all-black school? No. Would I like it if the racial mix was more proportionate? Yes, whatever the percentage of the makeup. That's an honest answer, from my soul. Is it hypocritical for parents to say, "We're sending our kids to public school," but they're sending them to an all-white gifted and talented program? But it's not our fault. We want the best for our children.[52]

Are you a bad person—not murderer bad, but still worthy of loathing and self-loathing bad—if you send your children to a public school, but then maneuver to get them into one of its academically challenging but demographically disproportionate programs? Wouldn't truly compassionate parents insist that *all* students not only go to public schools but receive the same education there, even if it meant their own children would study with tougher kids from the projects reading at grade level or below? A political persuasion that leads those who endorse it to apologize—anonymously, for fear of reprisal—about wanting the best for their children has two options. It can either become a cult that demands its members devote themselves to self-abnegation, or reassess whether the reconciliation of interest and duty it has formulated is either as morally compelling or as realistic as its adherents have long supposed.

WITH LIBERTY AND COMPASSION FOR ALL

I have, so far, not only relied on the distinction between empathizers and empathizees in assessing the politics of kindness, but treated that distinction as one with a clear boundary upon which all agree. That stipulation, though analytically useful for certain purposes, is also clearer than the truth. A better understanding of liberal compassion requires attending to the fact that the citizenry is *not* neatly divided between those who feel sorry and those who are felt sorry for.

This ambiguity is especially important in a democracy. One way to assemble a governing majority in such a polity would be if sufferers, united by the demand for policies to alleviate their suffering, constituted a majority of the voters, and refused to let any other political consideration distract them from voting on the basis of that one, overriding interest. This is the logic that governed the political career of Huey Long or Venezuela's Hugo Chavez. The compassion operative in such political calculations would be the solidarity of the suffering majority, motivated to secure what it believes it is rightfully owed and has been wrongfully denied. Empathy from others may be appreciated or resented but will not alter the movement's goals or progress toward them.

Since its founding in 1865, every issue of the *Nation* magazine has heralded the imminent arrival of a Chavez-like majority coalition of America's dispossessed, but the United States continues to dismay those who harbor such hopes. In 1932, when the unemployment rate was 25 percent according to some economists' retrospective estimates, the socialist presidential candidate, Norman Thomas, received 2.2 percent of the popular vote, and all other leftist parties combined for another 0.5 percent. Despite FDR's rhetorical invocations of altruism, and Eleanor Roosevelt's fusion of politics and social work, the New Deal coalition depended more on self-sufficiency, collectively pursued, than on compassion. Labor union activists in that era spoke of "rescuing" members "from demoralization at the hands of sentimental almsgivers."[53]

The greatest New Deal achievement, the Social Security Act of 1935, was structured and promoted as social insurance, a more encompassing version of private insurance but operating on the same principles. Benefits, accordingly, were paid for reasons having nothing to do with pity or charity. As Vincent Miles, a member of the original Social Security board, explained in a 1936 speech, Social Security benefits will be paid "by the United States Government in monthly checks—like the installments on annuities from an insurance company." And, "Like an insurance company policy, the worker's old-age benefit from the Government must be paid for in advance. Instead of weekly, monthly, quarterly, or yearly premiums, however, the Government collects weekly or monthly payments which are called taxes."[54] Another Social Security architect, J. Douglas Brown, spelled out the insurance paradigm's political rationale in a 1955 speech celebrating the program's twentieth anniversary:

The first and foremost element in our philosophy of social insurance, is that the system must provide protection as a matter of
right and not as a benevolence of a government, an institution
or an employer. In establishing social insurance, our Federal and
State governments reversed the presumption that a payment to
an eligible individual was a generous act of mercy by a sovereign,
to the presumption that such a payment, under social insurance,
was the honest fulfillment of a contract between citizen and
state.[55]

Eight decades of social insurance in America have demon-
strated that benefits constantly outpace the "contributions" set aside
and supposedly sufficient to pay for them. The programs were explained so misleadingly and beguilingly, however, that Americans
cannot be dissuaded from supporting them. The programs, that is,
combine the political strength of welfare with the moral strength
of insurance. Voters believe they're getting only what they paid for,
but regularly receive a great deal more than they paid for. Without running payroll taxes through a wealth augmentation machine,
this formula generates bad logic and bad policy but impregnable
politics.

Compassion of empathizers toward empathizees became important to the Affluent Society liberal coalition: the poor in their
pockets of poverty could not amount to a majority, so the majority
had to be assembled by combining the poor with other voters who
would gain moral validation rather than material benefits from
the War on Poverty. Even under exceptionally favorable economic
circumstances, however, this was a political challenge. For Robert
Kennedy to tell medical students, none of whom would be as comfortable for one week as he had been his entire life, that funds for
a bigger welfare state were going to come "from you," wins points
for candor but not political judgment. His strategy presupposed a
large number of voters would feel both prosperous and empathetic

enough to welcome, rather than resent, political campaigns based on the theme "Let's talk about what you're going to do for them." Lyndon Johnson, who had secured ten electoral victories on his own over the course of a political career that spanned four decades, had a better grasp of what voters would and would not tolerate when he promised that the War on Poverty would require very little of them—and, even then, its modest burden would quickly be repaid by rising prosperity for everyone.

The slight chance for appeals like Robert Kennedy's to secure a majority vanished after the 1973 Arab oil embargo marked the end of the Affluent Society boom. A more precarious economic era, continuing to this day, finds most Americans unable to recall or believe the bland postwar confidence about readily securing and maintaining a place in the broad middle class. In the Affluent Society's aftermath, liberalism faced a political problem: middle-class Americans viewed their obligations to help the poor through the prism of their own economic anxieties, which argued against sacrifices more painful than the ones LBJ had promised. As Kaus contended, "If citizens believe the welfare state is a big charity drive, they will naturally stop contributing when they feel they have nothing left over to give."[56]

In the era since the Affluent Society's sunset, liberals have struggled to adapt the rhetoric of compassion. Securing a Democratic majority by contending that *we* should feel sorry for *them* is impossible. Assembling one by saying we should feel sorry for ourselves, or they should feel sorry for us, suits the economic realities better but remains awkward. In 1972 Democrats challenged an incumbent Republican president they loathed, during an unpopular war. There had been inflation, resulting in wage and price controls, and a recession that began in 1969. Still, they chose to make their case in Affluent Society terms. Their party platform used the term "middle class" just once. There were six other uses of "middle income," all in the context of discussing housing programs for the continuum encompassing the poor and the less poor, as in "the lack of housing is particularly critical for people with low and middle incomes."[57]

In 2004 Democrats were, again, seeking to defeat a Republican incumbent they despised during an unpopular war. The party's platform *that* year went on and on about the middle class, using the term twenty times. An entire section was devoted to "Standing Up for the Great American Middle Class," which it hailed as a source of pride and prosperity, both the "heart of the American promise" and "the greatest engine of economic growth the world has ever known." Under Republicans, however, the "bottom line" is "Instead of working hard to get ahead, the middle class is working hard just to get by."[58]

Old habits die hard, however, and Democrats found it easier to change their language than their focus. In the summer of 2010, as the Tea Party was on the verge of recalling the GOP from an unexpectedly brief political exile, journalist Joshua Green explained that Democrats had suffered by offering an ersatz middle-class agenda: "Most Democratic policies, such as the earned income tax credit or increasing the minimum wage, were geared not toward the middle class but the poor. When middle-class Americans heard Democrats describe their problems, it did not resonate because they were actually the problems of the working poor." Green interviewed Senator Charles Schumer of New York, who took over the Democratic Senatorial Campaign Committee after the 2004 election and masterminded a comeback as the number of Democratic senators grew from 45 to 60 over the next two election cycles. Schumer said the key to securing middle-class votes for the liberal agenda was offering "aspirational policies" carried out by "a government active on behalf of the middle class." Schumer never brought into focus the qualities that define such an agenda, but does make clear how far the Democrats retreated in the four decades since Robert Kennedy sought the presidency by upbraiding the middle class for their callous indifference to the poor. "People will choose a government that helps them over no government at all," according to Schumer. "But they'll choose no government over one they believe is helping somebody else."[59]

The arc of former senator John Edwards's political career, prior to its laughingstock denouement, shows the intricacies of this political situation. Edwards set out to win the 2008 Democratic presidential nomination as the one candidate who sought, forty years later, to recapture the moral passion of Robert Kennedy's crusade for the poor. Edwards soon realized, however, that hunting where the ducks are meant, even in Democratic primaries, seeking votes from those who were not poor. "I'm not just talking about the rich and the poor," he said after retooling his campaign's rationale. "I'm talking about the very rich, and *everybody* else."[60]

Similarly, the Occupy Wall Street movement, with its "We Are the 99 Percent" slogan, showed a good grasp of majoritarian politics, whatever else it may have misunderstood. According to the World Top Incomes Database, every American household with a 2012 income below $371,689 was a prospective candidate for the Occupy coalition. It could, therefore, have suffered a fair number of defections from proletarians scraping by on $350,000 a year, and still assembled a dominant voting majority.

OPRAHFICATION

The fact that the Edwards and Occupy Wall Street majorities have not yet materialized does not guarantee they never will. With Bill de Blasio in Gracie Mansion and Elizabeth Warren in the United States Senate, committed egalitarians believe their long-awaited triumph may finally be at hand. The fact that such a majority would rest on dubious empirical foundations does not preclude its emergence. The New Deal coalition rested on dubious logical foundations, after all, about social insurance programs' magical ability to make every household a net importer of governmentally redistributed dollars, yet proved formidable and resilient.

A coalition forged by inducing mainstream Americans to feel sorry for themselves would, nevertheless, be predicated on alarmism. A study by the Pew Charitable Trusts' "Economic Mobility Project" followed a sample of children born in the 1950s and 1960s for three decades and found that "67 percent of Americans who were children in 1968 had higher levels of real [inflation-adjusted] income in 1995–2002 than their parents had in 1967–1971." Adjust the data for the smaller households at the end of the century— more singles, later marriages, fewer children—and the proportion of Americans who had a higher income by 2000 than their parents did some thirty years earlier rises to 81 percent.[61]

The Manhattan Institute's Scott Winship, former manager of the Pew project, points out, "Even after the Great Recession, we live in larger houses and own more cars than previous generations. . . . Air-conditioning and air travel, once considered luxuries, are now available to virtually all of us." Middle-class Americans of today are not worse off than middle-class families from the Affluent Society, but may feel worse off by virtue of the fact that average incomes, though still increasing, are rising about half as rapidly as they did from 1947 to 1979.[62] Furthermore, the standard of comparison today is of midcentury affluence and optimism, while the midcentury standard was the Depression. We have more than our parents did, but expect *much* more. As a result, the home movies in our heads about middle-class Americans' lives during the Affluent Society years exaggerate the prosperity. "A ranch-style tract house, a Chevrolet, and meat loaf for dinner will not do any more as the symbols of a realized dream," Nicholas Lemann wrote in 1989.[63]

The long arc of the history of social justice—from proudly defying sentimental almsgivers, to compassion for the downtrodden, to the conviction that nearly every American is among the downtrodden deserving compassion—bends toward self-absorption. As journalist Matt Bai recounts, at a "2004 book party for the liberal pundit Arianna Huffington, hosted by the billionaire Lynda Resnick and attended by Hollywood celebrities like Rob Reiner, Aaron Sorkin, and Larry and Laurie David . . . Resnick, an agribusiness titan and the owner of the Franklin Mint, ascended the spiral staircase of her legendary Sunset Boulevard mansion and declared, to great applause, 'We are so tired of being disenfranchised!'"[64] As life on earth demonstrates repeatedly, the perfection of self-absorption is the obliteration of self-awareness.

This shift—from a republic where the many are supposed to feel sorry for the few, to one where all are supposed to feel sorry for one another *and* for themselves—has political ramifications but is a sociological phenomenon. Inevitably, the axiom that empathizing with others is the paramount duty decent people are obliged to fulfill has engendered a corollary: being empathized *with* is the affirmation ordinary people are most entitled to receive. The danger is that when we are commanded to care for distant strangers with an intensity indistinguishable from the love we feel for our own families, what we get is not a nation of Albert Schweitzers and Mother Teresas, but one of frauds and hysterics.

What we get, in fact, is the Oprahfication of America, evident in the way political conventions now aspire to be empathy-fests that can hold their own with daytime talk shows. As Lee Siegel has argued, "The reverse side of a democracy based on exchangeable feelings is the creation of a kingdom of mere sensations, in which no experience has a higher—or different—value than any other experience." Oprah Winfrey dominated daytime television for two decades, during which she fortified and legitimized a social transformation that "turned living vicariously into living authentically." Winfrey taught America to "weep and empathize" with celebrities struggling with substance abuse or paparazzi, writes Siegel, and with ordinary Americans turned into celebrities for a day as they discussed their travails, from ghastly tragedies to mundane frustrations, for a studio and national audience. "The fungibility of feeling is really a reduction of all experience to the effect it has on your own quality of feeling." Because democracy means all have suffered and all deserve compassion, a republic created to secure inalienable rights becomes a continental support group to salve psychic wounds.[65]

Consider the victim impact statements offered during the sentencing phase of criminal trials, an innovation that became commonplace in America in the late twentieth century. Those who have survived a crime, or the friends and relatives of those who did not, are given an opportunity to tell the court (or parole board) about how they have been scarred by the experience. It is, then, exactly the kind of practice likely to be routinized in the Age of Empathy, but one raising problems unique to any such epoch. Historian Pamela Haag points out the corollary implied by inviting victims to entreat, on the basis of their suffering, the government to impose harsh punishments on those who wronged them: a criminal should receive "a more lenient sentence if his victim was someone of so little charm or social worth that he had no one to testify movingly for him."[66]

Blurring the distinction between the courtroom and a support group or talk-show set is a solution that legitimizes the problem it is meant to solve, bringing us closer to the visceral, unprincipled frontier justice Mark Twain derided. The reason criminal cases have titles like *Wisconsin v. Smith* or *United States v. Jones* is that violations of criminal law are considered transgressions against the entire community—against its safety and tranquility, its constitutive moral convictions, its capacity for efficacious self-government—not simply against a particular crime's victim. A national community with the moral confidence to punish criminals sternly would not need weeping relatives to clarify the intolerable wickedness of the criminal act. America was not, when victim impact statements became routine, such a nation. A 1995 Bureau of Justice Statistics report found that prisoners convicted of violent crimes and released from prison in 1992 had served, on average, sentences of 43 months. Convicted murderers received, on average, sentences of 149 months but had actually spent only 71 months in prison. For rapists, the corresponding numbers were 117 and 65 months; for kidnappers, 104 and 52 months; and for robbers, 95 and 44 months.[67]

The claims made for compassion by its most ardent publicists appear, in this light, highly suspect. A nation increasingly dependent on heartrending anecdotes to focus and activate its sense of justice is one that's losing the capacity for moral and abstract reasoning. Such a society, Jean Bethke Elshtain worried, will discover that "undifferentiated, unmediated emotion cannot sustain an ethical commitment to others." The question before the United States in 1787, wrote Alexander Hamilton in Federalist No. 1, was a question of urgent importance to the whole world: whether good government could be established by "reflection and choice," or would always rest on "accident and force." It is not just the founding, however, but the perpetuation of republics that makes reflection and choice imperative, and accident and force dangerous. If we agree the prospect of global empathy, felt for all without distinction, is ludicrous and hideous, then the politics of kindness will always rest on accidents. Wherever my expansive soul alights will be the place where an arbitrarily, randomly chosen sad story makes me tend to my well-being and self-regard by tending to the sufferer I happen upon. Such a nation, Elshtain contends, abandons the ideal of being a republic "sustained by ethical formation in and through our basic institutions" in favor of becoming "the United States of feeling good about ourselves."[68]

FATTER, SLOWER, AND DUMBER

For humans, feeling good about ourselves always takes place in a social context. We feel good, that is, not just about conforming to some abstract standard, but about emulating or validating the standards of the groups we care about, and surpassing or spurning the standards of groups we dislike. According to *The Righteous Mind*, Jonathan Haidt's widely discussed book on "why good people are divided by politics and religion," we appear to be citizens and voters who are weakly selfish but strongly "groupish." Individuals' political opinions often contradict their objective interests, but more reliably conform to the views of the groups they feel most strongly attached to. We "can believe almost anything that supports our team," he argues, because political opinions serve as "badges of social membership." Thus, people make sense of political reality by asking, "What's in it for my group?" rather than "What's in it for me?"[69]

Often, however, whether my group is in fact a group where I'm a member in good standing is not a clear, settled question. What I think of as "my" group may say more about what I aspire to, or how I see myself and want others to see me, than about the person I really am, who often turns out to be less well regarded by those whose good opinion I seek most avidly. "We are obsessively concerned about what others think of us," Haidt writes, "although much of the concern is unconscious and invisible to us." We formulate and express opinions not only to "support our team," but to "demonstrate commitment to our team."[70]

Thus, Garrison Keillor's description of what the politics of kindness means to its adherents sounds like a market research report about the National Public Radio audience, or at least on how those listeners like to think of themselves. "Liberals stand for tolerance, magnanimity, community spirit, the defense of the weak against the powerful, love of learning, freedom of belief, art and poetry, city life, the very things that make America worth dying for."[71]

The notion that the list of things that make America worth dying for includes art, poetry, and high-density living sounds like Keillor in his standard mode of gentle self-deprecation. Light irony is not the tone favored by syndicated columnist Dan Savage, however, who reacted to Republican victories in November 2004 by declaring, "Liberals, progressives, and Democrats" are "citizens of the Urban Archipelago," united by their rejection of "heartland 'values' like xenophobia, sexism, racism, and homophobia, as well as the more intolerant strains of Christianity that have taken root in this country." Savage went on to demonstrate his commitment to the liberal team in strident terms. Though he cautioned denizens of the urban archipelago against indulging fantasies of exile or secession in reaction to the 2004 election, internal defiance was still possible:

> We can secede emotionally, however, by turning our backs on the heartland. . . . We can create a new identity politics, one that transcends class, race, sexual orientation, and religion, one that unites people living in cities with each other and with other urbanites in other cities. The Republicans have the federal government—for now. But we've got Seattle, Portland, San Francisco, Chicago, Los Angeles, San Diego, New York City . . . and every college town in the country. We're everywhere any sane person wants to be. Let them have the shitholes, the Oklahomas, Wyomings, and Alabamas. We'll take Manhattan. . . .
>
> To red-state voters, to the rural voters, residents of small, dying towns, and soulless sprawling exburbs, we say this: Fuck off. Your issues are no longer our issues. We're going to battle our bleeding-heart instincts and ignore pangs of misplaced empathy. . . .
>
> In short, we're through with you people. . . .
>
> From here on out, we're glad red-state rubes live in areas where guns are more powerful and more plentiful, cars are larger and faster, and people are fatter and slower and dumber. This is not a recipe for repopulating the Great Plains. . . .[72]

Novelist Jane Smiley was only slightly more restrained in her reaction to the 2004 election results. "The error that progressives have consistently committed over the years is to underestimate the vitality of ignorance in America," she wrote in *Slate*. "[R]ed state types, above all, do not want to be told what to do—they prefer to be ignorant. As a result, they are virtually unteachable." Republican leaders, she continued, "are predatory and resentful, amoral, avaricious, and arrogant. Lots of Americans like and admire them because lots of Americans, even those who don't share those same qualities, don't know which end is up." In short, "red state types love to cheat and intimidate, so we have to assume the worst and call them on it every time. We have to give them more to think about than they can handle. . . ."[73]

The liberalism revealed by Smiley and Savage—smiley toward those deserving compassion, savage toward those who fail to extend empathy or are unworthy of receiving it—validates the assessment Christopher Lasch made ten years before their tirades in his posthumously published *The Revolt of the Elites*. "Upper-middle-class liberals," he wrote, do *not* regard their agenda or worldview as matters about which decent and reasonable people can disagree.

> When confronted with resistance to [their] initiatives, they betray the venomous hatred that lies not far beneath the smiling face of upper-middle-class benevolence. Opposition makes humanitarians forget the liberal virtues they claim to uphold. They become petulant, self-righteous, intolerant. In the heat of political controversy, they find it impossible to conceal their contempt for those who stubbornly refuse to see the light—those who "just don't get it," in the self-satisfied jargon of political rectitude.

> For such liberals,

"Middle America" . . . has come to symbolize everything that stands in the way of progress: "family values," mindless patriotism, religious fundamentalism, racism, homophobia, retrograde views of women. Middle Americans, as they appear to the makers of educated opinion, are hopelessly shabby, unfashionable, and provincial, ill informed about changes in taste or intellectual trends, addicted to trashy novels of romance and adventure, and stupefied by prolonged exposure to television. They are at once absurd and vaguely menacing—not because they wish to overthrow the old order but precisely because their defense of it appears so deeply irrational that it expresses itself, at the higher reaches of its intensity, in fanatical religiosity, in a repressive sexuality that occasionally erupts into violence against women and gays, and in a patriotism that supports imperialist wars and a national ethic of aggressive masculinity.[74]

Speaking at a 2008 campaign fund-raising event in San Francisco, unaware his remarks were being recorded, then-senator Barack Obama managed to express empathy and disdain for Middle Americans at the same time. "You go into some of these small towns in Pennsylvania, and like a lot of small towns in the Midwest, the jobs have been gone now for twenty-five years and nothing's replaced them. And they fell through the Clinton administration, and the Bush administration, and each successive administration has said that somehow these communities are going to regenerate and they have not." So far, so good: one more item on the endless roster of suffering situations liberalism exists to ameliorate.

Obama went on, however, to explain the situation in a way that wounded his campaign and reputation. Either he shared the worldview of the urban liberals seated before him, or understood that he needed to frame his point for this audience as an anthropologist would report on an exotic though primitive tribe. In any case, Obama asserted that he understood the red-state voters better than they understood themselves, and reduced their opinions and concerns to economic epiphenomena: "And it's not surprising then they get bitter, they cling to guns or religion or antipathy to people who aren't like them or anti-immigrant sentiment or anti-trade sentiment as a way to explain their frustrations."

For a century, going back to the Progressive era, the reactor core of American liberalism has been an "alliance of experts and victims," according to political scientist Harvey Mansfield.[75] The experts and victims may not add up to a majority, however, the basis for gaining power in a democracy. There are two ways to deal with this political problem. The first, which Occupy Wall Street took to its outer limit, is to argue that nearly all Americans are victims, and therefore depend for relief on the experts' ministrations. The difficulty with this course, as Smiley discerned, is that many Americans really don't like to be told what to do, and understand that self-pity will lead to being the objects of others' pity, and then to the objects of their directives. "No idea has deeper roots in American history and culture," writes Walter Russell Mead, than the "belief in the ability of the ordinary citizen to make decisions for himself or herself without the guidance or 'help' of experts and professionals."[76] The second response to this problem, if experts plus victims (self-identified and willing to be rescued by experts) is less than 50 percent of the voters, is to gain the votes needed to secure a majority by persuading or intimidating enough voters who are neither experts nor victims to vote for the alliance of those who are. The key argument for this purpose is that those who do not recognize the expertise of the experts are stupid, preferring ignorance, and those who do not recognize the victimhood of the victims are wicked, lacking compassion.

Despite their cognitive limitations, the Americans reviled by Savage and Smiley, and patronized by Obama, have figured something out. Even people so ignorant they happily remain in Oklahoma rather than relocate to Seattle infer, with good reason, that the alliance of experts and victims is not on the up-and-up. The experts are not always as expert or as disinterested as they like to think. In particular, the victims are not necessarily as helpless as the experts posit, as the latter are endlessly eager for venues to apply their expertise, assert the authority it bestows, and demonstrate their compassion. Red-state rubes who haven't heard of Goethe are smart enough to share his fear of a world that turns into one big hospital, where each is the other's humane nurse. Blue-state types may know something about Goethe, but not enough to grasp why a republic of wards and wardens might be a problem.

According to one 2012 exit poll, Mitt Romney won clear victories among the three-fourths of the electorate who believed a presidential candidate's most important quality was either his "vision for the future" (54 percent to President Obama's 45 percent), whether he "shares my values" (56 percent to 42 percent), or was "a strong leader" (61 percent to 38 percent). Obama carried the one remaining category so decisively, however, as to win reelection. Of the 21 out of every 100 voters who believed the most important quality in a presidential candidate was that "he cares about people like me," 17 voted for Obama and 4 voted for Romney.[77] Red-state primitives join with Goethe in their apprehensions about a nation that chooses its leaders on this basis, fears prefigured by Barbara Walters beseeching President-elect Carter, "Be wise with us, Governor. Be good to us." A vigorous republic should be defined, not by how much its public officials care for people like (or even unlike) me, but by how well people can and do care for themselves, their families, and their communities. The greater our capacity and determination to assert that prerogative and take advantage of the opportunities it defends, the less the quality of our lives will depend on presidential empathy.

Apart from the civic debilitation begotten by the politics of kindness, the correlation between politicians who care about people like me and policies that benefit people like me is, as I'll discuss in the next chapter, highly tenuous.

Chapter 4

HOW LIBERAL COMPASSION
LEADS TO BULLSHIT

H ead Start, a War on Poverty initiative, provides federal funds for preschool programs intended to prepare three- and four-year-olds from impoverished families for elementary school. Democrats constantly extol and promise to expand the program, and attack Republicans for criticizing and seeking to diminish it. The 1988 Democratic platform, for example, declared that few federal programs were more successful than Head Start.[1]

If that praise is accurate, all Americans should be apprehensive, liberals especially. "Head Start simply does not work," according to Joe Klein's summary in *Time* magazine of a long-term study released in 2010 by the Department of Health and Human Services, which administers the program.[2] The official HHS reaction to its Head Start Impact Study shed more light on why it was a failure than on how it might be improved. According to the department, the study showed that Head Start "positively influenced children's school readiness"—but only if you tested them after they finished Head Start but before they started kindergarten. On this basis the assistant secretary for children and families declared, "Head Start has been changing lives for the better since its inception." The department acknowledged, however, that "measured again at the end of kindergarten and first grade," children who went through Head

Start "were at the same level on many of the measures studied" as ones who did not.[3]

Less vaguely, the Cato Institute's Andrew Coulson sifted through the study's data to discover that when researchers gave both Head Start participants and an economically and socially similar control group of students never enrolled in the program "44 different academic tests at the end of the first grade, only two seemed to show even marginally significant advantages for the Head Start group. And even those apparent advantages vanished after standard statistical controls were applied."[4] HHS subsequently released data showing there were no latent benefits from Head Start, either, ones that manifested themselves as its graduates proceeded through their school years. Thus, by the end of the third grade children who had been enrolled in a program were no better off than those in a nonparticipating control group.[5]

Head Start, in other words, did a good job preparing children for school—right up until the day they started school, when it quickly became clear they were no more academically ready than children from outside the program. That HHS could, nonetheless, congratulate itself on improving the "readiness" of Head Start participants, who turned out not to be ready for the thing Head Start was supposedly getting them ready for, helps explain how a program that costs the federal government $8 billion a year, and has run up more than $180 billion in outlays since its inception in 1965, could spend so much and accomplish so little. Liberals' speeches and editorials routinely insist Head Start must be "fully funded," which means Congress should appropriate enough funds for the program to permit every eligible child to enroll.[6] But serious concern for the program's ostensible beneficiaries—as opposed to concern for its providers and administrators, who might be rewarded irrespective of children's progress—would make it more important for Head Start to be fully *functional* than fully funded.

Speaking in 2011 at a Head Start center in Pennsylvania, President Obama referred obliquely to the report chronicling the program's deficiencies. "I firmly believe that Head Start is an outstanding program and a critical investment," Obama insisted before criticizing Republicans for their plans to cut its budget. Nevertheless, he announced new rules to ensure for "*the first time in history* that Head Start programs will be truly held accountable for performance in the classroom" (emphasis added). The president did not explain the basis on which, other than its good intentions, a forty-six-year-old program that had never been held accountable for delivering on those intentions could be judged outstanding. The historic rules Obama announced would require Head Start programs to meet "clear, high standards" and allow new providers to bid for grants going to agencies that fell short.[7]

IMPLEMENTATION

That it can be characterized as a bold departure for the federal government to give money to social service providers only if—as opposed to whether or not—they do what they're supposed to with it is a more damning indictment of liberal government's business-as-usual than anything you'll read in the most scornful *Wall Street Journal* editorial. According to journalist James Fallows, conservatives believe "government is simply evil, that it is wasteful, oppressive, misguided and inefficient."[8] It would follow logically that American conservatives govern badly when given the opportunity because they don't really want to govern at all. A 2006 essay by social scientist Alan Wolfe argued that this contradiction explained how the Republican president and Congress in power that year "imploded, not despite their conservatism, but because of it." The fundamental problem is that conservatives confront an irresolvable tension inherent in "managing government agencies whose missions—indeed, whose very existence—they believe to be illegitimate." They fail when in power due to a "learned incompetence," resulting from their conviction that government has no business undertaking many of the tasks it now discharges.[9]

This theory of the case, resting on motive, has a corollary. If conservatives govern badly because they stand outside the boundary of the modern state yelling "Shrink!," then liberals should govern brilliantly. The mission that defines liberalism, after all, is to vindicate the activist state's right, duty, and capacity to handle all the responsibilities entrusted to it over the past century, and then assign it new ones. Mitch Daniels, Republican governor of Indiana from 2005 to 2013, told an interviewer in 2009 that disciplining government according to "measured provable performance and effective spending" ought to be a "completely philosophically neutral objective." For a green-eyeshade conservative, who wants the government to throw nickels around like they're manhole covers, getting the most bang for the fewest bucks is an obvious way to lighten the burden of taxes and regulations. Daniels went on, however, to voice a second implication: "I argue to my most liberal friends: 'You ought to be the most offended of anybody if a dollar that could help a poor person is being squandered in some way.' And some of them actually agree."[10]

Daniels sounds surprised that even some liberals emphasize performance and effectiveness, suggesting that such obvious criteria are *not* that big a deal to most. For a conservative politician to question liberals' sincerity may prove little, but Daniels is not alone. Philosophy professor Daniel Shapiro criticized his famous peer, John Rawls, on the same basis: stipulating that justice requires government policies guaranteeing the worst-off person in society be as well off as possible is all well and good, but it won't do to collapse the distinction between setting up government programs for the purpose of pursuing that goal and actually achieving it. In fact, writes Shapiro,

Institutions cannot be adequately characterized by their aims. In the real world, political decision makers do not simply have intentions to achieve a just society that they can simply implement. They have agendas and interests of their own.

Moreover, even the most dedicated, selfless public officials "face informational constraints, such as their ignorance about most of the facts that are relevant for a decision, the difficulties in evaluating the relevant evidence, and our uncertainty about predicting the consequences of various policies."[11]

Implementation—translating good and usually vague intentions into specific achievements—is not necessarily an insurmountable problem. (It is sometimes, though, which means we should choose the crusades we embark on with caution and humility.) But it's usually a big problem, which means that calling for and creating government programs to effect some social reform doesn't really mean much unless we overcome the barriers to successful implementation, thereby making sure a government program actually achieves its goals. Joe Klein argues forcefully that liberalism's deepest flaw is exactly its disregard for implementation, which leads activist government's practitioners and advocates to judge their efforts too leniently by equating good intentions with concrete achievements. The "liberal project cannot survive," he contends, "unless liberals take the lead in weeding out programs that aren't working, and either reforming them or closing them down." There are people who really do need help, and government programs that can improve their lives. But, Klein cautions, "if supporters of collective action are going to have any credibility at all, they have to focus perpetually on the efficiency of the programs they support."[12]

Let's consider whether Head Start's meager results, and liberals' complacence about them, are outliers or indicate a deeper problem.

BULLSHIT

"Bullshit" is American English's assertion, maximally succinct and vigorous, that a contention is factually preposterous or logically absurd. According to philosophy professor Harry Frankfurt, however, the "essence of bullshit is not that it is *false* but that it is *phony*." His slender volume devoted to the subject, *On Bullshit*, invites us to think of a Fourth of July orator "who goes on bombastically about 'our great and blessed country, whose Founding Fathers under divine guidance created a new beginning for mankind.'" The speaker's point is not "to deceive anyone concerning American history." Rather,

> What he cares about is what people think of *him*. He wants them to think of him as a patriot, as someone who has deep thoughts and feelings about the origins and the mission of our country, who appreciates the importance of religion, who is sensitive to our history, whose pride in that history is combined with humility before God, and so on.[13]

It's difficult to banish the glum suspicion that life in the twenty-first century, for all its economic and technological benefits, necessitates putting up with *much* more bullshit than our ancestors had to. One cause for this is that it's increasingly uncommon to make a living by rendering a good or service that can be judged directly, the way a carpenter or barber does. Instead, more and more of us perform work where, as political theorist Matthew Crawford argues, "you have to spend a lot of time managing what others think of you." Where reputation management is a dominant concern, "Survival depends on a crucial insight: you can't back down from an argument that you initially made in straightforward language, with moral conviction, without seeming to lose your integrity. So managers learn the art of provisional thinking and feeling, expressed in corporate doublespeak, and cultivate a lack of commitment to their own actions."[14]

Bullshit, writes Frankfurt, is defined by its "lack of connection to a concern with truth." In some circumstances, a lack of concern with truth is not simply the result of a speaker's phoniness, but is a shared communicative premise. For example:

> What tends to go on in a bull session [such as in a college dormitory] is that the participants try out various thoughts and attitudes in order to discover how others respond, without its being assumed that they are committed to what they say: it is understood by everyone in a bull session that the statements people make do not necessarily reveal what they really believe or how they really feel. The main point is to make possible a high level of candor and an experimental or adventuresome approach to the subjects under discussion.[15]

The bull session, in this account, partakes of the willing suspension of disbelief crucial to various art forms, especially the dramatic. Knowing that the actor portraying Hamlet is neither Danish nor indecisive does not cause us to consider his performance a betrayal. Even Frankfurt's Fourth of July orator avails himself of the considerable latitude extended by his listeners: they discount, as excesses inherent in the rhetorical context, his efforts to signal allegiance to national characteristics he thinks especially admirable.

The bullshit hits the fan when a speaker tries to have it both ways: to speak with the freedom of one who is not necessarily committed to what he says, while encouraging his listeners to take what he conveys seriously. Bullshitting, writes Frankfurt, culminates in "a retreat from the discipline required by dedication to the ideal of correctness to a quite different sort of discipline, which is imposed by pursuit of an alternative ideal of sincerity."

Rather than seeking primarily to arrive at accurate representations of a common world, the individual turns toward trying to provide honest representations of himself. Convinced that reality has no inherent nature, which he might hope to identify as the truth about things, he devotes himself to being true to his own nature.[16]

This subordination of accuracy about verifiable objective realities to sincerity about unverifiable subjective ones explains how Oprahfication renders bullshit safe for modernity. As Lee Siegel observes, Winfrey "has made the sincerity of a statement more important than the content of it. Which is to say, she has made it virtuous to be amoral." Under the dispensation of this ethic,

> You are not responsible for what you do because your truth as a person lies in the future as your "goal." You don't tell lies, because what might seem like a fabrication to other people is the expression of your genuine feeling, which is authorized by who you know you really are and can be in the future.[17]

It will be noted that what historian Daniel Boorstin discussed as the "language of anticipation" has a long, albeit equivocally honorable place in American discourse. Nineteenth-century go-getters, transforming a wilderness into a superpower, began availing themselves of "a new linguistic confusion of present and future, fact and hope." Under this dispensation, statements that otherwise would have stood condemned as fabrications were extenuated as descriptions of events that had not *yet* undergone the "formality of taking place."[18]

Unfortunately, Frankfurt argues, "sincerity itself is bullshit" since it is hard—much harder than the gospel of sincerity prepares us to comprehend—to know ourselves so well as to meet the standard of honest self-presentation, given that our natures are "elusively insubstantial."[19] He does not elaborate two other difficulties his argument suggests. First, very few of us have enough objectivity or self-discipline to meet the challenge of providing complete, revealing representations of ourselves without succumbing to the temptation to offer, instead, highly flattering representations of ourselves. As the saying goes, sincerity is so important because once you've mastered faking *that*, you can get away with anything.

Second, sincere bullshit not only cheapens and distorts our interpersonal communications, but threatens our individual psychological integrity. Holly Golightly in Truman Capote's *Breakfast at Tiffany's* is both a phony and not a phony because she's "a *real* phony," someone who genuinely "believes all this crap that she believes." A mere phony holds in reserve some part of his soul that never participates in the charade, realizing cynically but at least clearly that it *is* a charade. A real phony, however, *becomes* the part he's playing, so that the consummation of falsity yields a new, higher honesty. "To thine own self be true," commands me not to a journey of discovery but one of creation. If I can be anything I really want to be, then just by wanting to be something I have already fulfilled the essential requirement for actually being it. Those who would dispute my aspirations or authenticity are asserting that my transformation has not yet gone through the formality of taking place, a judgment resting on their objective assessments, which are necessarily less informed than my subjective one.

And if we can be *anything* we want to be, then we can be *many* things we want to be—serially, simultaneously, or even contradictorily. The perils inherent in exalting sincerity were the gravamen of the late Michael Kelly's indictment of Bill Clinton, delivered during the second year of the latter's presidency:

> The President's essential character flaw isn't dishonesty so much as a-honesty. It isn't that Clinton means to say things that are not true, or that he cannot make true, but that everything is true

for him when he says it, because he says it. Clinton means what he says when he says it, but tomorrow he will mean what he says when he says the opposite.[20]

PRESCRIPTIVE BULLSHIT

Frankfurt limits his discussion of bullshit to descriptive statements, analyzing and regretting our departure from the standard of truth. He does not take up the question of prescriptive statements, the mainstay of politics. Criticizing Republican proposals to cut spending on Head Start and other educational programs, for example, President Obama said, "We know that three- and four-year-olds who go to high-quality preschools, including our best Head Start programs, are less likely to repeat a grade, they're less likely to need special education, they're more likely to graduate from high school than the peers who did not get these services."[21] The first part of Obama's statement is not bullshit, because it does nothing worse than employ the politician's constant companion, the selectively revealed half-truth. Children who attend the *best* Head Start programs show positive results but, as we have seen, Head Start attendees *overall* are no better off than peers not enrolled in the program. Obama invokes the sunny side of the law of averages without acknowledging its grim side: if children who attend the best Head Start programs do better than their peers, children who attend the worst programs must, necessarily, have developmental problems even more severe than those afflicting children in a control group who never enrolled in the program at all.

The more interesting part of Obama's statement, for our purposes, is the generic political prescription, the assertion that government program X will solve problem Y. Prescription lends itself to bullshitting if, following Frankfurt, the prescriber has a lack of connection to a concern with *efficacy*. Both kinds of bullshitters, describers and prescribers, are more concerned with conveying their ideals, of which idealized understandings of their true selves are a central component, than with making statements that correspond scrupulously to empirical or causal reality. A bullshit description may be, at least in part, factually accurate, but any such accuracy is inadvertent. The accurate data was incorporated into the spiel not for the sake of correctness, but because it helped express the speaker's "values" or "vision."

A bullshit prescription, by the same token, might actually work to some degree, but any such efficacy is inadvertent and tangential to the central purpose: demonstrating the depths of the prescriber's concern for the problem and those who suffer from it, concerns impelling the determination to "do something" about it. As the political project that exists to vindicate the axiom that all sorts of government program X's can solve an endless list of social problem Y's, liberalism is always at risk of descending into prescriptive bullshit. Liberal compassion lends itself to bullshit by subordinating the putative concern with efficacy to the dominant but unannounced imperative of moral validation and exhibitionism. I, the empathizer, am interested in the sufferer for love of myself, Rousseau contended. Accordingly, an ineffectual program may serve the compassionate purposes of their designers and defenders as well as or better than a successful one.

Thus, while a particular program X *may* alleviate problem Y, it is hard for neutral observers to conclude efficacy is all that important, given that liberal programs are so rarely dropped from the lineup or sent down to the instructional leagues, even if their batting slumps continue for decades. In calling for "bold, persistent experimentation" in 1932, Franklin Roosevelt said, "It is common sense to take a method and try it: If it fails, admit it frankly and try another. But above all, try something."[22] "Experimentation" clearly implies that failed efforts will be discontinued, but logic and experience show the formidable difficulty of doing so. At the dawn of the Great Society the sociologist Nathan Glazer wrote, "How one wishes for the open field of the New Deal, which was not littered with the carcasses of half-successful and hardly successful programs, each in the hands of a hardening bureaucracy."[23] The practice of liberalism would be much easier without the legacy of liberalism.

And without the logic of liberalism. The acquiescence in wasteful and ineffective programs—so strikingly at variance with the earnest, often fervent, expression of solicitude for the sufferers who are supposed to benefit from those programs—persists not only because implementation is administratively and politically difficult, but because the liberals who create, perpetuate, defend, and expand social welfare programs are devoted to them less because they care about helping than because they care about caring. This fundamental flaw connects the theory of liberalism to the malpractice of liberalism. It explains why—in the words of Joe Klein, whose sparsely populated spot on the political spectrum may be described as rigorous, skeptical liberalism—the "special responsibility to make sure that federal programs are effective and well managed," which ought to be liberals' highest priority, is instead one they regularly subordinate to campaigns for "getting massive new programs passed." By embracing those priorities and allowing misconceived, mismanaged programs to shamble along endlessly, rarely reformed and never replaced, liberals confirm rather than refute conservatives' conviction that, as he writes, "government can mess up a one-car parade."[24]

Even columnist E. J. Dionne Jr.—a better team player than Klein, meaning a less rigorous and skeptical liberal—conceded that 2013's incompetent rollout of the Affordable Care Act, after the Obama administration had been given three and a half years following the law's passage to prepare for it, showed "[t]here's a lesson here that liberals apparently need to learn over and over: Good intentions without proper administration can undermine even the most noble of goals."[25] That such an elementary lesson is one liberals need to learn over and over suggests a fundamental flaw in liberalism, one that cannot be fixed by exhortations from friendly journalists. Obamacare's debut moved Franklin Foer, editor of the *New Republic*, to worry that the program's failure would erode "the public's willingness to give liberalism another shot," the kind allowing it to "replicate its greatest victories," since it has always been the case that "[i]f liberals wanted the federal government to take on big new projects—more to the point, if liberals wanted taxes to pay for them—they needed the public to believe that the money would be well spent."[26]

That Dionne and Foer place such concerns front and center inadvertently confirms Klein's point: liberals instinctively stress the importance of political victories over the need for successful policies. The perverse determination to assign government new social welfare responsibilities, rather than focus like a laser on discharging existing ones as effectively as possible, makes sense if the welfare of the people whom government programs were created to help was never really the main point of those programs. Rather, it was secondary, irrelevant, or even contrary to the more pressing need: embarking on humanitarian endeavors that, however much or little suffering they alleviated, reassured those who demand, enact, administer, and uphold all such programs that *they* are admirable people and their political adversaries are not.

In *Meditations on Hunting*, José Ortega y Gasset wrote that "one does not hunt in order to kill; on the contrary, one kills in order to have hunted." More generally, "when an activity becomes a sport, whatever that activity may be, the hierarchy of its values becomes inverted." When a failed hunt meant starvation, the hunter's "true purpose" was to kill his prey. For the sportsman who will be well nourished in any case, the "demonstration of effort and skill," which had been merely a means to the end for the "utilitarian" hunter, becomes an end in itself.[27]

Liberalism's concern with moral self-validation, tacit though pervasive, does indeed signal an inversion of the hierarchy of values. Conservative critiques of liberalism sometimes concede that liberals' aspirations are laudable before insisting that the means liberals favor are insufficiently practical and at least potentially destructive. The way liberal compassion lends itself to liberal bullshit, however, argues for a less forgiving interpretation. Liberals' ideals make them more culpable, not less, for the fact that government programs set up to *do* good don't reliably *accomplish* good. Doing good is often harder than do-gooders realize, but doing good is also more about the doing and the doer than it is about the good. Too often, as a result, liberals are content to treat gestures as the functional equivalent of deeds, and intentions as adequate substitutes for achievements.

GUN BULLSHIT

Consider gun control. The issue had been dormant in American politics after many Democrats concluded their party's commitment to that cause was costing its candidates votes they could not afford to lose. (If Al Gore had carried his home state of Tennessee, for example, he would have won the presidency in 2000, regardless of any court's rulings about Florida's hanging chads.) Even after a gunman shot seventy people, twelve fatally, in an Aurora, Colorado, movie theater in July 2012, less than four months before Election Day, Democrats addressed the question with great caution. The presidential press secretary, Jay Carney, went out of his way to signal the Obama administration's lack of interest in new legislation, telling reporters that "the President's view is that we can take steps to keep guns out of the hands of people who should not have them under existing law. And that's his focus right now."[28] Obama did not mention guns in his convention acceptance speech seven weeks after the shootings, and the party platform devoted a single modulated paragraph to the issue.

The month after Obama's reelection saw the perpetration of another massacre, this time in Newtown, Connecticut. An unhinged young man named Adam Lanza used guns his mother had acquired and kept at their home to murder her, twenty schoolchildren, and six school employees, before killing himself. Campaigning now for a place in history rather than a second term, President Obama was less circumspect after Newtown than he had been following Aurora, no longer willing to confine the discussion to the unrealized possibilities afforded by existing laws. Instead, in a news conference five days after the shootings, he aligned himself with the "majority of Americans" who support new laws banning assault weapons and high-capacity ammunition clips, and "requiring background checks before all gun purchases."[29]

By the time Congress began considering the issue in 2013, however, Democratic leaders concluded they had no way to secure the votes needed to ban any particular type of weapon or ammunition, and concentrated on legislation that would expand background checks. Their efforts had to overcome not only a political problem, the National Rifle Association and other opponents of gun control, but a logical one: explaining how Adam Lanza's crimes made it imperative to enact legislation that would not have prevented those crimes. "It's true," wrote the *New Yorker*'s Margaret Talbot, "that a background check would not have stopped Adam Lanza, who had no criminal record, and whose mother had bought the guns and ammunition he used in Newtown.

> But laws influence culture, just as culture influences laws, and if Congress enacted *a* serious piece of gun-control legislation *perhaps that might initiate a subtle shift* in American attitudes toward guns, and that *might eventually lead some parent* with a deeply troubled, deeply isolated son fascinated by violence to think

twice before turning the family home into a munitions depot. [Emphasis added.][30]

Or, as William Buckley liked to say, if we had some ham we could make a ham sandwich. If we had some bread.

With champions who declare it doesn't really matter what new laws say or do, gun control barely needs detractors. According to Talbot's argument, any gun law, as long as it is perceived to be serious, has the potential to catalyze the revaluation of all values relating to firearms. Talbot's moralizing on behalf of vague gestures we can all feel hopeful about—thereby sparing us the need to attend to the boring details about what conduct new regulations will actually proscribe and require, how these commands will be enforced, and the plausible cause and effect between the enforcement of their provisions and the realization of their intended goals—presents liberal bullshit as self-caricature.

Not all gun control advocates rely so heavily on wishful thinking about legislating morality. Even the more grounded arguments partake, albeit less flagrantly, of liberal indifference to efficacy. It is, in the first place, a hollow victory for a policy to "succeed" if it is endorsed and enacted according to terms by which it could not possibly fail. This kind of unfalsifiable proposition is essential to the argument that even if new gun control laws might not make much difference, they will make some. And some is better than none. "If there is even one step we can take to save another child or another parent or another town" from the kind of agony Adam Lanza inflicted on Newtown, President Obama said in a memorial service there, "then surely we have an obligation to try."[31] In April 2013, after legislation expanding background checks fell short of the sixty votes needed to end debate in the Senate, effectively scuttling the bill, the president pressed the same argument in a Rose Garden appearance, where he was accompanied by several parents whose children were among the Connecticut murder victims:

One common argument I heard was that this legislation wouldn't prevent all future massacres. And that's true. As I said from the start, no single piece of legislation can stop every act of violence and evil. . . . But if action by Congress could have saved one person, one child, a few hundred, a few thousand, if it could have prevented those people from losing their lives to gun violence in the future while preserving our Second Amendment rights, we had an obligation to try. And this legislation met that test. And too many Senators failed theirs.[32]

Politicians, as a class, are not legendarily meticulous when characterizing ideas they dispute and wish to defeat. Even judged by the norms of his profession, however, Obama's resort to straw man arguments is remarkably facile and shameless about ascribing idiotic views to those with whom he disagrees. In February 2009, during his first press conference as president, Obama congratulated himself for taking a tone with congressional Republicans "that has been consistently civil and respectful," before lamenting that based on what an unspecified "some in Congress" had been saying about his proposals to stimulate the critically wounded economy, "there seems to be a set of folks who—I don't doubt their sincerity—who just believe that we should do nothing." Even the *New York Times* and *Washington Post*, newspapers that exert themselves to give Obama the benefit of every doubt, made plain that *no one* on Capitol Hill contended, sincerely or otherwise, that the government's best response to the economic crisis was utter passivity.[33]

By the same token, Obama did not identify anyone who made the "common argument" that expanded background checks prior to gun sales were useless at best because they "wouldn't prevent all future massacres," much less "stop every act of violence and evil." Having disposed of the ludicrously high standard gun control opponents allegedly insisted on, Obama could adopt one of his favorite poses, the grown-up in the room, by invoking a ludicrously low standard, our duty to try policies that could save even one child from gun violence. In doing so the president employed a logical fallacy he was no doubt warned against while a law student: the argument that proves too much. If the government has an obligation to try anything that might save even one life, then it is going to be hyperactive in discharging an infinite workload.

This logical failure brings us to a prudential one, another hallmark of prescriptive bullshit: the failure to weigh a proposed course of action in light of possible alternatives, troubling implications, and foreseeable impediments, political and administrative. The *Atlantic*'s Conor Friedersdorf criticized Obama's rhetoric by pointing out that any list of options that might plausibly reduce the likelihood of the next Newtown massacre would have to include dramatically lower barriers to monitoring or even institutionalizing people with mental illnesses. Adam Lanza, though clearly troubled, had never run afoul of the law before the last day of his life, nor had he been placed under clinical supervision. Vigorous intervention by the authorities to treat or even confine him might well have prevented his killing spree—but would also require assigning government officials sweeping powers regarding weird, pathetic misfits in general. A few assailants may well be interdicted as a result, but a vastly larger number of troubled though harmless people will have their freedom curtailed and their lives diminished. To recoil from this prospect is not the moral equivalent of chortling during the Newtown funerals.[34]

The obligation to try anything that might save even one child's life would also, in short order, require contemplating stern social or government sanctions against violent movies and video games. (Lanza spent hours absorbed in the latter, according to some accounts.) The *New Yorker*'s Adam Gopnik, a gun control supporter, saluted the "liberal creed of open inquiry and presentation," before raising a troubling question:

It's difficult to believe that a hundred years from now historians are going to say, "America had a terrible curse of gun violence. It also had entertainments of all kinds, which depended on the use and glorification and a fetishization of guns, but these two things had no connection. They ran on completely different cultural circuits."

Strident demands for more gun control were numerous in the weeks following Newtown. By contrast, new laws and attitudes that would place a heavy burden of proof upon those whose movies and video games normalize and even celebrate lethal violence, thereby requiring them to demonstrate their products were socially benign, were peripheral to the national debate. No one suggested that to demur from calling to account the purveyors of those entertainments was to become complicit in the murder of schoolchildren.[35]

Gun violence, after all, does not exhaust the list of tragedies a civilized nation should strive to reduce. According to the National Highway Traffic Safety Administration, 32,367 Americans were killed in vehicular crashes in 2011, 1,341 of whom were under the age of sixteen. (By contrast, the Centers for Disease Control and Prevention found that firearms killed 350 Americans under the age of fifteen in 2010. Of these, 62 were accidental shootings, 208 were homicides, and 80 were suicides, all of the latter committed by children between the ages of ten and fourteen.) Collisions at intersections account for one-fifth of all traffic fatalities, according to a 2007 study by the Federal Highway Administration, and left turns were responsible for the majority of those accidents. We could, it follows, save the lives of thousands of Americans, many of them children, by reengineering busy intersections to allow for left turns without crossing in front of oncoming traffic, and by prohibiting left turns at less busy but still dangerous intersections. Doing so would entail large financial outlays, borne collectively, and millions of small time outlays, borne individually, as drivers avoided left turns by taking longer routes, including ones that require three right turns to go around a block. The certain result of such efforts, however, would be a reduction in the number of funerals attended by grief-stricken parents.[36]

Must we, QED, relegate left turns to the dustbin of transportation history? Most of us would hold that truth to be contestable, at best, rather than self-evident. That position, in turn, rests on another: our obligation to attempt measures that would save the life of even one child goes only so far. We weigh even the most dreadful prospects in balance against other considerations, some profound—such as the need to curtail preventive detentions ordered by psychiatric officials, or to uphold the free speech rights of those who make movies and video games—and others mundane—like the need to limit the taxes devoted to highway construction, or to prevent time-consuming trips to workplaces and stores from being even more time-consuming. A politician who invoked any such offsetting considerations could count on being spared accusations that his refusal to pursue the safety of children to whatever policy conclusions it required was "morally repulsive," "craven," "sickening," and "cowardly," proving him to be a "whore" with the blood of dead children on his hands. The liberal journalist Michael Tomasky threw all these bouquets in the course of a single article denouncing the senators who voted against expanding the number of gun purchases subject to background checks.[37]

How is it possible to accept that lifesaving measures certain to curtail personal liberties, cost exorbitant amounts, or cause major inconveniences pose trade-offs that decent, reasonable people can disagree about, while ascribing opposition to any particular gun control measure to shocking moral depravity? Only by assuming the rights and benefits associated with gun ownership are too slight to outweigh any benefits, however modest or unlikely, from curtailing guns. Such an assumption is, in the first place, culturally biased: blue-state gun control advocates don't grasp the red-state insistence on private ownership of firearms. Gopnik concedes, then proves, the point by describing guns as "ego-accessories" providing "the illusion of power."[38]

In urging us to be "as tolerant as humanly possible about other people's pleasures, even when they're opaque to us, and try only to hive off the bad consequences from the good," Gopnik restates rather than clarifies the problem. Friedersdorf admits to sharing Gopnik's blue-state sensibilities, but is more rigorous and less self-indulgent about applying them to the question of regulating guns: "The fact that it's a very different subculture than mine makes me *more* wary of insisting that the preferences of its members ought to be paid very little mind in shaping future public policy."[39]

There is also a constitutional impediment to restricting guns in order to do anything that might save the life of even one child. In a 1989 law journal article, Sanford Levinson warned against cultural assumptions' power to distort constitutional reasoning. Thus, "the absence of the Second Amendment from the legal consciousness of the elite bar, including that component found in the legal academy, is derived from a mixture of sheer opposition to the idea of private ownership of guns and the perhaps subconscious fear that altogether plausible, perhaps even 'winning,' interpretations of the Second Amendment would present real hurdles to those of us supporting prohibitory regulation." Levinson deplored the "happy endings" approach to constitutional exegesis: a jurist who invariably discovers that the Constitution's requirements and prohibitions align perfectly with his own political preferences is engaged in ventriloquism, not interpretation. Levinson does not try to settle the question of the Second Amendment's true meaning, and certainly does not align himself with the position that whatever individual rights it protects are absolute. He does, though, argue that however much those who favor gun control would prefer to read the Constitution as though its meaning without the Second Amendment would be exactly the same as its meaning with it, the historical and textual basis for treating the right to bear arms as protecting individuals' rights is, in fact, too formidable to ignore.[40]

Levinson's article was a bracing communication from one anti-gun liberal to others. It appeared at a time—1989—when the default assumption among the enlightened was that the Second Amendment concerned only "a well-regulated militia" and, therefore, was not even the smallest impediment to government regulations restricting individuals' rights to acquire or retain firearms. "Levinson's article inspired a wave of complementary scholarship in the 1990s," according to Randy Barnett, another law professor. This new interpretation not only culminated in Supreme Court decisions upholding individual gun rights, but in gun control advocates' abandoning their advocacy for the older, narrower interpretation of the Constitution. The president of the Brady Campaign to Prevent Gun Violence, one of the leading gun control organizations, told a reporter in 2012 that he considers the debate on the Second Amendment "closed" and has no interest in reopening it.[41]

There is, finally, a practical impediment to the idea that more gun control will have some kind of beneficial effect, however tenuous the assumptions of efficacy may appear under interrogation: Americans already own millions of guns. It isn't clear exactly how many, due in part to the limited monitoring of gun purchases. The *Atlantic*'s Jeffrey Goldberg estimated in 2012 that there were between 280 and 300 million privately owned guns in America, with 4 million new ones being acquired each year. He cites a 2011 public opinion survey indicating that 47 percent of American households possess at least one gun. Since politics is not a graduate seminar, and history does not present blank sheets of paper to those who want to shape the future, discussions about gun policy that disregard this enormous fact on the ground are a waste of everyone's time.[42]

One anti-gun argument that takes account of this reality is that our extraordinary level of private gun ownership is intolerable, and therefore must not be tolerated. It seems "positively ludicrous," to the *New Republic*'s Noam Scheiber, that we put up with thousands of gun-related homicides, suicides, and accidental deaths each year, not to mention wounds that result in agonizing pain or cruel debilitations, because "we accept these things as a kind of cost-of-business for widespread gun ownership." Even allowing for the great difficulty of arriving at the ultimate goal, he insists on clarity and candor about what that goal is: "If it were up to me, gun licensing would be so strict that only people who use guns professionally—cops, soldiers, firearms instructors, farmer and rancher types—could own them and store them at home. Everyone else could rent them if they wanted to go hunting or to a shooting range."[43]

Scheiber deserves credit for endorsing a clear, maximalist position that other gun control advocates may share, but don't advertise. They are reticent because his logic not only directs us to a distant goal but its political effect makes the goal even more distant. One sympathetic critic, journalist Joel Mathis, pointed out that if liberals are to have any hopes of enacting "modest, smart, commonsense changes to gun ownership rules" it's imperative for them to avoid saying *anything* that vindicates anxious gun owners' fears of a slippery slope leading to prohibition and confiscation. Advocates of politically feasible measures must, instead, repeat over and over, "We're not going to take your guns away."[44]

The trouble with modest, commonsense changes to our gun laws, such as background checks, waiting periods, or restrictions on the capacity of ammunition clips, is that there's no persuasive reason to believe that any reduction in gun violence such measures might effect, in a nation with nearly as many guns as people, would be distinguishable from statistical noise. And if the rejoinder is that we "have to start somewhere," the question of what exactly we're starting and how we'll know when it's completed reenters the debate. Such arguments suggest that red-state rubes who cling to their guns may be perceptive rather than paranoid about blue-state sophisticates' determination to treat private gun ownership as a privilege the government can confer or withhold, rather than a right it is obligated to respect.

They suggest, as well, the reluctance to fashion policies that take account of distasteful facts. Goldberg argues that given the remote possibility of effecting an enormous reduction in the number of privately owned guns in America—it would be a miracle of politics and policy if that number were cut in half, and the 150 million or so remaining guns would still be consistent with a high level of gun violence—a prudent objective would be to make the best of the existing situation rather than indulge dreams of transforming it. He points out, for example, that more states allow citizens, through "concealed-carry permits," to carry firearms outside the home than in the past, and there's no evidence this policy has increased crime and some it has reduced it. "Today, the number of concealed-carry permits is the highest it's ever been, at 8 million, and the homicide rate is the lowest it's been in four decades—less than half what it was 20 years ago." Before Ohio enacted a concealed-carry law in 2004, opponents predicted it would turn the state into a free-fire zone. After it became law, crime rates involving firearms stayed the same.[45]

After the U.S. Senate thwarted laws to expand gun control in 2013, the Obama administration announced it was going to follow the course first indicated after the Aurora, Colorado, shootings in 2012: make existing federal laws work rather than enact new ones. The Associated Press reported that gun laws passed in 1968, 1993, and 2007 pointed to the creation of a database for delaying or preventing gun purchases by those deemed to have mental health issues. Many states had forwarded fewer than ten records to the database, however, because of concerns compliance with *that* law would require violating other laws protecting health privacy. The administration committed to any legislative action that might save even one person, one child from gun violence had not, during its first four years in office, gotten around to the executive actions that would make the existing legal strictures created for that purpose operate effectively.[46] In January 2014, nearly five years after Obama's first inauguration, the administration announced executive actions that would clarify the particular mental health determinations that would prohibit a firearms purchase, while also clarifying how health care providers could report on these issues without violating protections of medical privacy.[47]

Green Bullshit

An America without guns is a fantasy, but it is at least a fantasy we can imagine government officials in the United States securing and maintaining. The planet's 6.8 billion non-Americans could not, however, nullify our gun control regime by their gun- and trigger-happy actions.

An America that reduces carbon dioxide emissions to the point that global warming decelerates and reverses is, however, far less plausible than a gun-free America. The world's non-Americans could, through economic growth driven by availing themselves of the most readily available forms of energy, easily negate America's enactment of every item on the Sierra Club's agenda. After declaring that "the health of the planet we inhabit" required President Obama to make the environment the highest priority of his second term, *New Yorker* editor David Remnick lamented that America's "paltry attempts to reduce global warming are being overtaken elsewhere by the attempt to raise hundreds of millions of people out of abject poverty. Advances in living standards in China, India, and Africa will radically increase the demand for cars, televisions, air-conditioners, washing machines—in short, the demand for power and the burning of fossil fuels."[48]

Though noting the existence of arguments rebutting the contentions that (a) global warming is real; (b) its effects will be harmful, if not devastating; and (c) it is largely caused by human actions and can, therefore, be largely remedied by such actions, I stipulate these propositions in order to pursue a different inquiry. To borrow another David Mamet line, this time from Brian De Palma's movie *The Untouchables*: what are you prepared to do? "Climate change is the single biggest environmental and humanitarian crisis of our time," according to the Natural Resources Defense Council (NRDC), a leading advocacy group. If global warming presents a grave or even existential threat, it demands a response that will accomplish as much good as possible, as distinguished from one that makes its advocates feel as good as possible.

The environmentalist movement has long indulged a penchant for preening over efficacy, however. John Tierney, for some years the *New York Times*'s token libertarian/contrarian, wrote an article for its magazine in 1996, "Recycling Is Garbage." It contended that mandatory recycling programs—such as municipal regulations requiring households to put glass and plastic garbage in this bin, yard waste in that one—"may be the most wasteful activity in modern America: a waste of time and money, a waste of human and natural resources." The programs are based on the false premises that America is running out of landfill space, and that landfill is inherently dangerous. But America had a population density of 104 people per square mile if we exclude Alaska and Hawaii from the equation, according to the 2010 census. If America needs radical changes to meet its waste disposal needs, then the Netherlands (400 inhabitants per square mile), South Korea (500), and Taiwan (650) would have to devote all their political energies to dealing with a permanent garbage crisis. As for their safety, "there's little reason to worry about modern landfills, which by Federal law must be lined with clay and plastic, equipped with drainage and gas-collection systems, covered daily with soil and monitored regularly for underground leaks."[49]

Apart from the cost to the cities of running several trucks on each route, and sorting garbage that usually has little market value for recycling, there is the unquantifiable cost of residents' time spent sorting their own garbage. For the many Americans who treat recycling as "an act of moral redemption . . . a rite of atonement for the sin of excess," however, the inconvenience is not a cost but a benefit. Tierney learned the importance of that sacrament after the publication of his essay, which elicited more letters of condemnation than any other article in the newspaper's history.[50]

By the same token, the imperative to save the planet by reducing carbon dioxide emissions argues for reaching attainable goals and relying on available technology. Instead, environmentalists prefer to talk about transforming human civilization by relying on technology that has not yet undergone the formality of being invented or made feasible. In the *Index of Leading Environmental Indicators, 2008*, published by the Pacific Research Institute, Steven Hayward examined one of the key transformational aspirations: America's carbon dioxide emissions in 2050 should be 80 percent lower than they had been in 1990, a goal endorsed by former vice president Al Gore and all the leading contenders for the 2008 Democratic presidential nomination. What would it mean to reduce carbon dioxide emissions from 1990's 5 billion metric tons to 1 billion over a sixty-year span? Hayward calculated that if the Census Bureau's projection that the U.S. population reaches 420 million by 2050 proves correct, the 2.4 tons of CO_2 emissions per capita required to meet the overall goal would give America per capita emissions 75 percent lower than they were in 1910, and about equal to what they were in 1875. Of course, in either 1910 or 1875 all but a handful of Americans were living below today's poverty line. Twenty-first-century nations that emit less than 2.4 tons of CO_2 include Grenada and Botswana, both of which have per capita GDPs about one-tenth of America's.[51]

In 2006, according to Hayward, the United States had CO_2 emissions of 19.4 tons per capita, much higher than those in Europe. Some of these differences have less to do with energy efficiency than with affluence (Americans have more cars and larger homes than Europeans), climate (cooler summers in Europe lead to less air-conditioning than in America), and geography (a bigger, more sparsely populated nation consumes more energy transporting people and goods than a smaller, more densely populated one). Even prosperous countries with much lower CO_2 emission rates than America's have ones more than twice as high as the 2050 goal of 2.4 tons per capita, however. Switzerland's rate was 6.1 tons per capita and France's was 6.6, but Switzerland generates most of its electricity from nuclear and hydroelectric power, while France derives 80 percent of its electric power from nuclear energy.

The low-hanging fruit for the reduction of carbon dioxide emissions is to replace coal with cleaner sources for generating electricity. One kilowatt hour generated by coal causes 2.1 pounds of CO_2 emissions, while the figure for natural gas is 38 percent less, 1.3 pounds. And the development of hydrological fracturing—"fracking"—has made that substitution even more attainable, since America turns out to have enormous reserves of natural gas not recoverable before the advent of that means of extraction.

The urgency of doing something *right now* about the biggest humanitarian crisis of our time should lead environmentalists to encourage the development of nuclear power and fracking in order to decommission as many coal-fired power plants as possible, as quickly as possible. "One cannot logically claim that carbon emissions pose a catastrophic threat to human civilization and then oppose the only two technologies capable of immediately and significantly reducing them," argue Ted Nordhaus and Michael Shellenberger of the Breakthrough Institute. Given the still more compelling force of liberal bullshit, however, unyielding opposition to these two alternatives "is precisely the position of Al Gore . . .

the Sierra Club, NRDC, and the bulk of the environmental movement."[52]

Environmentalists oppose nuclear power and fracking in part because they believe reliance on imperfect improvements will postpone the adoption of superior alternatives, such as wind and solar power. But if there were a linear relation between how ardently a scientific breakthrough is desired and how quickly it materializes, cancer would have been cured long ago. According to the U.S. Energy Information Administration, all forms of renewable energy accounted for 12.4 percent of America's electrical output in 2011. Two-thirds of that total was from "conventional hydroelectric power"—dams, that is, which environmentalists have come to revile. Wind power contributed 3 percent of the total, and solar power accounted for less than half of one percent. Coal accounted for 43 percent, natural gas for 24 percent, and nuclear energy for 20 percent.[53] Because large-scale electrical storage is also among the technologies that have not yet gone through the formality of being invented, increasing reliance on variable energy sources like wind and solar necessarily means perpetuating reliance on conventional sources of energy as a minute-to-minute supplement.

To some extent, the environmentalist agenda aligns with the sociology of the gun control agenda. The difference is that while the majority of NPR listeners and donors are already in complete compliance with the most stringent gun control laws that might be enacted, they *would* be affected by enacting the entire Sierra Club agenda, albeit less profoundly than most NASCAR fans. The blue-state types who own few guns and want to restrict the red-state types who own many are also more likely to reside in cities or inner-ring suburbs than in exurbs or sparsely populated rural areas. They can, therefore, readily endorse policies that would favor public transit over private transit, and smaller multiple-family dwellings over larger, single-family ones. The red states also have, as a rule, hotter summers, so would be more affected by regulations that rendered electricity and, in particular, air-conditioning more expensive.

The knottier problem is that the NPR listeners are disposed to think as they have been encouraged to think: the sacrifices needed to arrest and reverse global warming are comparable to sorting trash for recycling, duties that leave behind the warm glow that comes from advancing a sacred cause through noble but not onerous deeds. Journalist Megan McArdle refers to "the preferred Democratic politician mode of pretending that [the actions needed to halt global warming] will be some minor adjustment."[54] In fact, as Michael O'Hare, a professor of public policy at the University of California, Berkeley, argues, "Climate stabilization advocates, members of my intellectual and political tribe," routinely delude themselves about how easily the burdens needed to reverse carbon dioxide emissions will be borne. "If I thought it would work, I might join this chorus and preach that we will all get rich making windmills, but it won't fly." The reality, O'Hare contends, is that "climate stabilization will be very expensive."

> We will have to liquidate enormous capital investments in car-dependent suburbs and coal plants, and we will have to learn to live with less stuff of every kind, and we will deny people who never got to drive cars a future they have every right to. Then we will have to buy enormous amounts of expensive stuff like a smart electric grid and trains. Habits and aspirations that almost reach the level of identity definition will have to be abandoned, like driving wherever we want alone and parking free when we get there, and living in a big house with rooms we hardly ever sit in.[55]

The items O'Hare leaves off his list make the task of cooling the planet sound even more daunting than the ones he mentions. McArdle gives one example: divide the carbon a jet airplane emits over the course of a single round-trip commercial flight from San Francisco to New York by the number of customers on board, and each passenger ends up adding between two and three tons of carbon to the atmosphere. By contrast, the average annual carbon emission of an American passenger car is 5.1 tons. If you drove your Prius to the airport even one time during the course of the year, in other words, you would have been kinder to the planet if you had skipped the plane trip, driven away from the airport, and traded the hybrid in for a SuperPolluter SUV on your way back home.[56]

None of these obstacles factor in an even more daunting impediment: abating greenhouse gas emissions is the collective action problem from hell. Absent mechanisms never yet seen in human history to develop and then enforce multilateral agreements among all nations that pollute, each nation will plausibly fear that its own sacrifices will be pointless. Unlike many pollutants, whose "neighborhood effects" do indeed stay localized, a ton of greenhouse gases emitted anywhere has effects on global warming that are felt everywhere in roughly the same way. Because (a) slightly less than 5 percent of the world's people live in America; and (b) American democracy militates against policies that burden large numbers of people without providing offsetting benefits, the politics are extremely difficult. Since 95 percent of the benefits of an American program to reduce greenhouse gases are going to be enjoyed by people outside the United States, in other words, the costs of that program are going to be electorally feasible only if its benefits to America are twenty times greater than its costs. The list of options meeting that criterion is not long.[57]

And, to recall our friend Mpinga Bomboku, any global regime that allows poor countries to pursue economic growth by relying on cheap but carbon-intensive sources of energy is going to require even more stringent controls on energy usage by already prosperous countries. Offsetting new coal-fired power plants in the Global

South, however, would require America to find policies with a benefit/cost ratio exceeding 20:1. If, as will almost certainly be the case, such a challenge proves politically impossible, the implementation of less ambitious but politically attainable policies will be a net plus for the global environment only if poor countries can be induced to stay poor longer, or get rich slower, than they would by relying on fossil fuels.

Environmentalists who disdain the trade-offs of mitigations like nuclear energy and fracking, which would buy time for the development and adoption of less problematic technologies, traffic in liberal bullshit, preferring to feel good than to do good. The hazy, hopeful agenda they endorse instead, consisting of ineffectual gestures on the one hand and political, administrative, and technological nonstarters on the other, is akin to the "politician's syllogism" popularized by the BBC program *Yes Minister*.

> *Major Premise* (uttered with gravity): "Something must be done."
> *Minor Premise*: "This [with a wave of the hand to indicate whatever policy alternative happens to be under discussion] is [resigned shrug of the shoulders] . . . something."
> *Conclusion* (again with gravity and finality): "*This* must be done."

As with gun control advocates who want to abolish the private ownership of firearms in America, the maximal environmentalist position also has an intellectual coherence and moral integrity not discernible among the "realistic" incrementalists. Seeking, against formidable odds, a position more provocative that Susan Sontag's declaration that whites are the cancer of human history, Paul Watson, founder of the Sea Shepherd Conservation Society, wrote in 2007 that human beings are the "AIDS of the Earth." That is to say, "Our viral like behaviour can be terminal both to the present biosphere and ourselves."[58] Fortunately, there may be human solutions for the human problem, redemptive choices we can make that will, to some extent, roll back the voracious depredations that have defined the history of our species. "We need to re-wild the planet," Watson believes, which "will require a complete overhaul of all of humanity's economic, cultural, and life style systems." For starters, "We need to radically and intelligently reduce human populations to fewer than one billion," from its present level of 7.1 billion. The last time fewer than one billion people lived on earth, demographers think, was around 1800. The drastic revision of human population must be accompanied by a revolution in human consciousness. "We need to eliminate nationalism and tribalism and become Earthlings," Watson writes. "And as Earthlings, we need to recognize that all the other species that live on this planet are also fellow citizens and also Earthlings."[59] This characterization of the challenge amounts to the terrestrial outer limit to the project of taking care of our own.

In this brave new/old world, "No human community should be larger than 20,000 people," because we need "vast areas of the planet where humans do not live at all and where other species are free to evolve without human interference." Those communities will be distant from one another and surrounded by wilderness. In effect, "people should be placed in parks within ecosystems instead of parks placed in human communities."

"Communication systems can link the communities," Watson writes. Such systems will be imperative because his agenda is going to make travel between communities extremely difficult. For one thing, "We need to stop flying, stop driving cars, and jetting around on marine recreational vehicles. The Mennonites survive without cars and so can the rest of us." For another, "Sea transportation should be by sail," which would return nautical transport to the state of the art that prevailed the last time the world's population numbered one billion. We should re-create the clipper ships of that era, supplemented by a technology that was then—and is still—unavailable: "Air transportation should be by solar powered blimps when air transportation is necessary."

Transportation will be largely superfluous, in any case, because our communities of twenty thousand or fewer people will be autonomous and self-sustaining. "All consumption should be local. No food products need to be transported over hundreds of miles to market. All commercial fishing should be abolished. If local communities need to fish the fish should be caught individually by hand." Watson's consumption agenda will facilitate his energy agenda. "We need to stop burning fossil fuels and utilize only wind, water, and solar power with all generation of power coming from individual or small community units like windmills, waterwheels, and solar panels."

It goes without saying that to reverse two centuries of population growth, reducing the number of humans by 85 percent, will require having fewer children. Watson spells out one implication: most people won't have any children at all, and the criteria for determining which ones are worthy (and permitted?) to procreate will be more exacting than any standards humanity has ever recognized.

> Who should have children? Those who are responsible and completely dedicated to the responsibility, which is actually a very small percentage of humans. Being a parent should be a career. Whereas some people are engineers, musicians, or lawyers, others with the desire and the skills can be fathers and mothers. Schools can be eliminated if the professional parent is also the educator of the child.[60]

"The only future more expensive and painful than a carbon-free one," O'Hare writes, "is the *only other one on the table*," which the planet will endure if humans' use of fossil fuels makes the world hotter and hotter. Watson's future is highly unlikely to be realized, but one can plausibly describe how it would be better than the climate change apocalypse. What is the less drastic alternative, the one *more* likely to be realized than Watson's, while still averting the catastrophe O'Hare and most environmentalists believe is upon us? In the continuing absence of a clear answer to that question, environmentalists' opposition to fracking and nuclear power is an exercise in fecklessness.

DIVERSITY BULLSHIT

The defining characteristic of prescriptive bullshit, as I've been using the term here, is a strong preference for political stances that demonstrate one's heart is in the right place, combined with a relative indifference to whether the policies based on those stances, as actually implemented, do or even can achieve their intended results. Liberalism's diversity agenda qualifies, on these grounds, as meta-bullshit, prescriptive bullshit in the service of descriptive bullshit.

"Diversity" became, after the 1978 Supreme Court's *Bakke* decision, synonymous with "affirmative action" or the concept of social justice in general. It's rare to find an institution of higher education or large business enterprise in twenty-first-century America that does not have a diversity mission statement and staff members whose professional responsibility is to make the organization more diverse, and then make that diversity more successful and rewarding. The *Economist* noted in 2014, "The closest thing the business world has to a universally acknowledged truth is that diversity is a good thing: the more companies hire people from different backgrounds the more competitive they will become."[61] A Rip van Winkle who went to sleep six months before *Brown v. Board of Education* in 1954 and woke up six months after *Regents of the University of California v. Bakke* in 1978 would conclude that diversity had been the whole point of the civil rights movement.

In fact, the great diversity crusade came about through happenstance, and a determined rush to exploit it. *Bakke* was the Supreme Court's first big affirmative action case, brought when Allan Bakke filed suit after the University of California, Davis, medical school denied him admission. Bakke claimed he had been the victim of racial discrimination by the medical school since (a) he was white; and (b) several applicants who were members of minority groups were admitted to the program, despite having lower grades and test scores than his. This result came about because the school had set aside a certain number of positions in its entering class for nonwhites only.

Four of the Court's nine justices (Warren Burger, William Rehnquist, John Stevens, and Potter Stewart) ruled in favor of Bakke: the law prohibiting institutions and programs that receive federal funds from discriminating on account of race was applicable, they said, and the University of California broke it. Four other justices (Harry Blackmun, William Brennan, Thurgood Marshall, and Byron White) ruled in favor of the university: the importance of increasing the number of black and Hispanic doctors, improving medical care in minority communities, and overcoming the legacy of racial discrimination in general were sufficient reasons to justify the medical school's racial classification policy, and the harm it inflicted upon Bakke. Affirmative action policies were legal and constitutional, they contended, provided their purpose is "not to demean or insult any racial group, but to remedy disadvantages cast on minorities by past racial prejudice." In a concurring opinion Blackmun wrote, "[I]n order to get beyond racism, we must first take account of race. There is no other way. And in order to treat some persons equally, we must treat them differently."

The ninth justice, Lewis Powell, charted a middle course. He agreed that UC Davis had discriminated against Allan Bakke, and joined with the justices who ordered the university to admit him. He also, however, agreed with the four justices who ruled in the university's favor—up to a point. Educational institutions were justified in taking race into account, Powell contended, but *not* for the sake of remedying disadvantages resulting from past prejudice, or getting beyond race by taking account of race. The only permissible justification for race-conscious admissions policies, wrote Powell, is that universities have a compelling interest in "the attainment of a diverse student body," which may take precedence over the applicant's right to have his credentials considered in a nondiscriminatory manner. Thus a medical school could legally enroll a student whose grades, test scores, and other credentials might not otherwise secure his admission if the applicant's "particular background—whether it be ethnic, geographic, culturally advantaged or disadvantaged—may bring to a professional school of medicine experiences, outlooks, and ideas that enrich the training of its student body and better equip its graduates" to discharge their professional duties. Powell ruled in Bakke's favor because he opposed quotas: every applicant should have the right to compete for every opening, rather than just for the ones not set aside in advance for members of a particular demographic group. But he ruled in favor of affirmative action, provided that demographic status was only a "plus" factor in the admissions process, "where race or ethnic background is simply one element—to be weighed fairly against other elements—in the selection process."

With the endorsement of exactly one Supreme Court justice, then, diversity suddenly became affirmative action's raison d'être. (Not until 2003, in a case involving the University of Michigan's law school, did a majority of the Court finally endorse the diversity rationale.) One irony of the situation is that, even as in the 1950s editorialists all deplored conformity in interchangeable terms, America's leading public and private institutions embraced diversity after 1978 in exactly the same way. Diversity, it seems, is too important to abide diverse opinions about diversity, such as ones that might sanction some institutions' idiosyncratic commitment to homogeneity.

Furthermore, whether Powell intended it or not, his argument about plus factors had the primary effect of making the admissions process more opaque and hypocritical. A quota system explicitly discriminates against certain applicants. A "holistic" system, the term Sandra Day O'Connor employed in the Michigan case, uses race only as a plus factor, while leaving open the possibility it will be such a big plus factor as to be operationally indistinguishable from a quota. A study by sociologist Thomas Espenshade found that identifying yourself as a black applicant to three highly selective private universities was as valuable to your chances of gaining admission as a 230-point increase on your Scholastic Aptitude Test score, measured on a 400-to-1,600-point scale. Hispanic applicants got what amounted to a 185-point boost, while Asian-American applicants were assessed the equivalent of a 50-point penalty. Take away those plus (and minus) factors, and black and Hispanic acceptance rates would decline by more than 50 percent, with Asians receiving four out of every five acceptance letters that would have otherwise gone to black or Hispanic applicants. (Whites' acceptance rates would stay almost the same.)[62]

Well, wouldn't the more-Asian, less-black, less-Hispanic, and equally white freshman class created by abandoning affirmative action be as diverse as the less-Asian, more-black, and more-Hispanic one rendered by using it? According to *Slate*'s Dahlia Lithwick, an affirmative action defender, Powell's diversity rationale was regarded as bullshit from day one, in that it invoked one goal for the purpose of promoting a different one:

> What Justice Powell was calling race-neutral diversity was always known to be a code word for racial diversity. Powell wasn't really interested in filling colleges with Alsatian goat herders. He was looking for some neutral-sounding reason to give minority candidates a small "plus" in the admissions office.[63]

Moreover, diversity, as explained by Powell and championed by the subsequently created diversity-industrial complex, purports to be for the benefit of the entire student body, not just the students who get in because of it and would have been rejected in the absence of affirmative action. Students on campuses who wear T-shirts proclaiming "I'm not here to be your black experience" express an unimpeachable sentiment, but one totally at odds with the diversity rationale. Applicants who get a demographic-based bonus exceeding one standard deviation of the SAT score distribution are there precisely, according to Powell, to provide "experiences, outlooks, and ideas" that broaden and enhance their classmates' educational experience. "In other words," writes Lithwick, "some white students are refused so that other white (and nonwhite) students may be enriched. This is the core of the 'diversity' defense."

As with guns or carbon emissions, the maximalist position on affirmative action, captured by Harry Blackmun's Orwellian formulation about treating people equally by treating them differently, has the virtue of making goals and standards reasonably clear. Whether any kind or amount of affirmative action would make race and ethnicity trivial factors in America's class structure may be doubted, but at least we would know that result if we saw it. By contrast, the goal of diversity does not admit of successful completion, even in theory. Institutions' compelling interest in having a variety of backgrounds and perspectives in the ranks of their students and employees is permanent, so the departure from race neutrality, the ostensible goal of the civil rights movement and legislation, is not just protracted but eternal.

Pursuing one goal by appealing to a different one will also be permanently dodgy, however. The *New York Times* reported in 2004 that of the 520 black Harvard undergraduates, 8 percent of the student body, "the majority of them—perhaps as many as two-thirds—[are] West Indian and African immigrants or their children, or to a lesser extent, children of biracial couples." That leaves "only about a third of the students from families in which all four grandparents were born in this country, descendants of slaves." It's a sensitive topic, so much so that the *Times* had to say "perhaps" and "about"—Harvard was among the many schools that did not gather this type of information about its students. "You need a philosophical discussion about what are the aims of affirmative action," said the chairman of Harvard's sociology department. "If it's about getting black faces at Harvard, then you're doing fine. If it's about making up for 200 to 500 years of slavery in this country and its aftermath, then you're not doing well."[64]

But the whole point of making diversity the justification for affirmative action was that liberals did not want to have, because they did not think they could win, a philosophical discussion about using affirmative action to make up for slavery and Jim Crow. Such a debate would have squarely confronted the question of reverse discrimination, which the one about diversity circumvented. Should Allan Bakke have been kept out of medical school because stifling his ambitions was a necessary and fair price to pay for getting beyond racism by taking race into account? Four life-tenured justices wanted to go down that road, but few politicians facing voters were prepared to follow. The safer argument called for rejecting applicants like Bakke for the sake of student bodies and workforces that would be gorgeous mosaics providing an eclectic array of perspectives.

One defense of affirmative action was that while its costs might seem high, and even unfair, to the individuals denied educational and career opportunities for the sake of diversity, these costs were not particularly heavy for society overall, considered in light of affirmative action's benefits. Allan Bakke completed medical school, and went on to read in the *New York Times Magazine* in 1995 that he did not "appear to have set the world on fire as a doctor," since he "has no private practice and works on an interim basis, rather than as a staff physician" at a hospital. The article, written by Nicholas

Lemann, contrasted Bakke's career with that of Patrick Chavis, one of the black UC Davis medical students admitted under the affirmative action program struck down by the Supreme Court in 1978. Chavis "freely admits," wrote Lemann, that "he would not have been admitted strictly on the basis of his grades and test scores. . . ." But while Bakke didn't set the world on fire, America was clearly a better nation for having gone out of its way to give Chavis a medical education, since he went on to become an obstetrician-gynecologist whose practice was devoted to the poor and underserved. "If Chavis hadn't gotten into medical school," Lemann stated, "his patients wouldn't be treated by some better-qualified white obstetrician; they'd have no doctor at all and their babies would be delivered the way Chavis was—by whoever happened to be on duty at the emergency room of the county hospital."[65]

Affirmative action became a central controversy of the 1996 election when California considered (and ultimately passed) a ballot initiative, Proposition 209, severely restricting it. Senator Edward Kennedy relied on the feel-good story about Dr. Chavis in telling a Senate committee in April 1996, "He is the supposedly less qualified African American student who allegedly displaced Allan Bakke at UC Davis and triggered the landmark case. Today, Dr. Chavis is a successful ob-gyn in central Los Angeles, making a difference in the lives of scores of poor families." Unfortunately, in June 1996 Patrick Chavis also made a difference in the life of Tammaria Cotton, on whom he performed liposuction surgery, a sideline taken up to increase revenue for his medical practice. Cotton went into cardiac arrest while still at the clinic where Chavis had performed the surgery, after the doctor had left to check on another liposuction patient who was recovering in Chavis's home. Because of his absence and failure to leave adequate instructions for the clinic's nurse on caring for Cotton, she died later that day in the hospital. Other Chavis liposuction patients suffered severe infections and massive blood loss, according to the California Medical Board, which suspended Chavis's license to practice medicine in 1997 and revoked it in 1998. "Defenders of the policy said affirmative action should not be judged by one man's performance," the *Los Angeles Times* reported after Chavis's medical career had collapsed. That's a prudent reminder, but an unpersuasive one coming from the same quarters that had so recently told the more encouraging parts of the Chavis story in order to argue that affirmative action *should* be judged by one man's performance.[66]

Diversity, finally, qualifies as meta-bullshit not only because it is a benign-sounding though problematic stalking horse for reverse discrimination, but because there's a strong argument that the net effect of implementing diversity is to harm, not help, members of minority groups. Affirmative action, a vehicle for feeling good while doing bad, is in that sense a paradigmatic case of prescriptive bullshit. According to Richard Sander and Stuart Taylor Jr., the primary consequence of plus factors in college admissions as hefty as those discovered by Thomas Espenshade is to mismatch students and institutions. The "beneficiary" of affirmative action "finds himself in a class where he has weaker academic preparation than nearly all of his classmates. The student who would flourish at, say, Wake Forest or the University of Richmond, instead finds himself at Duke, where the professors are not teaching at a pace designed for him—they are teaching to the 'middle' of the class, introducing terms and concepts at a speed that is unnerving even to the best-prepared student." Civil rights activists denounced the reduction in the number of black and Hispanic students enrolled at the very competitive University of California, Los Angeles (where Sander is a law professor) after Proposition 209 curtailed affirmative action. What they did not mention was that while fewer students served the function of being others' black and Hispanic experience, or imparted the warm glow throughout the university of furthering the cause of diversity, the number of UCLA *degrees awarded* to black and Hispanic students in the five years after Proposition 209 was the same as the number awarded in the five years before it. The students missing on account of 209 were mostly ones who would not have graduated from UCLA, having been induced to attend it rather than one of the many institutions where they might well have flourished.[67]

Comprehensive Bullshit

If the alliance of experts and victims is to prevail in a democracy, as many voters as possible must (a) either regard themselves as victims or feel sorry for others they believe to be victims; and (b) respect and defer to experts to solve the victims' problems. For their part in advancing the alliance's political arguments and cause, experts need to demonstrate their expertise not just by solving problems, but by characterizing the problems they propose to work on as big, urgent, and complex. To do otherwise, and suggest that some problems are small, manageable, and straightforward, would undercut the argument for relying on experts.

A vital term in the experts' rhetorical inventory is "comprehensive." Big problems need big solutions. But when the experts are, in effect, getting paid by the hour, small solutions are never recommended because small problems are never detected. During the debate over President Obama's health care proposals, advocates for comprehensive reforms repeatedly deplored the fact that 47 million Americans lacked health insurance. Balamurali Ambati, a University of Utah ophthalmologist, contended that statistic did not mean what it seemed to. It included, for one thing, 14 million people who were eligible for existing government health programs, such as Medicare, Medicaid, or veterans' programs, but for one reason or another had not enrolled. Of the remaining 33 million without insurance, nearly 10 million were noncitizens. During the frightening economic reversals of 2009, Democrats insisted they

were not interested in reforms that would give taxpayer-subsidized
health care to people who came to the country voluntarily, and in
some cases in violation of American immigration laws. Another
9 million uninsured Americans had household incomes exceeding
$75,000. These were people who hadn't secured health insurance
as opposed to people who couldn't. Subsequent policy debates and
experience would make it hard to see these uninsured people as
victims of America's health care system. They were, instead, the
heedless "young invincibles" who were willfully exacerbating its
problems by refusing to throw their healthy selves into the national
risk pool. Of the remaining 14 million people without health insurance, somewhere between 3 and 5 million were, at any given
moment, uninsured for a period of two months or less, mostly as
a result of being between jobs or just beginning new ones. "That
leaves about 10 million Americans who are chronically without
insurance," wrote Ambati, or some 3 percent of the population, a
problem that should not "require a wholesale overhaul" of American health care.[68]

Sweeping solutions for what turn out to be discrete problems,
however, elevate the status and importance of expert findings, and
of expertise itself. No expert, as a result, is put in the embarrassing
position of saying, "The fact is, we don't really understand this problem very well, or have any particularly encouraging ideas of how to
solve it. Rather than try something big and bold, which would be
reckless under the circumstances, we should make modest, incremental changes and carefully study their consequences."

In 2009, during the debate over health care reform, the president's Council of Economic Advisers cited studies by the Dart-
mouth Institute for Health Policy and Clinical Practice in a report
claiming that "nearly 30 percent of Medicare's costs could be saved
without adverse health consequences." Moreover, if the changes
that would capture those wasted expenditures could be applied to
all health care outside of Medicare, the result would be to reduce

health care spending from 18 to 13 percent of GDP. Journalist Virginia Postrel asked why "a report that claims that Medicare is wasting 30 percent of its spending thinks it's making a case for making the rest of the health care system more like Medicare." In other words, if we *are* wasting 30 percent of our Medicare outlays, why don't we apply a new set of reforms to Medicare *first*, and *see* whether or not they work, rather than just *assume* they'll work and apply them to the entire health care system? Peter Orszag, President Obama's first director of the Office of Management and Budget, responded to Postrel's question by saying that making Medicare efficient was politically impossible, since interest groups like AARP would oppose even the prospect of savings that might someday involve benefit reductions unless they were preceded by clear, irrevocable expansions in health care coverage.[69]

In a 2009 address to Congress, President Obama said that the "commitment" to "quality, affordable health care for all Americans" is "a step we must take if we hope to bring down our deficit in the years to come."[70] The face-value meaning of that declaration was that expanding health care to all Americans was going to save the federal government more money than it would cost, so much so that getting federal borrowing under control would be impossible without the commitment to health care for all. One assumption widely touted by advocates of what became Obamacare was that making sure no one lacked health insurance would cut down on the use of the expensive care offered by emergency rooms, especially by the uninsured who could not otherwise afford to see a doctor, even for medical problems that were not emergencies. A study released in 2014, however, showed people newly enrolled in Medicaid were 40 percent *more* likely to go to emergency rooms than socioeconomically similar people not covered by Medicaid. It turns out "covering people with health insurance doesn't save money," economist Jonathan Gruber, who had advised the Obama administration on health care policy, told the *Washington Post*. Showing skills that would have served him well in diplomacy or public relations, he continued, "That was sometimes a misleading motivator for the Affordable Care Act. The law isn't designed to save money. It's designed to improve health, and that's going to cost money."[71]

Comprehensiveness serves another political purpose. Insisting that comprehensive reform is the only path forward has the effect of stipulating that changes nonexperts might find sensible are ones that cannot be disaggregated from, and are going to be held hostage to, changes the experts deem necessary. Securing the nation's borders and enforcing its immigration laws, accordingly, is not a "viable" stand-alone option. It can only work, reform advocates have stated over and over, as part of a package that "normalizes" the status of "undocumented" workers, giving them a way "out of the shadows" and toward full citizenship. As with health care, the notion that we can address one issue *and then* another, taking our bearings by analyzing the practical consequences of incremental steps rather than implementing entire systemic theories, is ruled to be somehow out of order.

The cult of complexity responds to that political challenge by enacting simple reforms in a complicated manner. Discovering complexity where it may not exist is always a useful way for experts to undermine policy measures they opposed but couldn't thwart. Thus, complaints that the border between Mexico and America was unacceptably porous led to an elaborate project for an $8 billion electronic "fence" relying on radar, cameras, and satellite signals. In 2010, after years of testing and futility, the director of the project at the Department of Homeland Security told the *Los Angeles Times*, apparently with a straight face, "It was a great idea, but it didn't work." When Homeland Security secretary Janet Napolitano ordered "a department-wide assessment" of the project, a spokesman for the Federation for American Immigration Reform, a restrictionist group, said, "Instead of spending a lot of time reassessing, they should get out there and do the sorts of things we know work effectively to get control of the border, such as double fencing and more manpower."[72]

GENEROSITY BULLSHIT

In proclaiming "our credo" to the 1984 Democratic national convention, Mario Cuomo began by saying, "We believe in only the government we need, but we insist on all the government we need." On the occasions when liberals rhetorically engage the question of how much government we need, they usually operate at such a high level of abstraction that the answer could mean almost anything. "All the government we need," for example, is open to debate, which means citizens across the ideological spectrum could conclude their various, incompatible answers are each consistent with Cuomo's standard.

Liberals prefer to make the case for their position—we need much more government—by particularizing rather than generalizing. This means, above all, depicting suffering situations and imploring Americans to respond compassionately by demanding government programs that aid the sufferers. Liberals frequently connect programs with categories of sufferers. Nicholas Kristof of the *New York Times*, for example, wrote in 2013, "[S]lashing food stamp benefits—overwhelmingly for children, the disabled and the elderly—wouldn't be a sign of prudent fiscal management by Congress. It would be a mark of shortsighted cruelty."[73]

An even more effective argument, judging by the frequency with which it is employed, is to connect a specific suffering situation to the absence or underfunding of a government program. Paul Waldman invented Betsy Wilson, but Kristof discovered Richard Streeter, a forty-seven-year-old truck driver with "a tumor in his colon that may kill him because Obamacare didn't come quite soon enough." Lacking health insurance, Streeter put off seeing a doctor, until he learned that economizing on medical expenditures had put his life at risk.[74]

Liberals say these things so often because they're advantageous as well as gratifying. As I've noted, framing the liberal agenda as the politics of kindness is an attempt, often very effective, to put conservatives on the defensive at the outset of every policy debate. The politics of kindness is even more useful to liberalism, however, by virtue of the subjects it excludes. The sufferer and the mechanism by which the government might alleviate his suffering if only we were a bit more compassionate and generous are always at the top of the agenda, while several awkward questions are ruled out of order. Indeed, even to raise them is to evince the callousness that permits so much suffering in the first place.

So, for example, conservatives never tire of pointing out that a cut in government social welfare spending means . . . a cut, which is not the same as a reduction from some past or anticipated rate of growth. Liberals, for their part, never tire of disregarding this simple fact. The California journalist Peter Schrag declared in 2011 that in both Sacramento and Washington, D.C., "government and government services are being taken down piece by piece," because the "paucity of revenues has become an immutable political absolute." It's a story with a villain, one as mendacious as it is malign: "The GOP may not acknowledge that it wants to privatize public schools or drive students of limited means out of the universities, or eliminate tax-funded health care and social services for the poor, or destroy the last vestiges of publicly supported transit or shut the parks. . . . But that clearly is what it's accomplishing."[75]

In 2010, however, the last full fiscal year before Schrag issued his indictment, California's state and local governments combined to spend $11,621 for each state resident on all government functions. Adjusted for inflation, those per capita outlays were 52 percent higher than they had been eighteen years earlier. In 1992, it will be noted, California operated schools and universities.

Eighteen years later public spending on education was 48 percent higher, adjusted for inflation and population growth, and education advocates complained constantly about how the schools were running out of money. State and local governments also provided health care in 1992. By 2010, when California's conservatives were marshaling the forces of greed and selfishness to deny vital funding to those endeavors, public outlays on hospitals and health programs were 39 percent higher. Spending on public welfare programs, the ones being dismantled as a result of fiscal austerity, went up 47 percent. The parks being forced to close had 36 percent more money, while the housing programs being eviscerated received 83 percent more. In short, ever-bluer California spent two decades increasing outlays on all the causes most important to liberals, at rates far faster than the combined effects of inflation and population growth would dictate. The result, somehow, is a public sector that has gotten worse rather than better at meeting California's basic needs . . . for which conservatives are to blame.[76]

Liberalism without bullshit, if such a thing is conceivable, would take up Mitch Daniels's challenge to make sure the programs liberals have created over the past century operate so effectively and efficiently that no government dollar capable of benefiting a poor person is being wasted in any way. There's a reason so few liberals sign up for this crusade: acknowledging the importance of making government programs more effective requires admitting they are not, presently, as effective as they can or should be. Such an admission could lead reasonable people, not to mention vicious right-wingers, to conclude that before we turn our attention to creating new government programs and increasing funding for existing ones, we should—both for the sake of taxpayers who fund social welfare programs and for clients who depend on them—make sure the existing array of programs is working as well as can reasonably be expected. Putting the liberal political project on hold until the liberal governmental project is in good repair, however, could involve a long, enervating delay. During it, parading one's compassion and denouncing the empathy-deficient will give way to the useful but less gratifying drudgery of making stuff work right. And if protracted, earnest, but unsuccessful efforts to improve implementation demonstrate that some stuff cannot be made to work right, the political project will endure not just a delay but a defeat, as it becomes clear that conservative opposition to the government program in question had a basis in something more substantial and admirable than greed and cruelty.

Better, then, for liberals to debate the welfare state in terms of whether we're putting as much into it as we're obliged to, rather than whether we're getting as much out of it as we deserve to. All the government we need is not only a great deal of government but always a great deal *more* government than we have at any particular moment, no matter how much government has grown. Liberal rhetoric in default mode, demanding more and bigger government programs, proceeds as though ongoing and even long-established initiatives addressing this or that intolerable problem did not exist. Suffering situations are depicted with harrowing detail, while the efficacy of the government programs to alleviate them is posited. Examining a website where artists explained their preference for reelecting President Obama, the *Weekly Standard*'s Andrew Ferguson concluded that liberals invest the words "program" and "funding" with "talismanic power." They enthuse over programs that "will rescue the environment or curb domestic violence or teach civility or help the disabled or train the jobless. The proper program can do everything but play canasta. And it can be advocated without wondering how it might work or whether it would work or what other programs would not be funded so it could be."[77]

Democratic presidents cannot be as blithe about the question of efficacy as citizens venting their opinions. Each of the three most recent has felt the need to say and do something about it. In his 2011 State of the Union address, President Obama acknowledged that wasteful, inconsequential government was a problem for the party *of* government. He urged Congress to give the people "a government that's more competent and more efficient," because "We can't win the future with a government of the past." Noting that "the last major reorganization of the Government happened in the age of black-and-white TV," Obama promised his administration would "develop a proposal to merge, consolidate, and reorganize the Federal Government."[78]

With this declaration Obama was inadvertently or slyly disparaging his most recent Democratic predecessor. In a 1993 speech announcing the creation of the National Partnership for Reinventing Government, President Bill Clinton said, "Our goal is to make the entire federal government less expensive and more efficient, and to change the culture of our national bureaucracy away from complacency and entitlement toward initiative and empowerment. We intend to redesign, to reinvent, to reinvigorate the entire national government."[79]

For the president in 2011 to state that one must go back half a century to find a government reorganization worthy of the name is to signal, implicitly but unmistakably, that very little came of Clinton's ambitious goals and the council that spent eight years working on them. In a sense, however, it's only fair for Obama to slight Clinton, given that Clinton's vow to upgrade the expensive, inefficient, complacent governmental apparatus *he* inherited signaled just as clearly that Jimmy Carter's promises in 1976 to make government as good and competent as the American people, through innovations like sunset laws and zero-based budgeting, had yielded little of durable value.

Obama's promised transformation was completely forgotten months after he introduced it. The boldest, most visionary proposal toward the goal of merging, consolidating, and reorganizing the federal government was to transfer the Office of the United States Trade Representative from the Executive Office of the President to the Department of Commerce. Congress wasn't interested and, it became clear, neither was the White House.[80] Having made no changes that anyone hails or even recalls, the Obama crusade to make the government more competent and efficient leaves the next Democratic president free to make the same promise yet again, and well positioned to achieve the same result. The fate of a chronic problem, evidently, is to have a chronic solution. If any recent Democratic administrations' bold proclamations about transforming American governance had produced tangible outcomes that turned out to be even quasi-transformative, successive Democratic presidents would not keep finding it necessary to push what sounds like the very same boulder up what sounds like the very same hill. These serial futilities suggest either that activist government's flaws are irremediable, or that liberals' efforts to address them are exercises, deluded or cynical, in going through the motions. It is fitting that the problem of government programs that are busy but inconsequential, doing much but accomplishing little, elicit periodic government reform crusades that are also busy, or at least noisy, and inconsequential.

There are, then, many arguments about the unnecessary suffering that people—preferably, specific people, ones with sad stories that can be told in affecting detail, who'll struggle not to but ultimately cry on camera in a way that makes television viewers want to cry, too—will endure because of the failure to create this government program or "adequately" fund that one. (That not a single well-intentioned government program has ever been adequately funded is axiomatic.) One possible response is that rather than talk about this sufferer and that program, we need, like the diversity professionals in college admissions offices, to consider the question holistically. Doing so would argue that, in the context of America's overall efforts to alleviate suffering situations, the problem is not that the amount of money the government spends is insufficient but that the manner in which it spends money is ineffective. Frame the issue in that way and the key issue cannot be inputs, such as how much money is spent on a program; or outputs, such as how many people it employs or how many beneficiaries it enrolls; but out*comes*, the measured, provable performance Governor Daniels called for. And if outcomes matter—indeed, if they're the only thing that matters—then it's a mistake to put demands for more social welfare spending on the national agenda before we establish beyond a reasonable doubt that the money we're presently spending is being spent well. To proceed otherwise, to increase spending now and demand effectiveness at some indeterminate point in the distant future, deals in bad faith with Americans in their capacity as (1) people who do or might depend on a government program; (2) taxpayers who fund the programs; and (3) citizens of a republic, since the refusal to talk about programmatic efficacy until that fine day we achieve budgetary adequacy means we'll *never* make efficacy a high priority. The engineers who build the social welfare machine can, as a result, eternally postpone a day of reckoning about the design and operation of their marvel by insisting on the need to build a bigger, better, more expensive one before we judge them or their creation.

In 2012, for example, the federal government spent $7,085 per American on the five major areas of what the Office of Management and Budget categorizes as the Human Resources "superfunction." (These "functions" include: [1] Social Security; [2] all other income support programs, such as unemployment or disability insurance; [3] Medicare; [4] all other health programs, such as Medicaid; and [5] all programs for education, training, employment, and social services. I exclude the sixth OMB human resources function, programs for veterans of the armed services, since the moral basis on which we discharge those obligations is sui generis.) Spending on these five functions in 2012 represented 63 percent of federal outlays, and one-seventh of GDP. That level of human resources spending also amounted to $28,340 of resources per four humans; in 2012 the "poverty guideline," known colloquially as the poverty line, was $23,050 for a family of four.[81] According to the Census Bureau, state and local governments spent an additional $728 billion in 2011 (the latest year available) for "social services and income maintenance," which is roughly another $2,300 per American.

Federal spending on human resources, on a per capita, inflation-adjusted basis, was 57 percent larger when Barack Obama took office in 2009 than it had been sixteen years earlier when Clinton was inaugurated, and 57 percent larger when Bill Clinton took office in 1993 than it had been in 1977, when Jimmy Carter was sworn in. After compounding, this means that human resources spending was nearly two and a half times greater in 2009 than in 1977. Meanwhile, the proportion of families living in poverty in 1977, according to the Census Bureau, was 9.3 percent. In 1993 it was 12.3 percent, and in 2009 it was 11.1 percent. That figure was 13.9 percent in 1965, when the War on Poverty was launched, and has never been higher since then, nor lower than 8.7 percent.

It requires a deeply eccentric computer program to crunch such numbers and produce the conclusion that America's main problem is that it's not devoting enough resources to the alleviation of suffering. William Galston contends that America did not lose the War on Poverty but, rather, "fought poverty to a draw" over the course of half a century during which changes in the world's economy and the nation's sociology "became increasingly unfavorable for lower-wage workers and their families."[82] Even this tempered conclusion leaves Johnson's War on Poverty looking like his war in Vietnam, one to which the nation devotes escalating resources in the service of a strategic goal that grows increasingly distant and amorphous the more aggressively we pursue it. In both cases, good governance demands reassessing the goals and conduct of the war, rather than making the lazy, inertial assumption that deploying one more increment of resources in the service of the same strategy will make it succeed, even though all the previous increments that were supposed to secure victory did not.

Leave aside the interpretation of poverty statistics. For the better part of a century the political reality has been that the more the government spends on social welfare programs, the more liberals insist it needs to spend. If their agenda is succeeding, liberals are the last people to know or admit that fact. People who care about caring demand more government spending but eschew rigorous interrogations about the efficacy of past and present spending. Their expansive souls desire their own well-being in whatever suffering situations where they feel their existence, and the best, most direct way to feel better is to demand more ameliorative government spending. Complacency about whether social welfare spending is doing any good for the people it is supposed to be helping is completely consistent with liberal compassion, as such questions would only complicate the main focus, the empathizer's capacity to feel like a good person. Whether we can achieve a more beneficial, admirable configuration of empathizer, empathizee, and government is the subject of the next and final chapter.

Chapter 5

How Conservatives Have Countered the Arguments Put Forward in the Name of Liberal Compassion, and Might Rebut Them More Effectively

---

L iberals believe compassion is the quality that defines liberalism, certifying its moral excellence. This belief corresponds to their conviction that a shocking lack of compassion, manifested in callous indifference to human suffering, is the quality that defines conservatism, certifying its moral depravity. In reply, conservatives complain constantly, to little avail, that the liberal project vitiates the qualities that make compassion admirable by practicing generosity with other people's money, made available to the government through the exertions of tax collectors and regulators, who operate at the front of a phalanx of police officers, judges, and prison guards. The American social scientist William Graham Sumner made this case in an 1883 essay, "The Forgotten Man."

> As soon as A observes something which seems to him to be wrong, from which X is suffering, A talks it over with B, and A and B then propose to get a law passed to remedy the evil and

help X. Their law always proposes to determine what C shall do for X or, in the better case, what A, B and C shall do for X. As for A and B, who get a law to make themselves do for X what they are willing to do for him, we have nothing to say except that they might better have done it without any law. . . . [C] is the man who never is thought of. He is the victim of the reformer, social speculator and philanthropist, and . . . he deserves your notice both for his character and for the many burdens which are laid upon him.[1]

Forty-nine years later, Franklin Roosevelt took a step toward the White House with a speech endorsing policies "that build from the bottom up and not from the top down, that put their faith once more in the forgotten man at the bottom of the economic pyramid."[2] FDR's forgotten man, thus, was Sumner's X, who is suffering from some wrong, which liberals propose to alleviate by enacting laws and creating government programs. He was *not* Sumner's C, who will foot the bill run up by the reformers and humanitarians determined to relieve X's suffering.[3]

In 2011 performer and commentator Penn Jillette expressed Sumner's argument in the idiom of modern libertarianism:

It's amazing to me how many people think that voting to have the government give poor people money is compassion. Helping poor and suffering people is compassion. Voting for our government to use guns to give money to help poor and suffering people is immoral self-righteous bullying laziness.

People need to be fed, medicated, educated, clothed, and sheltered, and if we're compassionate we'll help them, but you get no moral credit for forcing other people to do what you think is right. There is great joy in helping people, but no joy in doing it at gunpoint.[4]

The dominant mode of Jillette's politics is neither liberalism nor conservatism but skepticism. (His article was titled "I Don't Know, So I'm an Atheist Libertarian.") His disposition regarding political compassion conforms to that of another famous American skeptic, H. L. Mencken, who wrote, "The urge to save humanity is almost always only a false-face for the urge to rule it. Power is what all messiahs really seek: not the chance to serve."[5]

STATISM

With the rise of the Tea Party, conservatives have recommitted to their master narrative: preserving freedom requires eternal resistance to liberalism's relentless, reckless expansion of the state. In this view, liberals' good intentions are at best subordinate to, and at worst a spurious pretext for pursuing, their bad ones: the endless expansion of government's power and scope, corresponding to an inexorable reduction of human liberty. On this point they line up with Sumner, Mencken, and Jillette, who mentions government force once and its guns twice in brusquely dismissing liberal compassion. The 1936 Republican platform, for example, charged that the New Deal's purpose was to extinguish the liberties the people had known under the Constitution: "We dedicate ourselves to the preservation of [Americans'] political liberty, their individual opportunity and their character as free citizens, which today for the first time are threatened by Government itself."[6]

A decade later an Austrian economist teaching at the London School of Economics wrote an improbable American bestseller, *The Road to Serfdom*. Friedrich Hayek's title admirably distilled his thesis: totalitarianism, both fascist and communist, was the inevitable consequence when government supplanted markets. "We have progressively abandoned that freedom in economic affairs without which personal and political freedom has never existed in the past," Hayek wrote. Abandoning laissez-faire economics is a grave mistake, but the lesser part of the menace. Hayek believed that collectivism and central planning imperiled "one of the salient characteristics of Western civilization as it has grown from the foundations laid by Christianity and the Greeks and Romans. Not merely nineteenth- and eighteenth-century liberalism, but the basic individualism inherited by us from Erasmus and Montaigne, from Cicero and Tacitus, Pericles and Thucydides is progressively relinquished."[7]

Conservatism's leading polemicist and its leading politician of the past half century each affirmed that attenuating freedom is liberalism's ultimate purpose, and fortifying it conservatism's. In 1959's *Up from Liberalism* William Buckley wrote:

> I will not cede more power to the state. I will not willingly cede more power to anyone, not to the state, not to General Motors, not to the [Congress of Industrial Organizations]. I will hoard my power like a miser, resisting every effort to drain it away from me. I will then use my power, as I see fit. I mean to live my life an obedient man, but obedient to God, subservient to the wisdom of my ancestors; never to the authority of political truths arrived at yesterday at the voting booth.[8]

And in his farewell address in 1989, summarizing not just an eight-year presidency but an entire public career, Ronald Reagan said, "I hope we have once again reminded people that man is not free unless government is limited. There's a clear cause and effect here that is as neat and predictable as a law of physics: As government expands, liberty contracts."[9]

"I think Ronald Reagan changed the trajectory of America in a way that . . . Richard Nixon did not and in a way that Bill Clinton did not," Barack Obama said during his 2008 campaign for president.[10] That is, Nixon ("I am now a Keynesian in economics") and

Clinton ("The era of Big Government is over") merely acceded to the political realities they inherited. Reagan, by contrast, altered them, and for Obama to alter them in the opposite direction requires, above all, refuting the allegations of liberal statism. Obama attempted to do so most directly in a commencement address at Ohio State University in 2013. "Unfortunately," he told the graduates, most of whom were born after Reagan left office, "you've grown up hearing voices that incessantly warn of government as nothing more than some separate, sinister entity that's at the root of all our problems. . . .

> They'll warn that tyranny is always lurking just around the corner. You should reject these voices because what they suggest is that our brave and creative and unique experiment in self-rule is somehow just a sham with which we can't be trusted.
>
> We have never been a people who place all of our faith in government to solve our problems; we shouldn't want to. But we don't think the government is the source of all our problems either. Because we understand that this democracy is ours. And as citizens, we understand that it's not about what America can do for us, it's about what can be done by us, together, through the hard and frustrating, but absolutely necessary work of self-government.[11]

In Obama's telling, the American experiment was conceived less to prevent government from doing harmful things than to enable it to do splendid ones. "The Founders trusted us" with "awesome authority," by leaving Americans with "the keys to a system of self-government, the tools to do big things and important things together that we could not possibly do alone. . . ." Therefore, "We should trust ourselves with it too."

Conservative rhetoric about the fragility of liberty, and the determination of social reformers to diminish it, is notable for its high level of abstraction. There are concrete examples, however—not of free citizens reduced to serfdom by tyrannical government, but of officials who believe wielding power in the public interest entitles them to harass a private citizen as they see fit. In Chapter One we met Marty Hahne, the magician preparing disaster plans, to be filed with the U.S. Department of Agriculture, for the rabbit in his show. His predicament resembles that of Chantell and Michael Sackett, who bought a 0.63-acre parcel of land in Priest Lake, Idaho, and started to build a vacation home. "In May 2007, three days after workers started clearing the property," according to the *Wall Street Journal*, "officials from the [Environmental Protection Agency] and the Army Corps of Engineers showed up to ask if the Sacketts had a permit to fill in wetlands. . . . Nearly seven months later, the agency sent the couple a compliance order directing them to restore the property to its original condition," despite the Sacketts' protest that the "wetlands" were located in a residential subdivision. The EPA contended that the Clean Water Act gave it the authority to "issue an administrative compliance order directing a property owner to stop discharging pollutants or restore a damaged wetland" on the basis of "any information," including "a newspaper article or an anonymous tip."[12]

The Sacketts took the EPA to federal court, where they were initially told they had no right to file such a lawsuit. Both the district court and the Ninth Circuit appellate court, that is, upheld the EPA's position that a dispute between it and a private citizen about whether a parcel of land qualified as wetlands, making it subject to EPA enforcement, was a question the property owner could pursue in an EPA administrative hearing, but not in the court system. Had that opinion prevailed, the sole recourse for a citizen who believed the EPA had wrongly designated his property as wetlands subject to its jurisdiction would be to beseech one part of the EPA to rebuke another part of the EPA. James Madison's fears—that the "accumulation of all powers, legislative, executive, and judiciary, in the same hands . . . may justly be pronounced the very definition of tyranny"—are more pertinent to the Sacketts' dilemma than Obama's confidence about a government equipped to do big, important things.

Only if the agency sued the Sacketts for failing to satisfy the terms of its compliance order would a member of the judicial branch, as opposed to a referee on the EPA payroll, be in a position to hear their side of the story. And the risks they ran by defying the EPA could do nothing but increase, since the costs of losing a lawsuit filed by the agency could do nothing but grow. While the EPA was attempting to get the Sacketts to comply with its orders, it could assess them a fine. Every day the dispute was unresolved was a day the Sacketts were out of compliance, so the meter would stop running only if they settled or ultimately won a lawsuit the agency brought against them.

How big could the fine become? When the case went before the U.S. Supreme Court in 2012 the justices initially believed that the maximum was $37,500 per day, a sum designed to get the attention of corporate polluters. The EPA's sense of restraint in using its discretion, however, was all that guaranteed smaller fines against homeowners. The solicitor general, defending the EPA, helpfully informed the Court that the maximum was actually $75,000 per day—$37,500 for violating federal environmental law, and another $37,500 for violating the compliance order. Justice Samuel Alito asked the solicitor general whether an "ordinary homeowner," presented with the facts of *Sackett v. Environmental Protection Agency*, wouldn't say, "this kind of thing can't happen in the United States?"

> You buy property to build a house. You think maybe there is a little drainage problem in part of your lot, so you start to build the house and then you get an order from the EPA which says: You have filled in wetlands, so you can't build your house; remove the fill, put in all kinds of plants; and now you have to let

us on your premises whenever we want to. You have to turn over to us all sorts of documents, and for every day that you don't do all this you are accumulating a potential fine of $75,000. And by the way, there is no way you can go to court to challenge our determination that this is a wetlands until such time as we choose to sue you.[13]

The Court ruled unanimously in favor of the Sacketts. The 9–0 vote meant that even the four justices appointed by Democratic presidents—Stephen Breyer and Ruth Bader Ginsburg, nominated by Clinton; and Sonia Sotomayor and Elena Kagan, nominated by Obama—ignored clear instructions from Obama's Justice Department and the *New York Times*, both of which wanted the EPA's position vindicated. The *Times* editorial warned that "those supporting the Sacketts with friend-of-the-court briefs are corporate Goliaths like General Electric and real estate developers eager to weaken the EPA's ability to protect wetlands and waterways under the federal Clean Water Act." With a degree of understatement divorced from the facts of the case, and the realities of modern regulatory governance more generally, the *Times* contended that compliance orders private citizens cannot challenge in court "are useful because they allow the agency to press landowners to negotiate about mitigating harms."[14] The Court had the sense and decency to grasp that the negotiating leverage the *Times* urged it to preserve for the EPA was comparable to that wielded by an extortionist. In a concurring opinion Justice Alito called on Congress to revise the "notoriously unclear" Clean Water Act. As it stands, "Any piece of land that is wet at least part of the year is in danger of being classified by EPA employees as wetlands covered by the Act. . . ."[15]

What's scariest about stories like the Sacketts' or Marty the Magician's is that the villains come across as functionaries rather than tyrants. No one favors abused animals or dirty water, of course, so it makes sense for legislators to pass laws to mitigate those blights. Because the laws have to be enforced, and because Congress cannot anticipate every obstacle to achieving their stated goals, it confers both power and latitude on the agencies assigned to secure compliance from those in a position either to further or impede the laws' goals.

It's just that one thing leads to another, and then another. Laws enacted to prevent the big shot's damaging actions become the basis for policies superintending the little guy's innocuous ones. Having public officials telling citizens what they may and may not do is a means to an end, but it also appears that for at least a subset of those drawn to careers in government, bossing people around becomes an end in itself. Fortified with the moral self-confidence that comes from pursuing laudable aims, some bureaucrats view their demands on ordinary folks as justifiable measures that must be taken against recalcitrant obstacles to progress.

Furthermore, some theorists argue that apart from any broader social impacts, the best interests of the people being bossed around can justify issuing and enforcing edicts. Philosophy professor Sarah Conly, author of *Against Autonomy: Justifying Coercive Paternalism*, believes "sometimes we need to be stopped from doing foolish stuff" because "we often don't think very clearly when it comes to choosing the best means to attain our ends." There's no need to be overly worried, however, that coercive paternalism will lead to intrusive, bullying government. Enacting "successful paternalistic laws" on the basis of prudently weighed costs and benefits "is something the government has the resources to do," meaning not just the money and power but also the expertise and sagacity.[16]

Compassion figures into this equation in two senses. First, liberalism's alliance of experts and victims will call upon experts to alleviate the suffering endured by the victims of ambient social problems, but also of those victimized by the limitations of their own decision making. "In the old days we used to blame people for acting imprudently," writes Conly, "and say that since their bad choices were their own fault, they deserved to suffer the consequences." Now, however, the expertise of the experts encompasses an understanding of the difficulties nonexperts have in making smart decisions. Laymen are too optimistic to be prudent, too shortsighted to defer gratification, too inertial to relinquish an old way of doing things when a better one is presented to them. Because of such insights, "we see that these errors aren't a function of bad character, but of our shared cognitive inheritance. The proper reaction is not blame, but an impulse to help one another."[17] Helping one another does not mean reciprocity between experts and victims, of course, since the latter have nothing to offer the former in trade. Rather, it means the victims, of both social circumstances and their own decision-making insufficiencies, will come together to delegate power to experts who will spare each victim from suffering the consequences otherwise likely to be inflicted by forces beyond his control.

Second, because the welfare state socializes costs of individuals' bad decisions, costs formerly confined to the people who made those decisions, we all become victims of their mistakes. This encumbrance justifies state intervention to protect us from their follies. According to journalist Ben Adler, people who "fall ill from smoking or fatty food, cost the rest of us money. We pay their emergency room bill, their Medicare bills or their Social Security disability insurance." Those who bristle against such government experts protecting individuals and the society that underwrites their welfare from the risks of heedless lifestyles betray a fallacy, one that, in Adler's words, "clearly expresses a fundamental tenet of conservative/libertarian thinking: that engaging in risky behavior with serious social costs is an entitlement."[18] But since the elaboration of the welfare state means that there are fewer and fewer behaviors that do *not* have serious social costs, every augmentation of government power winds up strengthening the case for additional augmentations.

"It's not always worth it [for government experts] to intervene," writes Conly, "but sometimes, where the costs are small and the benefit is large, it is." This makes it sounds like we're confining the discussion to clear-cut cases, ones that rest lightly on individuals by curtailing their freedom in small ways, exercised at the margins of their lives. But perhaps not. Conly's next book project is *One: Do We Have a Right to More Children?* It will argue, "If population growth is sufficiently dangerous, it is fair for us to impose restrictions on how many children we can give birth to."[19]

Clearly, the humanitarian impulses to reform and elevate society lend themselves to other, more problematic motives. "It would be better to live under robber barons than under omnipotent moral busybodies," C. S. Lewis wrote. "The robber baron's cruelty may sometimes sleep, his cupidity may at some point be satiated; but those who torment us for our own good will torment us without end, for they do so with the approval of their own conscience."[20]

Another literary scholar, more strongly inclined to give social reformers the benefit of the doubt, reached the same gloomy conclusion about social engineering's capacity to validate abuse. In 1947 Lionel Trilling told a college audience that "the world is ripe" for "great changes in our social system." The alternatives were "greater social liberality" or "a terrible social niggardliness," and, "We all know which of those directions we want." Precisely because of this consensus, however, he thought it imperative to remind his listeners that "the moral passions are even more willful and imperious and impatient than the self-seeking passions. All history is at one in telling us that their tendency is to be not only liberating but also restrictive." Thus,

> we must be aware of the dangers which lie in our most generous wishes. Some paradox of our natures leads us, when once we have made our fellow men the objects of our enlightened inter-

est, to go on to make them the objects of our pity, then of our wisdom, ultimately of our coercion.[21]

COMPASSIONATE CONSERVATISM

For many conservatives—the ones who take a no-retreat, no-surrender approach to politics—"compassionate conservatism" sounded like a bad idea from the start. From the vantage point that regards governmentalized compassion as immoral, self-righteous bullying, it is imperative for conservatives to oppose that endeavor root and branch, *not* to fashion a compromise with it or devise a more benign version of it. In this view, once conservatives accept the idea that compassion is a political virtue, not just a moral one, they invite liberals to judge them according to liberal criteria, an invitation liberals will eagerly accept. What's left of compassionate conservatism today, some fifteen years after George W. Bush inserted it into America's political vocabulary, is indeed its use to taunt conservatives for opposing rather than supporting the liberal agenda. One journalist singled out a Republican senator who argued for extending unemployment benefits in 2014 as "the last compassionate conservative," a compliment that was really a vehicle for disparaging the GOP in general for being "wholly unconcerned with the struggles of working-class Americans."[22]

Despite this intra-Right dissension over compassionate conservatism, its champions and detractors agree (1) that the distinction between state and society is indispensable to making modernity coherent and feasible; and (2) that the effect, and perhaps the intent, of American liberalism since the New Deal has been to break down rather than build up the wall between the two. Recall Hubert Humphrey's declaration that how it treats the young, old, and suffering is the moral test of government. Make one change—substitute "society" for "government"—and most conservatives would endorse that proposition enthusiastically. What leaves conservatives apprehensive is the strong suggestion that liberalism treats the one question as the only part of the other that matters: the moral test of a society is how *its government* treats the needy, which trivializes every nongovernmental aspect of society that prevents and alleviates suffering. Deval Patrick, the Democratic governor of Massachusetts, said in 2012 that government is "just the name we give to the things we choose to do together."[23] The narrator's script in a video welcoming delegates to that year's Democratic National Convention in Charlotte, North Carolina, went farther:

> We *are* committed to all people. We *do* believe you can use government in a good way. Government is the only thing we all belong to. We're different churches, different clubs, but we're together as a part of our city, or our county, or our state, and our nation.[24]

Where the conservative opponent and proponent of compassionate conservatism differ is that the former's objections to liberal compassion are couched in terms of its aggrandizement of the state, while the latter's emphasize the danger of debilitating society. Compassionate conservatism's advocates make the further, practical point that conservative politicians have no choice but to appeal to voters as they are, rather than as conservatives think they should be. Decades of liberal speeches and journalism about heartless conservatives have altered popular assumptions, and any conservative who hopes to win a hearing, much less an election, does not have the option of ignoring charges in the electorate's expectations and assumptions, no matter how regrettable he considers those changes. As the late Michael S. Joyce, an influential conservative thinker and donor, told congressional Republicans in 1996, if budget and program cuts were the only item on the menu conservatives placed before voters, it will "play right into liberalism's caricature of us as heartless, uncaring conservatives."[25]

During Ronald Reagan's eight years in the White House, federal outlays on human resources programs increased (after adjusting for inflation and population growth) by 9.8 percent. They had always grown at a faster rate before 1981, however, so liberals spent the 1980s denouncing Reagan's "savage cuts" to social programs. Vice President George H. W. Bush understood the necessity to respond to these accusations and assumptions about harsh Republicans if his 1988 presidential campaign was to succeed. Michael Dukakis had said in his acceptance speech at the Democratic convention that the election that year was about competence, not ideology. It was Bush, however, who came to devote his presidency to the proposition put forward by the man he defeated. The famous line from *his* acceptance speech was the call for "a kinder, gentler nation." He elaborated this point in his inaugural address, contending that the "high moral principle of our time" is "to make kinder the face of the Nation and gentler the face of the world." The chastened response to this imperative, he continued, was to regard liberalism as well-meaning but unrealistic.

> The old solution, the old way, was to think that public money alone could end [social] problems. But we have learned that that is not so. And in any case, our funds are low. We have a deficit to bring down. We have more will than wallet, but will is what we need.[26]

Shortly after Bush finished his inaugural address, congressional Democrats, holding majorities in both houses and convinced that where there's a will there's a wallet, set out to make the new president break his campaign pledge not to raise taxes. Bush's capitulation to them in 1990 did more than any other decision he made to demoralize his political base and imperil his reelection. Conservatives, then and ever since, have disparaged Bush as a committed moderate who spent eight vice presidential years pretending to be a Reagan Republican in order to subvert the Reagan Revolution in his own presidency.

The seeds of the Gingrich Revolution, which delivered both houses of Congress to the GOP in 1994 for the first time in forty years, were sown in conservatives' denunciations of that tax increase. By the time George W. Bush announced his presidential campaign in 1999, political calculations once more dictated the need to rebut liberals' accusations of heartlessness, this time leveled against Newt Gingrich and his allies. (Because his genial persona blunted the criticism his domestic agenda was mean-spirited, Reagan's frustrated opponents had called him the "Teflon president." No one ever called Gingrich the Teflon Speaker.)

"I know Republicans—across the country—are generous of heart," Bush said in announcing his candidacy in 1999. "I am confident the American people view compassion as a noble calling." Bush not only insisted that conservatives were within America's moral mainstream, as his father had done a decade earlier, but conveyed the desire for a more ambitious, telling rebuttal of the charge—that conservatives were heartless—than was Bush 41's "thousand points of light." For Bush 43, compassionate conservatism would go beyond politicians praising and encouraging private organizations and volunteerism. Federal policy would seek to catalyze such efforts, and make *them*, rather than designed-in-Washington government policies, the vehicle for alleviating suffering and solving social problems. The goal was "prosperity with a purpose"—not just material advances but progress toward stronger character and communities. The relation between empathizers and empathizees Bush envisioned was, as a result, moral rather than nonjudgmental. What made compassionate conservatives compassionate was their concern for the poor. What made them conservative was their belief that because people who acquired certain dispositions and habits were highly unlikely to be poor—and, if so, briefly rather than protractedly—a society that failed to transmit and instill those dispositions and habits was condemning more people to poverty through an egregious sin of omission. "For our children to have the lives we want for them, they must learn to say yes to responsibility, yes to family, yes to honesty and work," Bush declared. "I have seen our culture change once in my lifetime, so I know it can change again."[27]

It remained unclear, throughout Bush's campaigns and presidency, what such intentions meant in terms of public policy. "Government can spend money," he said in 1999, "but it can't put hope in our hearts or a sense of purpose in our lives. This is done by churches and synagogues and mosques and charities that warm the cold of life." Bush promised to be a president who would usher in a "responsibility era" but this, too, is bully pulpit stuff, not policy. Bush said he would "lift regulations" that hampered nonprofits, and "involve them" in social policy pursuits like prison and welfare reform. In his 2000 acceptance speech, Bush said, "My administration will give taxpayers new incentives to donate to charity, encourage after-school programs that build character, and support mentoring groups that shape and save young lives."[28]

Once inaugurated, Bush created the White House Office of Faith-Based and Community Initiatives, but its first director, political scientist John DiIulio, returned to academia after less than a year. In October 2002 he wrote, "There is a virtual absence as yet of any policy accomplishments that might, to a fair-minded nonpartisan, count as the flesh on the bones of so-called compassionate conservatism."[29] DiIulio's complaint is more than if-only-they'd-listened-to-me carping by a departed government official: there remained no policy flesh on the bones for the duration of Bush's presidency. (The term "compassionate conservatism" does not appear in Bush's presidential memoir.)

One might conjure a counterfactual history of the Bush presidency, in which there was no terrorist attack on American soil, and no wars in Afghanistan and Iraq. The resulting domestic policy agenda could then have provided the focus and resources to demonstrate compassionate conservatism's operational meaning. Weighing against any such prospect, however, is the basic tension inherent in fashioning a *political* agenda for the purpose of catalyzing a *social* transformation, especially an agenda proposed by a party that proclaims itself the champion of limited government.

It is clear that social problems have policy implications. According to the Centers for Disease Control, for example, 18.4 percent of all babies born in 1980 had an unmarried mother, compared to 33.2 percent in 2000, and between 40 and 41 percent each year from 2008 to 2011.[30] The increase in divorces and out-of-wedlock births means a growing portion of American children live with one parent, almost always their mother. Nearly half of such children (45 percent) live in poverty, while only 13 percent of children residing with both parents do, a disparity with profound consequences for crime, education, welfare, and the labor force.[31]

It does not follow, however, that traffic on this street can be made to run in both directions. The desire for policies that correct the causes of social problems, as distinguished from policies that merely attempt to cope with their consequences, does not guarantee such policies will be formulated and successfully implemented. Indeed, it does not guarantee that any such policies are possible. That being the case, the compassionate conservatism George W. Bush invoked was an incongruous basis for securing and wielding political power. It seems Bush, who joined the United Methodist Church as an adult, embraced a Wesleyan conception of America's urgent need "to rally [the] armies of compassion that exist in every community" so that they could nurture, mentor, comfort, and "perform their commonplace miracles of renewal." This sounds like the work we would expect from moral and religious leaders—but not, as Bush called it, "one of the biggest jobs for the next *president*," since it is highly doubtful the remoralization of society can be reconciled with the tool kit or job description of a politician in a modern, plural, secular republic.

BEYOND COMPASSION

Does the failure of compassionate conservatism show that conservatism makes no sense without the insistence that the only good compassion is private compassion, on the grounds that giving it *any* political role guarantees self-righteous bullying by hectoring liberals? Milton Friedman, champion of market economics, cast a vote against that proposition in *Capitalism and Freedom*, published in 1962. He argued that government social programs, funded at gunpoint, as libertarians would say, address a collective action problem that private charity cannot, since "the benefits from [charity] accrue to people other than those who make the gifts."

> I am distressed by the sight of poverty; I am benefited by its alleviation; but I am benefited equally whether I or someone else pays for its alleviation; the benefits of others' charity therefore partly accrue to me. To put it differently, we might all of us be willing to contribute to the relief of poverty, *provided* everyone else did. We might not be willing to contribute the same amount without such assurance. In small communities, public pressure can suffice to realize the proviso even with private charity. In the large impersonal communities that are increasingly coming to dominate our society, it is much more difficult for it to do so.

Friedman finds this consideration adequate to justify "governmental action to alleviate poverty; to set, as it were, a floor under the standard of life of every person in the community."[32] The correlation of incentives, then, makes it unlikely that Sumner's A and B who want to help X would have done so, as he hoped, "without any law." But enacting a law will necessarily require C to help X, too, even if C would never have voluntarily contributed to A and B's charitable campaign.

It's important to note that Friedman's argument does not necessarily depend on the operation of compassion, either in Rousseau's sense of alleviating the distress your suffering causes me, or according to Kant's idea of enabling me to have a good opinion of myself by virtue of responding to your suffering in the way I would want you to respond to mine. The resident of a crowded city, for example, would probably desire that homeless people have a place to sleep other than the doorsteps or heating grates adjacent to his own home and business. According to Tom Wolfe's *The Bonfire of the Vanities*, the key to managing New York City life in the 1980s was to "insulate, insulate, insulate." Only so much insulation is feasible, however, beyond which addressing the problems one seeks insulation from becomes imperative. The motives for doing so would include: empathy; concerns about the quality of life; peace of mind for one's family; peace of mind *about* one's family and property; and (for business owners) the desire not to lose customers to competitors in locations where the homeless are not present. Different people will harbor these concerns in different proportions, ones that we and even they will struggle to define precisely.

Rather than treating compassion as the only decent basis for addressing the problem, self-interest well understood can encompass and reconcile altruistic considerations with self-interested ones. As Friedman says, a charity drive for a homeless shelter to address this urban problem faces doubtful prospects. If everyone responds to the incentives rationally, the shelter that everyone thinks would make the neighborhood more livable never comes into existence or, if it does, operates perpetually on a shoestring budget. The welfare state cuts that Gordian knot by making every taxpayer a "donor" to the program, and making government the vehicle for acting together to address problems that affect us together. In 1932 Franklin Roosevelt argued from self-interest rightly understood in praising the "wholly new science" of public health. Communicable illnesses give the healthy obvious reasons to heal the sick, but serious illnesses of all kinds curtail the productivity of both the afflicted and the family members forced to care for them. Thus, FDR said, "from the purely dollars and cents point of view that we Americans are so fond of thinking about, public health has paid for itself."[33]

There's no mistaking Roosevelt's disdain for his countrymen, who can be persuaded to do the right thing only if they're given a dollars-and-cents answer to the question "What's in it for me?" It would be far more edifying to secure popular support for liberalism by telling voters that virtue—in the form of supporting the liberal agenda—is its own reward, which was Robert Kennedy's approach with college audiences in 1968. The unremitting denunciations of greed and selfishness make clear that liberal politicians speak like Roosevelt did in 1932, which is most of the time, because they think they have to, and like Kennedy did in 1968 because they want to.

In that speech, Franklin Roosevelt rejected "the philosophy of 'letting things alone,'" because it "has resulted in the jungle law of the survival of the so-called fittest." This rationalization of passivity, he said, holds that "if we make the rich richer, somehow they will let a part of their prosperity trickle down to the rest of us." The only alternative to that reliance on spontaneous order is to pursue "the protection of humanity and the fitting of as many human beings as possible into the scheme of surviving." Embracing it will require initiatives that "make the average of mankind comfortable and secure." Instead of waiting and hoping for prosperity to trickle down, social action will cause it to "rise upward, just as yeast rises up, through the ranks."[34]

The welfare state reconfigures the compassionate bonds among citizens, however. The sincere, spontaneous reaction to suffering, which propels the liberal project, is attenuated by the pursuit of that project. FDR's larger point in 1932 was to advocate "social justice through social action." He contended, "The followers of the philosophy of 'social action for the prevention of poverty' maintain that if we set up a system of justice we shall have small need for the exercise of mere philanthropy." Leon Wieseltier of the *New Republic* made the same point seventy-five years later: individuals' voluntary generosity "is not economic justice," since it is "the absence of economic justice that makes charity necessary."[35] It follows that the presence, or perfection, of economic justice will make charity unnecessary. That culmination will leave nothing for private citizens to donate to, or volunteer for, that isn't already being done better by a government agency. Whether it's possible to retain hearts full of compassion after all our empathetic impulses have been routed through the voting booth, tax collector's office, and government social welfare departments is highly doubtful.

Indeed, not only will the attainment of social or economic justice make mere philanthropy unnecessary. The pursuit of that objective renders philanthropy harmful. For one thing, the alliance of experts and victims will progress toward its goals more slowly and with greater difficulty if amateurs, hobbyists, and dilettantes are mucking about, trying to alleviate victims' suffering. They don't know what they're doing, and should keep out of the way of people who do. Furthermore, caring for others by any means other than supporting, with votes and taxes, welfare state programs to enact and adequately fund those programs postpones rather than hastens the realization of social justice. "I gave at the office" should mean just one thing: the taxes withheld from my paycheck are funding government programs, the only path to social justice. If it means, instead, charitable contributions or activities that endorse the efficacy and virtue of extragovernmental efforts to ameliorate suffering situations, the pursuit of social justice is thwarted.

According to the Organisation for Economic Co-operation and Development, realizing a social democratic conception of economic justice in America would make ours a more statist and less charitable country. The OECD social expenditure database found that in 2009 more than one-third of all social welfare spending in the United States came from private sources, compared to less than a tenth in Denmark, France, and Sweden. Combine more extragovernmental spending in America on social welfare with the fact of our more productive economy, and the total social spending figures belie the notion of American meanness in contrast to other modern nations' liberality.[36]

The ability of governmentalized compassion to weaken all the other ties that connect a society's members works down to the most basic level. Alan Wolfe, a critic of what he considers conservatism's contradictions, has acknowledged this liberal one. "The Scandinavian welfare states which express so well a sense of obligation to distant strangers," he wrote in 1989, "are beginning to make it more difficult to express a sense of obligation to those with whom one shares family ties." They do so most directly by imposing the high, widely applicable taxes needed to fund generous government programs. Such taxes make it extremely difficult for married couples to be other than two-career couples, even if their preference would be for one parent, usually the mother, to stay home full- or part-time to care for children, or to take an active role in caring for an aging parent. The great difficulty of maintaining a middle-class standard of living, after the taxes have been paid, necessitates two paychecks from two full-time workers. As a result, family obligations are outsourced to state-supported caregivers, whose own salaries depend on the same heavy taxes that drive customers to their door. "Socializing the young and caring for the sick, viewed traditionally as women's work," Wolfe writes of Scandinavia, "are still women's work, but now they are carried out for a government wage rather than within a family setting." Nearly two-thirds of the Danish women who left domestic life for the paid workforce in the 1960s and 1970s, he reports, wound up working in day-care centers, old-age homes, hospitals, or schools. As a result, "the Scandinavian welfare states organize through taxation and public services activities for all of society that were once undertaken intimately and privately." The danger is that "as intimate ties weaken, so will distant ones, thus undermining the very moral strengths the welfare state has shown."[37]

This feature of the liberal project is not a surprising, unforeseen development, but a direct consequence of its logic. As George Lakoff contends, "We're in this together. We bear joint responsibility for one another and all our children." To understand and accept that joint responsibility means rejecting in all its wicked manifestations the conservative ideology that prizes individual liberty as a license to heedlessly pursue our own self-interests.[38] Any result *other than* the attenuation of families, churches, civic groups, and all other nonpolitical human bonds, while the ties that bind the "national family" get stronger and stronger, would be the real anomaly. Bertrand de Jouvenel argued in *The Ethics of Redistribution* that as ever higher taxes fund ever more governmentally dispensed provisions, individuals' exertions to provide for their immediate and extended families are ultimately restricted to funding hobbies and amusements.[39]

The political effect of liberal compassion is, then, doubly constricting. First, it makes clear that the only motives and considerations that are wholly welcome in the public square are disinterested, selfless ones. Liberals in a democracy must often stoop to advocating their plans in the self-interested, dollars-and-cents terms the benighted voters are so fond of. They do so, however, only to conquer that atavistic, contemptible outlook, steadily and someday completely replacing it with a wholly enlightened one. Second, once we situate our empathetic concerns and aspirations in the public realm, they can have one and only one decent expression: support for government social welfare programs to alleviate suffering. The attainment of social justice will obviate mere philanthropy, so the pursuit of it must repudiate charity.

As I've argued throughout, however, liberal compassion does not banish selfishness from politics, as its advocates assume. Rather, the advance of the belief that compassion is the moral and political consideration that should prevail against all others merely displaces one kind of selfishness—largely concerned with material well-being, family advancement, community respectability, and patriotic pride—with another, which is preoccupied with emotional, psychological, and status gratifications. Viewed in this way, the debate between conservatives and liberals is not an argument between the champions and enemies of selfishness. It is, instead, an argument between conservatives who endorse self-interest well understood, and liberal advocates of selflessness cynically or stupidly misrepresented.

The futile, pernicious quest to extirpate selfishness from politics makes *Bleak House*'s Mrs. Jellyby, devoted practitioner of "telescopic philanthropy" on behalf of the suffering natives of Borrioboola-Gha, a liberal paragon rather than a liberal cartoon. She does Marian Wright Edelman and Melissa Harris-Perry one better, not merely refusing to discriminate between her own and other people's children, but caring for theirs *more* attentively than hers. There can be no compelling moral duty to accomplish that which it is impossible to accomplish, however. We cannot devote our lives to widening the ambit of our concern, all the while effacing the self at the center of that ambit. "Compassion fatigue" is the inevitable result, not of moral deficiencies but of moral and political standards badly chosen. Pete Hamill wrote in 1986 that after the upheavals and disappointments of the 1960s, many burned-out liberals "pulled back to tend private gardens, to raise children, to build careers, to eat and live well. . . ." One told him:

> I just gave up and I'm not ashamed of saying it. I did everything I could in my day and then realized I really couldn't make any difference. I couldn't change the welfare system. I couldn't create a half-million jobs. I couldn't teach people how to get up in the morning, every day of the week, and go to work. I couldn't make dumb people smart. Most of all, I couldn't help people who wouldn't help themselves.[40]

Liberals need to wise up so this guy can lighten up. Selflessness, the never-ending quest to eradicate every trace of self-regard, is not a rational political standard. Selflessness *has* been the ideal for the devoutly religious aspiring to sainthood. "For whosoever will save his life shall lose it: and whosoever will lose his life for my sake shall find it," according to the New Testament. Nontheocratic republics cannot operate by demanding a corresponding secular sainthood, however, where the only path to find one's life is to lose it for the sake of the children of Borrioboola-Gha or the endangered tropical rainforest.

Liberalism calls on us to deny the undeniable fact that we live our lives in concentric circles of regard and obligation. My own children matter more to me than do my neighbor's kids, who matter more to me than my neighbor's cousin's plumber's kids. My embrace of the duty to nurture these children changes and diminishes as we move from inner circles to outer ones, a tendency liberals view as a moral failing betraying atavistic self-centeredness. By the same token, patriotism is not an embarrassing vestige of tribalism, one we should aspire to outgrow by evolving toward an empathy that extends an undiminished, undifferentiated solicitude throughout the world. Far sounder and healthier, according to the late political scientist Joseph Cropsey, is the conservative presupposition that it is "more human, surely more civil, to love what is near and similar, as such, than what is remote and strange, as such."[41]

The alternative to liberal compassion is not, as liberals have convinced themselves, insatiable greed. The normal, inevitable, and admirable desire to prefer my children to other people's, and my compatriots to foreigners, is not a failing to be overcome but a foundation on which to build. The duties and rewards of parenthood and patriotism don't detract from the possibility of treating other children or members of other nations respectfully and, when feasible, helpfully. It is, instead, the only possible human basis on which I can even begin to navigate the terrain between callous disregard and frantic sensitivity toward people to whom I am not related by bonds of family, community, country, or creed.

Liberalism, by resting on the belief that we can and must apply our moral sentiments and duties to infinitely wider circles, guarantees sociological inanities and governmental perversities. An example of the latter is the California Supreme Court's *Serrano v. Priest* decisions against relying on local property taxes to finance public education. (In subsequent years, other states' supreme courts have made similar rulings about the meaning of their state constitutions, though the U.S. Supreme Court rejected this interpretation of the Fourteenth Amendment's equal protection clause by a vote of 5 to 4 in 1973.) When it first ruled, in 1971, that the funding disparities between rich and poor districts were intolerable, the California legislature responded by directing additional state funds to school districts that had meager revenues from property taxes assessed within their boundaries. By 1976, according to economist William Fischel, "state aid accounted for the majority of the financing of the property-poor districts." In *Serrano v. Priest II*, a decision that would have confirmed Tocqueville's worst fears, the court then ruled that a high floor was not good enough: the egalitarian imperative also demanded a low ceiling to prevent communities from taxing themselves to provide their own children any educational advantages not available throughout California. The inevitable result was to equalize per-pupil expenditures throughout California and make the state government, rather than school districts, the nexus of educational finance.

It seemed like a good idea at the time, at least to liberals. They voiced the confident hope that as a result of the court decisions the general level of expenditures for education, statewide, would greatly increase. The thinking was that if no one can get excellent schools unless everybody gets excellent schools, then voters will approve the taxes needed to pay for excellent schools across the state. In 1980's *The Revolt of the Haves*, Robert Kuttner looked forward to *Serrano* logic's being applied to other public services: "If the state is paying the bill, how can huge disparities be justified in welfare, health, sanitation, or recreation any more than in education?"[42]

And if social justice demands eliminating every intrastate disparity in the funding of the entire range of public services, by what logic could it possibly countenance *interstate* disparities? Kids in Compton deserve not just good public schools, but schools every bit as good as the ones in Beverly Hills. Equalizing per-pupil expenditures across California was the response to that command, but achieving it does nothing for the kid in Salt Lake City whose school spends less than the ones in Compton and Beverly Hills. (In 2011, according to the Census Bureau, California's public schools spent 47 percent more per pupil than Utah's.)[43] The *logic* of *Serrano*, the logic of economic justice in general, is to make the national government, rather than state or local ones, the nexus of finance for all public services.

According to Fischel, however, "The genius of local property tax financing for schools is that it gives everyone in the community—

not just those with kids in the public schools—an incentive to favor efficiently run, high-quality schools." That is, it connects individual self-interest to a comprehensible community interest. Because good schools enhance property values and high taxes reduce them, prudent citizens will have a strong incentive to be mindful of the costs and quality of the public education offered in their district, giving them a basis for differentiating tax increases that are worth it from ones that are not. This willingness to pay taxes for schools one does not use directly rests on self-interest well understood rather than, as Melissa Harris-Perry imagined, the amorphous altruism of being "connected to a larger whole." By contrast, when a vast, populous, and diverse state like California centralizes school financing, citizens have a strong incentive to *dis*engage from schools, politically and financially. It is no longer possible to weigh the cost of a tax increase against any discernible benefit, since more money may—or may not—improve the schools, and those improvements that do occur may be manifested in distant parts of the state. The *Serrano* rulings, hailed at the time as a liberal triumph, paved the way for Proposition 13, the 1978 tax cut that assaulted the liberal project. Liberals assumed that Californians would easily redirect their concern for their local community to the entire state. When they refused, liberals did not question their own premises about human nature and motivations, but accused the Californians who enacted Proposition 13 of greed and bigotry.[44]

BEYOND BULLSHIT

The "sort of hope that characterizes modern liberal societies," wrote the late philosopher Richard Rorty, is "the hope that life will eventually be freer, less cruel, more leisured, richer in goods and experiences, not just for our descendants but for everyone's descendants."[45] According to the British journalist Geoffrey Wheatcroft, "almost all Americans are liberals," in the older, broader sense of the term, which means they "believe in an open society, in material progress, in individual fulfillment, in the pursuit of happiness. You believe in that. So do I."[46]

The debate since 1932 between conservatives and liberals (in the narrower, more modern sense) is about the means to the end of human flourishing, on which all disputants are in basic agreement. Throne-and-altar conservatism has long since disappeared, and no one on the Left can explain how socialism in the twenty-first century would surpass its dismal record in the twentieth. Mostly, no one even tries. As the Hoover Institution's Tod Lindberg wrote in 2013, there may be "a few aging radicals who still dream of sweeping the whole capitalist system away and starting over. But never in the history of the Left have such views been so marginal."[47]

A debate about means, though, entails a debate about the effectiveness and risks of alternative paths to the end: material progress, individual fulfillment, etc. There's still plenty of raw material for good debates, in other words. Conservatives, for example, object that liberals' history of the past century is one long post hoc, ergo propter hoc argument: the government launched noble, high-minded initiative X; desirable development Y ensued; therefore, X caused Y. This account ignores the possibility the progress occurred for other reasons.

The abatement of social problems in the absence of government programs established to relieve them, in particular, would call into question the programs' value. Thus, legal scholar Richard Epstein points out that child labor, Exhibit A in every argument for the necessity of an activist government to protect us from predatory capitalism, declined steadily when the economy was lightly regulated. In 1890, 6.4 percent of the labor force consisted of children between the ages of ten and fifteen, according to the Census Bureau. That proportion shrank to 6.0 percent in 1900, 4.3 percent in 1910, 3.3 percent in 1920, and 1.4 percent in 1930. This steady decline occurred despite the Ellis Island wave of immigration, which brought unprecedented numbers of the world's huddled masses to these shores. In 1916 Congress passed a law prohibiting the interstate sale of merchandise that children had been employed to manufacture, legislation struck down by the Supreme Court in 1918 on the grounds it exceeded the federal government's constitutional power to regulate commerce among the several states. (The Court overturned that precedent in 1941.) The decline in child labor, then, occurred despite the absence of federal legislation (and the states' very limited efforts) to curtail it. There were similar, measurable advances in those pre–New Deal decades toward a life with more leisure and opportunity: shorter workweeks, higher incomes, increased life expectancy. "The obvious explanation for these improvements," according to Epstein, "is that increases in technology and productivity redounded to the benefit of all, just as the 'obsolete' analysis of Adam Smith had predicted." Such prosperity undercuts progressives' "tendentious . . . view of social progress," which "equated active government with good government."[48]

When such equating does not rely on doubtful causality to connect liberalism to progress, it depends on tautologies. But declaring a public policy successful is meaningless if all the tests it passed are ones it could not possibly have failed. The liberal project consists in large measure of having the government give people stuff—money, goods, and services. And it cannot be denied that when the government gives people stuff, the people it gives stuff to wind up with more stuff than they had before the government started giving them stuff. I once sat in the audience for a campus forum on the welfare state where a heckler challenged a guest speaker opposed to it: "Does your mother like getting Social Security?" The necessary corollary of the assumption that such a rhetorical question weighs heavily against an austere social welfare policy is that the only government programs we may rightly curtail or eliminate are ones whose intended recipients scornfully refuse the proffered benefits.

This way of thinking has more prominent advocates. Journalist Peter Beinart, for example, argues that Barack Obama finally secured passage of the Affordable Care Act in 2010 because he "turned a theoretical debate into a tactile one." The tactile Obama succeeded when he came around to emulating his great Democratic predecessors. Franklin Roosevelt, Beinart records, waved aside a question about how he would explain the political philosophy behind his Tennessee Valley Authority with the answer, "I'll tell them it's neither fish nor fowl but, whatever it is, it will taste awfully good to the people of the Tennessee Valley." Lyndon Johnson was also tactile. Because he "had seen his Hill Country neighbors bent and broken by arthritis as the result of decades of near-medieval labor," LBJ "wasn't interested in what Friedrich Hayek said." He enacted Medicare and Medicaid because "[h]e knew that in the real world, government-funded subsidized health care, like government-subsidized electricity, didn't enslave people; it freed them."[49] We should not be surprised when arguments relying on unfalsifiable propositions turn out to be un-false. But neither should we be persuaded.

Modern political debates concern, above all else, how to augment, widen, and perpetuate the prosperity that, as Deirdre McCloskey argues, sets modern societies apart from the entire human experience before the past two centuries. The 1.5 percent economic growth rate McCloskey discerns since that inflection point would, if it continues, mean that America's $50,700 per capita GDP in 2012 would grow, in real terms, to $101,400 in 2059 and $202,800 in 2105. Long-term trends, even highly reliable ones, are not laws of nature, so this future cornucopia is not guaranteed. Economists discuss the backward-bending supply curve of labor: at some point those businesses with the happy problem of too many orders to fill realize that offering their employees bonuses and incentives to work overtime becomes counterproductive. Employees eventually stop signing up for additional shifts when their already elevated incomes permit them to consume the next increment of wealth in the form of more leisure time. If, as prosperity grows, the backward-bending supply curve becomes a more general phenomenon, the 1.5 percent growth rate will be increasingly difficult to sustain, assuming no society reaches the point where it can just turn on the prosperity machine and give every adult an open-ended sabbatical.

Therein lies the essential cultural contradiction of capitalism, made famous by sociologist Daniel Bell in his 1976 book of that title. An ethic of thrift, discipline, and deferred gratification generates unprecedented prosperity, he argued, but the prosperity then generates an ethic of consumption, indulgence, and instant gratification, which makes continuation of the economic expansion increasingly tenuous. It will be noted that for all the elegance of Bell's thesis, the four decades since its exposition offer more empirical evidence to challenge than to support it. Americans who want to ascend from poverty, or fear descending to it, seem to be working as hard as ever. Globalization means that more and more people performing fungible labor are competing with workers from around the world, many of whom immigrate to compete for service-sector jobs.

But people with little fear of poverty also work very hard. As David Brooks argued in *Bobos in Paradise*, published in 2000, the new "bourgeois bohemians" arrange to have their arugula and eat it, too. Instead of using their earning power to enjoy more leisure and perform less labor, they synthesize the two (and acquire the collateral benefit of social status) in careers where work "becomes a vocation, a calling, a métier. In the 1960s most social theorists assumed that as we got richer we would work less and less. But if work is a form of self-expression or a social mission, then you never want to stop. You are driven by a relentless urge to grow, to learn, to feel more alive."[50]

It remains to be seen whether we will ever be confronted by the cultural contradictions of capitalism, and how we'll respond if we do. In the meantime, we *are* confronted by the contradictions—cultural, economic, and political—of the liberalism that sets out to secure the nice parts of capitalism while eradicating the harsh parts. The liberal contradiction I've emphasized in this book, especially the previous chapter, is caring compassionately about victims of suffering situations while accepting complacently government programs that discharge their core mission—alleviating that suffering—ineffectively and inefficiently.

The main political reason this contradiction persists is that neither conservatives nor liberals have the capacity and desire to solve it on their own, or to negotiate a deal yielding a more successful welfare state. Conservatives embrace laissez-faire, a policy of having the government stand aside while individuals act upon their inclinations. Their argument is not that laissez-faire guarantees results better than any imaginable alternative, but that it's likely to produce outcomes better than any *available* alternative. If philosopher-kings, supremely wise and just, routinely directed government interventions in the economy, the liberal case would be very strong. It proves very little, however, when liberals contrast actual market failures with hypostatized government successes. The journalist Harold Meyerson, for example, wrote that "systemic failures," like the financial panic of 2008 or Gulf of Mexico oil spill in 2010, show "the human capacity for mistake and self-delusion, not to mention avarice and chicanery," thereby proving the need for "active, disinterested governmental regulation."[51] It's an argument that excludes the possibility that government officials, such as those at the Securities and Exchange Commission who spent sixteen years finding nothing amiss in Bernard Madoff's Ponzi scheme, might also be mistaken, deluded, or avaricious.

Given the correlation of political forces, conservatives are understandably reluctant to enter into discussions about how government can better perform activities they don't think it should be doing at all. Liberals, for their part, are understandably reluctant to address the shortcomings of the programs they have brought into existence if their adversaries will use such candor to demand repealing the programs, rather than to discuss reforming them. (Liberals have other reasons to leave well enough alone regarding their programs' efficacy. The Democrats are the party of government in two senses: as the home for the advocacy of activist government; and as the coalition that includes large numbers of government employees and dependents. Most measures that would make activist government work better would also complicate the lives of those employees and dependents, which means powerful constituencies within the party resist rather than welcome all such reforms.)

Attempts to break this stalemate have been rare. Liberals believe that activist government has one major flaw—there's not nearly enough of it—which, if corrected, would remedy any minor flaws it might have. Thus, Obamacare was supposed to be the corrective for Medicare's deficiencies, chief among them an incentive structure thought to benefit health care providers financially more than it benefits health care recipients medically. The corrective for Obamacare's deficiencies, in turn, is supposed to be single-payer health insurance—that is, Medicare for all.

Furthermore, liberals' worldview gives them no political reason to seek a deal with conservatives to make the welfare state work more efficiently and effectively. Unless liberals are in a position to dictate the terms of any such agreement, it will entail concessions, ones likely to reduce or reorganize the welfare state, as did the 1996 welfare reform law. But if liberals *are* in a position to dictate terms, they don't really need an agreement, and are certainly not interested in making the 1996 law a template for future policy making. Such anomalies aside, liberals in general don't believe they need to negotiate with conservatives over the size and operation of the welfare state. To be a "progressive," after all, is to believe you're on history's side and history is on yours. What history wants, according to its liberal oracles, is government programs that make life freer, less cruel, more leisured, and so forth. If a particular historical contingency, such as the Reagan presidency or the tax revolt, seems to be thwarting the realization of history's deepest desire, the zeitgeist will eventually reward liberals who wait for it to assert itself.

For this reason, conservatives believe that discussing domestic policy with liberals is, in general, as futile as discussing foreign policy with the Soviet Union: both adversaries take the posture that what's theirs is theirs, and what's yours is negotiable. Conservatives do from time to time send up trial balloons, all of which work from the premise that the perversity of spending more and more to eliminate poverty, even as poverty shows no sign of disappearing, calls for a wholly different approach. In *Capitalism and Freedom* Milton Friedman advocated a negative income tax: the government would pay people a percentage of the difference when their income fell below some specified level. Determining that percentage and income level would be a straightforward assignment for a deliberative democracy. That is, having agreed that we want to set a floor under the standard of living of every person in the community, the question would be the amount we think we can afford and our willingness to impose the necessary taxes on ourselves for that purpose. Citizens' sense about what the established rules of decency render necessary to the lowest rank of people would inform those deliberations; studies by experts purporting to speak and act on victims' behalf would not.[52]

In Our Hands, Charles Murray's book published in 2006, offered a detailed plan for implementing a negative income tax. It called for having the federal government give every American age twenty-one or older, and earning less than $25,000 a year, an additional $10,000, no strings attached. People who earn more than $25,000 but less than $50,000 would see their $10,000 stipend reduced by 20¢ for each dollar they earn in excess of $25,000, up to an earned income of

$50,000. Thus, someone with an earned income of $30,000 would receive $9,000 more from the federal government, a neighbor with an income of $40,000 would receive a payment of $7,000, and someone making $50,000 would receive $5,000. There would be no additional reduction for those making more than $50,000, so someone with an earned income of $500,000 or $5 million would also receive $5,000. (Murray's plan doesn't speak to tax policy, so the $5,000 grant to the affluent, under the existing or any imaginable tax system, would really amount to a tax rebate.) The government grant would go to individuals, regardless of their marital status or domestic arrangements. A couple consisting of two people each making $25,000 would receive $20,000 from the federal government, $10,000 apiece. A couple consisting of one person making $50,000 and one with no earnings would receive $15,000, $5,000 for the person who's in the workforce and $10,000 for the one who isn't.[53]

Murray's transfer system would abolish nearly every social welfare program: the book is subtitled *A Plan to Replace the Welfare State.* "Social Security, Medicare, Medicaid, welfare programs, social service programs, agricultural subsidies, and corporate welfare" are all zeroed out. An appendix lists ninety-eight federal programs to be eliminated, and the implementation of the plan calls for a constitutional amendment prohibiting not only the federal government but state and local ones from enacting any law or program that "provides benefits to some citizens but not others." It's not quite a libertarian Nirvana, in that Murray leaves in place existing arrangements for public education, the provision of transportation infrastructure, and the U.S. Postal Service.

A different approach to sweeping all the chess pieces off the board was put forward by William Buckley in his 1973 book, *Four Reforms.* Buckley relies on federalism to pare back and simplify the welfare state by limiting eligibility for federal social welfare and insurance programs to those Americans living in states whose median income was below the national average. We would all, as

American taxpayers, assist the poor in poor states, which would strain to pay for such assistance out of taxes raised within their borders. Having done so, those of us who are Californians, Virginians, or residents of some other prosperous state would rely entirely on state programs funded from state taxes to assist the poor within our state's borders. Under federalism, different states might try different approaches (perhaps even a negative income tax), and the most successful systems would be copied around the country. Because Buckley thought it was economically and politically debilitating to turn the "sky black with criss-crossing dollars," his proposal grounds a lot of those dollars. Federal welfare expenditures would shrink, as the number of people eligible for them was limited, and prosperous states would pay for their own welfare programs without the transportation and administrative fees of sending dollars to Washington and then back to the states.[54]

Apart from the fact there is no likelihood a policy resembling Friedman's, Murray's, or Buckley's will be enacted in the foreseeable future, the proposals have other similarities that clarify the argument between conservatives and liberals. First, all three treat the welfare state as an inevitability—Friedman for practical reasons, Murray and Buckley for political ones. In doing so, they move the debate away from whether to have a welfare state, pouring water on the hopes of those conservatives who want to see it completely dismantled someday, to the question of how to organize and operate it.

Second, by radically simplifying the welfare state, all their proposals speak to liberalism's efficacy failures. In general, simple tasks are completed more successfully than complex ones, and the welfare state is no exception. When it gives people money, people receive the money it gives them. When it gives them Head Starts or Model Cities, they often wind up with something less than a head start or a model city.

Third, simplicity is conducive to efficiency as well as to effectiveness. Writing in 2006, Murray argued that the day was fast approaching when it would be cheaper to inaugurate a transfer state than to perpetuate the existing welfare state. That day has arrived. There were 222 million Americans at least twenty-one years of age in 2012. The federal government spent $2.224 trillion on human resources programs that year. (And, as noted in Chapter Four, state and local governments spent an additional $728 billion on social services and income maintenance in 2011.) Giving each American adult $10,000 would have cost $2.22 trillion, less than what we spent on scores of federal, state, and local government programs to fight poverty and alleviate suffering. Murray's plan, however, does not give *every* adult $10,000: those who earn more than $50,000 receive $5,000, and those who earn between $25,000 and $50,000 receive a total between $5,000 and $10,000, as determined by the formula described above. Using Census Bureau data for 2002, he calculated that those provisions for reducing the transfer payment would lower the cost of the program by 14 percent from its theoretical maximum.

Apply that reduction to the facts of 2012, and the program would have cost $1.913 trillion, or about one-third less than actual federal, state, and local outlays on the welfare state that year. Because of inflation and economic growth, a larger proportion of Americans in 2012 had earnings in excess of $50,000 than in 2002, so the reduction of the program's cost from its theoretical maximum would have been greater than 14 percent. Even if the basic amount of the government stipend had been $11,170, the HHS poverty guideline for an individual in 2012, the theoretical maximum of the program would have been $2.48 trillion, leaving a net cost in the neighborhood of $2 trillion, still far below the actual cost of all welfare state programs in 2012.

Fourth, the simplicity these conservatives propose would clarify not only the welfare state's administration, but also its politics. Doing so, by no coincidence, creates problems for liberals. The more complex the welfare state, the more difficult it is for any citizen to know whether he is a net importer or net exporter of the wealth it redistributes. Large parts of the welfare state are organized to take advantage of this ambiguity by encouraging the illogical belief that nearly every citizen, except for the very richest, is a net importer of the enormous but finite amount of money it redistributes, and is *entitled* to come out ahead in his dealings with the welfare state. Social Security benefits are paid by ~~check or~~ direct deposit; Social Security is funded by payroll taxes imposed on employees and employers. The former is palpable, the latter is subtle, neither of which is by happenstance. Simplify the welfare state, take billions of crisscrossing dollars out of the sky, and we address the issue in terms of how much help the poor need and how much the rest of us can afford, banishing all ambiguity about who the poor are and are not.

Fifth, the plans (Murray's in particular) challenge liberals in another sense: "Do you want to eliminate poverty? This eliminates poverty. Our democracy takes up the intertwined questions of our duty to the poor and our definition of what it means to be poor. People who find the democratically determined answers insufficiently compassionate are free to argue for a higher income floor or a different schedule for reducing transfer payments . . . *and* for the higher taxes those changes will require.

"Do you, on the other hand, want an endless, eternal supply of venues for demonstrating your empathy? That's your problem—not ours, and not America's. If you want to prove, to the world or yourself, how noble and sensitive you are, do it on your own time and your own dime. The fundamental obligation to one another's economic welfare that connects us as fellow citizens has already been discharged through the transfer program. All other acts and feelings of solicitude will connect Americans in extra-political ways, as neighbors, co-religionists, etc."

Sixth, a negative income tax will enable the great-sapping-nullity lifestyle, and some will avail themselves of that opportunity. But the existing welfare state enables the great-sapping-nullity lifestyle, and any conceivable configuration of the welfare state will do the same. There is no *policy* that precludes this moral hazard, the cultural contradiction of the welfare state. If government mitigates the consequences that follow from a lack of discipline, initiative, providence, and self-respect, some people will respond to those incentives by discarding those habits and dispositions. If we, as a republic, believed upholding those habits and dispositions was so important that it would be worth the risk that some people might starve or freeze to death (or be spared from doing so only by private charity), there wouldn't be a welfare state. The fact that every nation prosperous enough to fund one has created a welfare state argues that no modern society is prepared to order its moral priorities in this fashion. We would rather live with the irresponsibility of some than with the abject misery of others, even if we believe that the irresponsible and the miserable are often one and the same because more responsibility leads to less misery.

To be spared from misery is not the same as flourishing, however. "Here's the money," Murray's plan says to every American, whether their ambitions are grand or meager, noble or base. "Use it as you see fit. Your life is in your hands."[55] In other words, once we turn the welfare state into a transfer state, people are on their own. We don't care, in our capacity as citizens dealing with other citizens through the medium of government, whether people use their basic income to go to night school, save for retirement, or buy vodka. Some people are going to make bad choices, and they will "own" those choices, as pop psychology has taught us to say. We'll still have moral duties to reach out to the suffering through churches and volunteer organizations, but will have already discharged our civic duty to them. George W. Bush's armies of compassion will perform their commonplace miracles of renewal, that is, but through channels distinct from government rather than intertwined with it.

Indeed, replacing the whole crowded roster of welfare programs with a guaranteed income could have the effect of invigorating society while establishing firm boundaries for the state. The sort of voluntary organizations that played a vital role in social welfare prior to the New Deal would have important new responsibilities.[56] Not only would volunteered charity help people who are poor, but joint, voluntary action can keep people from becoming poor. Replacing huge middle-class entitlement programs like Social Security and Medicare with a negative income tax would require individuals to tend to their own financial security. They would not have to do it *as* individuals, however, if fraternal societies or faith-based associations assumed a central role in offering and vetting the necessary investment and insurance products that will replace the entitlement programs. Rather than the enervation that comes from the cultural contradictions of capitalism, these kinds of arrangements would enable economic and social capital to fortify one another.

Finally, the bullshit of a liberal project indifferent to its own efficacy is inseparable from the bullshit of liberalism's lack of a limiting principle. (The latter is descriptive bullshit, in the sense that discussions purportedly concerning how expansions of the welfare state will bring us closer to the goal of social justice, inadvertently make clear that there *is* no goal, which renders the idea of getting closer to it meaningless.) If there is no end to the list of problems government should address, then there is no urgency about addressing any one of them successfully. In liberals' eyes, the welfare state's failures always result from insufficient elaboration, never from inadequate performance.

By stipulating that the welfare state should not get indefinitely smaller, conservatives would gain new leverage in debates and negotiations to press liberals to stipulate it should not get indefinitely bigger. In particular, conservatives think the steadily rising GDP documented by economists like McCloskey should permit the welfare state to get smaller, rather than permit it to get eternally bigger, the liberal position and the historical pattern. Indeed, economic growth holds out the prospect of a welfare (or transfer) state that grows in absolute terms while shrinking in relative terms. The 9.8 percent increase in (per capita, inflation-adjusted) human resources outlays on Ronald Reagan's watch occurred mostly because of economic growth. Relative to GDP, such spending shrank from 11.1 percent in 1981 to 10 percent in 1989. This may look like a rounding error, but it deserves respect as a policy accomplishment. Over eight years Reagan saw the welfare state diminish by one-tenth of what it had been, relative to the entire economy, despite never having a Republican majority in both houses of Congress, and despite the fact that a large portion of social spending is in entitlement programs strongly fortified against mere elected officials. For conservatives to interpret the growth, in absolute terms, of human resources spending in the 1980s as proof that Reagan was a failure, or conservatism is futile, requires begrudging that decade's economic expansion.

By the same token, for liberals to insist that a compassionate society is obligated to devote a larger share of its economic output to social welfare spending—no matter how much the economy grows, no matter that prosperity alleviates suffering, no matter that prosperity allows social spending to shrink in relative terms while increasing in absolute ones, no matter how unreliably social spending has reduced suffering in the past—is to put the republic on a treadmill under the pretext of entreating the citizens to undertake a pilgrimage to social justice. And that's bullshit, too.

BEYOND LIBERALISM

From 1975 to 1977, sociologist Jonathan Rieder inhabited and carefully observed Canarsie, a predominantly Jewish and Italian middle-class neighborhood in Brooklyn. Many of its residents had grown up in families that honored Franklin Roosevelt as the hero who saved the country from depression and the world from fascism. By 1975, however, America's travails at home and abroad over the preceding decade had convinced Canarsie's voters that liberalism now stood for "profligacy, spinelessness, malevolence, masochism, elitism, fantasy, anarchy, idealism, softness, irresponsibility, and sanctimoniousness," according to Rieder's book about the neighborhood. Its residents were, at the same time, disposed to become "Reagan Democrats" a few years later because to them, "The term *conservative* acquired connotations of pragmatism, character, reciprocity, truthfulness, stoicism, manliness, realism, hardness, vengeance, strictness, and responsibility."[57] In other words, a sizable, crucial segment of the electorate came to view the fundamental differences between liberalism and conservatives the way conservatives always had. They came to believe that whether the challenge was a totalitarian superpower, international terrorism, riots in slums and on campuses, crime in the streets, or welfare fraud and abuse, Americans could count on liberals . . . to fashion a response that was conceptually fatuous and operationally feckless.

Based on this shift in public attitudes, conservatives dared to believe *all* the big political events a generation ago—the tax revolt started by the 1978 passage of Proposition 13 in California, Margaret Thatcher's victories in Great Britain, Ronald Reagan's election and reelection to the presidency, the fall of the Berlin Wall and disintegration of the Soviet Union, and the 1994 midterm elections—meant that long decades of liberal hegemony were giving way to a new, comparably enduring, conservative era. In fact, conservatism's political advantages in that era yielded victories far less formidable and durable than the ones liberalism secured in the middle of the twentieth century. It's clear that in a contest between "progressives" and "conservatives," both sides have embraced designations that assume the passage of time is likely to aid the former's cause and damage the latter's. Whatever else it encompasses, the term "conservative" conveys acceptance of a duty to safeguard a legacy, one that is vulnerable, therefore requiring conservation, and valuable, therefore deserving it.

This sense of resisting history's gravitational forces, woven into the conservative enterprise, has a specific focus. "Liberalism is the glue that cements the conservative movement," political scientist James Ceaser argues, "and if liberalism were to disappear tomorrow, the conservative movement as we know it would begin to disintegrate on the next day."[58] There is no prospect liberalism will disappear tomorrow, so in that sense conservatism's future is assured. It is doubtful for other reasons, however. The *National Journal*'s Ronald Brownstein has argued that Republicans are getting a larger percentage of the vote from exactly one segment of the electorate, white voters without a degree from a four-year college, a group in steady decline, accounting for 53 percent of the electorate in 1992 but only 39 percent in 2008. Democrats, meanwhile, are doing better with every other segment—white college graduates, blacks, Hispanics, and other minorities—all of which are a growing proportion of the population. What Brownstein calls the Democrats' "Coalition of Transformation" appears poised to gain strength, perhaps for many years to come, vis-à-vis the Republicans' "Coalition of Restoration." This means, he writes, that the days of "the political dominance of married, churchgoing white families" are "gone."[59]

Inevitably, conservatives are exerting themselves to devise political strategies that will prevail against these trends. There are certainly things conservatives can do to improve their fortunes, including some they've not done at all and others they've not done well. There may even be many such things . . . but there are only so many of them. In a democracy, the question of *how* to win future elections is so engrossing that it constantly threatens to efface the question of *why* to contest them. At some point, however, a political movement dishonors itself if it doesn't draw a line and say it's better to lose an election than to win by abandoning certain essentials. What a British conservative said of war is also true of politics: it being impossible to guarantee victory, one can strive only to deserve it.

Conservatives would deserve more victories, and might even secure more, if they clarified their mission. Conserving America's experiment in self-government does require opposing liberalism. Paradoxically, conservatives would oppose liberalism more effectively if they opposed it less fundamentally. Liberalism is *a* problem, but not *the* problem. The more basic challenge is to protect democracy from itself, since its strongest tendencies include some of its most self-destructive ones. Liberalism tells Democrats what they want to hear, that the cure for the ailments of democracy is more democracy. In calling for more democracy, liberals encourage the people to demand much from government, in the belief that its democratic character will suffice to make it responsive, efficacious, and benign.

Compassion emerges naturally from Democratic politics. The pervading axiom that people are fundamentally equal and alike engenders the belief that everyone has the capacity to understand everyone else's viewpoint and sorrows, whether (as on *The Oprah Winfrey Show*) they are movie stars or battered spouses. Compassion also reconciles us to the inescapable political inequality: even though the governors derive their just powers from the consent of the governed, we hope the power they exercise *over* us will be *for* us. To reassure us of their benign intentions, and that the power we entrust to them won't go to their heads, they offer constant pledges about feeling our pain, and testimonials about enduring suffering in their own lives that drive them to work night and day to spare us from similar distress.

Conservatism, by contrast, tells Democrats what they need to hear: the corrective for the harmful dispositions of democracy is better democracy. In calling for better democracy, conservatives summon Democrats to be cautious rather than zealous, farsighted rather than impulsive, apprehensive about democracy's fragility rather than complacent about its durability. As Lincoln said in his first inaugural address, "A majority held in restraint by constitutional checks and limitations, and always changing easily with deliberate changes of popular opinions and sentiments, is the only true sovereign of a free people." A democracy that resents and dismantles rather than honors and upholds the ways Democrats are restrained, checked, and limited is one that threatens the only basis for hoping that democratic government will reliably produce good government.

The politics of compassion jeopardizes democracy by disdaining such caution and consensus. The deliberate judgment of the people exercised through constitutional channels, from the perspective that makes compassion the supreme political virtue, yields nothing more than a government frozen in the ice of its own indifference, all for the sake of sparing us the occasional faults of a government that lives in a spirit of charity. Even if there had been no Progressive movement, then, no New Deal and no Great Society, democracy itself would give rise to an abiding need to cultivate the habits and dispositions—both public and private—that sustain self-government, while opposing the ones that erode it.

Compassion is not, in itself, one of the latter. We may even join with Nicholas Kristof in calling it a mark of civilization. It is not the only one, however. Another is an abiding sense of civilization's frailty. Evelyn Waugh voiced this concern in 1964 when reviewing a biography of Rudyard Kipling, whom he described as "a conservative in the sense that he believed civilization to be something laboriously achieved which was only precariously defended. He wanted to see the defences fully manned and he hated the liberals because he thought them gullible and feeble, believing in the easy perfectibility of man and ready to abandon the work of centuries for sentimental qualms." The sentiments Waugh ascribes to Kipling are ones he expressed in his own name in 1939: "Civilization has no force of its own beyond what is given it from within. It is under constant assault and it takes most of the energies of civilized man to keep going at all. . . . Unremitting effort is needed to keep men living together at peace; there is only a margin of energy left over for experiment however beneficent."[60]

To insist compassion must have its way because it is such a basic, noble emotional force; to insist that all who defy it are mean and greedy; to disdain the reality that governance's challenges will frequently impel decent nations to subordinate compassion's claims to those of justice, honor, liberty, and security—is to complicate and imperil self-government. It is nice, all things being equal, to have elected officials who feel our pain rather than ones who, like imperious monarchs, cannot comprehend or do not deign to notice it. Much more than their empathy, however, we require their respect—for us; our rights; our capacity and responsibility to feel and heal our own damn pains without their ministrations; and for America's constitutional checks and limitations, which err on the side of caution and republicanism by denying even the most compassionate elected official a monarch's plenary powers. Kindness may well cover all of Barack Obama's political beliefs, and those of many other self-satisfied liberals. It neither begins to cover all the beliefs that have sustained America's republic, however, nor amounts to an adequate substitute for those moral virtues and political principles indispensable to sustaining it further.

NOTES

INTRODUCTION: SUFFERING SITUATIONS

1. Christopher Reeve, 1996 Democratic National Convention Address, August 26, 1996, American Rhetoric, http://www.americanrhetoric.com/speeches/christopherreeve1996dnc.htm.

2. Clifford Orwin, "Compassion," *American Scholar*, Summer 1980, p. 324.

3. Al Gore, "Speech to the 1996 Democratic Convention," *New York Times*, August 29, 1996, http://www.nytimes.com/1996/08/29/us/gore-speech-america-is-strong-bill-clinton-s-leadership-is-paying-off.html?pagewanted=print&src=pm.

4. Kevin Sack, "Gore Forced to Make Hard Choices on Tobacco," *New York Times*, August 30, 1996, http://www.nytimes.com/1996/08/30/us/gore-forced-to-make-hard-choices-on-tobacco.html.

5. Erik Schelzig, "Al, Tipper Gore Kiss 40 Years of Marriage Goodbye," *Dallas Morning News*, June 2, 2010, http://www.dallasnews.com/news/20100602-Al-Tipper-Gore-kiss-40-5764.ece.

6. Glenn Kessler, "'The Road We've Traveled': A Misleading Account of Obama's Mother and Her Insurance Dispute," *Washington Post*, March 19, 2012, http://www.washingtonpost.com/blogs/fact-checker/post/the-road-weve-traveled-a-misleading-account-of-obamas-mother-and-her-insurance-dispute/2012/03/18/gIQAdDd4KS_blog.html?hpid=z2.

7. Barack Obama, "Remarks on Signing the Patient Protection and Affordable Care Act," March 23, 2010, American Presidency Project, http://www.presidency.ucsb.edu/ws/?pid=87660.

8. Louise Radnofsky, "Boy at Obama's Side Now in High School," *Wall Street Journal*, October 1, 2013, http://blogs.wsj.com/wash wire/2013/10/01/boy-at-obamas-side-now-in-high-school/. See also Kyung M. Song, "Boy Who Lost Mom Takes Health Care Story to D.C.," *Seattle Times*, March 8, 2010, http://seattletimes.com/html/localnews/2011292589_marcelas09m.html.

9. Sheryl Gay Stolberg, "To Promote Health Care Plan, Obama Talks About His Own Grandmother," *New York Times*, August 15, 2009, http://www.nytimes.com/2009/08/16/health/policy/16address.html?_r=0.

10. "Remarks by the First Lady on What Health Insurance Reform Means for Women and Families," September 18, 2009, http://www.whitehouse.gov/the-press-office/remarks-first-lady-what-health-insurance-reform-means-women-and-families.

11. Mark Evanier, "Bottom of the Barrel," *News from Me*, February 2, 2010, http://www.newsfromme.com/2010/02/10/bottom-of-the-barrel/.

12. Garrison Keillor, *Homegrown Democrat: A Few Plain Thoughts from the Heart of America* (New York: Viking, 2004), p. 20.

13. "President Obama Speaks on the Economy," November 26, 2013, http://www.whitehouse.gov/photos-and-video/video/2013/11/26/president-obama-speaks-economy#transcript.

14. Paul Bloom, "The Baby in the Well: The Case Against Empathy," *New Yorker*, May 20, 2013.

15. Kenneth Minogue, *The Liberal Mind* (Indianapolis: Liberty Fund, 2000), ch. 1, sec. 1, "Suffering Situations," http://oll.libertyfund.org/?option=com_staticxt&staticfile=show.php%3Ftitle=672&chapter=165210&layout=html&Itemid=27.

16. Remarks at the dedication of the Hubert H. Humphrey Building, November 1, 1977, *Congressional Record*, November 4, 1977, vol. 123, p. 37287.

17. Franklin D. Roosevelt, "Acceptance Speech for the Renomination for the Presidency, Philadelphia, Pa.," June 27, 1936, American Presidency Project, http://www.presidency.ucsb.edu/ws/?pid=15314.

18. Steven F. Hayward, *The Age of Reagan: The Conservative Counterrevo-*

lution, 1980–1989 (New York: Crown Forum, 2009), pp. 383–84.

19. Paul Krugman, "Hunger Games, U.S.A.," *New York Times*, July 14, 2013, http://www.nytimes.com/2013/07/15/opinion/krugman-hunger-games-usa.html?_r=0.

20. Jonathan Allen, "Grayson: GOP Wants 'You to Die,'" *Politico*, September 9, 2009, http://www.politico.com/news/stories/0909/27726.html.

21. "An Open Letter to Republicans: Your Country Isn't Coming Back," *ChicagoNow.com*, November 8, 2012, http://www.chicagonow.com/offhanded-dribble/2012/11/an-open-letter-to-republicans-you-are-not-getting-your-country-back/.

22. Charles M. Blow, "'A Town Without Pity,'" *New York Times*, August 9, 2013, http://www.nytimes.com/2013/08/10/opinion/blow-a-town-without-pity.html.

CHAPTER 1

1. Benjamin Adams and Jean Larson, "Legislative History of the Animal Welfare Act," National Agricultural Library, United States Department of Agriculture, Animal Welfare Information Center, http://www.nal.usda.gov/awic/pubs/AWA2007/intro.shtml.

2. David A. Fahrenthold, "Watch Him Pull a USDA-Mandated Rabbit Disaster Plan out of His Hat," *Washington Post*, July 16, 2013, http://www.washingtonpost.com/politics/watch-him-pull-a-usda-mandated-rabbit-disaster-plan-out-of-his-hat/2013/07/16/816f2f66-ed66-11e2-8163-2c7021381a75_story.html.

3. Joe O'Connor, "Magician Forced to Pull Rabbit Disaster Plan out of His Hat," *National Post*, July 18, 2013, http://news.nationalpost.com/2013/07/18/marty-the-magician-rabbit-disaster-plan/.

4. Arthur M. Schlesinger Jr., "The Perspective Now," *Partisan Review*, May–June 1947, p. 238.

5. John F. Kennedy, "The President's News Conference," March 21, 1962, American Presidency Project, http://www.presidency.ucsb.edu/ws/?pid=8564.

6. Edward M. Kennedy, Address at the Public Memorial Service for Robert F. Kennedy, delivered June 8, 1968, at St. Patrick's Cathedral, New York, http://www.americanrhetoric.com/speeches/ekennedy-tributetorfk.html.

7. Mario Matthew Cuomo, 1984 Democratic National Convention Keynote Address, delivered July 16, 1984, in San Francisco, http://www.americanrhetoric.com/speeches/mariocuomo1984dnc.htm.

8. Paul Waldman, "The Failure of Antigovernment Conservatism," August 7, 2007, *American Prospect*, http://prospect.org/article/failure-antigovernment-conservatism.

9. George Lakoff, "Empathy, Sotomayor, and Democracy: The Conservative Stealth Strategy," Truth-Out.org, May 31, 2009, http://www.truth-out.org/buzzflash/commentary/item/7319-empathy-sotomayor-and-democracy-the-conservative-stealth-strategy-by-george-lakoff.

10. See, for example, Leo Strauss, "Political Philosophy and History," *Journal of the History of Ideas* 10, no. 1 (January 1949): 30–50.

11. "Conservatively Speaking," *New York Times Magazine*, July 11, 2004, http://www.nytimes.com/2004/07/11/magazine/11QUESTIONS .html?ei=5070&en=a78be4479c624bcf&ex=1204952400.

12. Nicholas D. Kristof, "Where Is the Love?," *New York Times*, November 27, 2013, http://www.nytimes.com/2013/11/28/opinion/kristof-where-is-the-love.html?_r=0.

13. John Rawls, *A Theory of Justice* (Cambridge, MA: Harvard University Press, 1971).

14. Mark Lilla, "The Politics of God," *New York Times Magazine*, August 19, 2007.

15. Francis Fukuyama, "The End of History," *National Interest*, Summer 1989.

16. George F. Will, *The Pursuit of Happiness: And Other Sobering Thoughts* (New York: Harper & Row, 1978), p. 180.

17. George Orwell, *My Country, Right or Left, 1940–1943*, ed. Sonia Orwell and Ian Angus (Jaffrey, NH: Nonpareil, 2000), p. 14.

18. Alexis de Tocqueville, *Democracy in America*, ed. and trans. Harvey C. Mansfield and Delba Winthrop (Chicago: University of Chicago Press, 2000), p. 502.

19. Adam Smith, *An Inquiry into the Nature and Causes of the Wealth of Nations*, ed. Edwin Cannon, Book I, Chapter 2, Library of Economics and Liberty, http://www.econlib.org/library/Smith/smWN1.html.

20. Franklin D. Roosevelt, "Radio Greeting on St. Patrick's Day, Warm Springs, Ga.," March 17, 1937, American Presidency Project, http://www.presidency.ucsb.edu/ws/?pid=15379.

21. Pete Hamill, "Doing Good," *New York*, October 13, 1986, p. 39.

22. Learned Hand, "The Spirit of Liberty," speech delivered in New York City on May 21, 1944, in Diane Ravitch, ed., *American Reader: Words That Moved a Nation* (New York: HarperCollins, 1990), p. 288. For President Clinton's enthusiasm for Hand's argument, see William J. Clinton, Remarks Announcing the Nomination of Stephen G. Breyer to Be a Supreme Court Associate Justice, May 13, 1994, American Presidency Project, http://www.presidency.ucsb.edu/ws/index.php?pid=50164&st=&st1=. For President Obama's enthusiasm, see Larissa MacFarquhar, "The Conciliator," *New Yorker*, May 7, 2007, http://www.newyorker.com/reporting/2007/05/07/070507fa_fact_macfarquhar.

23. Jeffrey Peter Hart, *The American Dissent: A Decade of Modern Conservatism* (New York: Doubleday, 1966), p. 171; "After 50 Years of Covering War, Looking for Peace and Honoring Law," *New York Times*, December 16, 2001, http://www.nytimes.com/2001/12/16/weekinreview/16WORD.html.

24. Jean-Jacques Rousseau, *Emile or On Education*, translated by Allan Bloom (New York: Basic Books, 1979), p. 235n.

25. Barack Obama, *The Audacity of Hope: Thoughts on Reclaiming the American Dream* (London: Canongate Books, 2008), pp. 67–68. See Clifford Orwin, "Does He Feel Our Pain?," *In Character*, June 22, 2010, http://incharacter.org/observation/1does-he-feel-our-pain.

26. Hart, *The American Dissent*, p. 171.

27. Minogue, *The Liberal Mind*.

28. Arthur M. Schlesinger Jr., *The Vital Center: The Politics of Freedom* (Boston: Houghton Mifflin, 1949), pp. 245, 248, and 256.

29. Jimmy Carter, "Address to the Nation on Energy and National Goals: 'The Malaise Speech,'" July 15, 1979, American Presidency Project, http://www.presidency.ucsb.edu/ws/?pid=32596.

30. "Hillary Clinton's Politics of Meaning Speech," *Tikkun*, May–June 1993.

31. Schlesinger, *Vital Center*, pp. 251, 245.

32. Michael Kazin, "What Liberals Owe to Radicals," *Liberalism for a New Century* (Berkeley and Los Angeles: University of California Press, 2007), p. 123.

33. Max Ways, "Don't We Know Enough to Make Better Public Policies?," *Fortune*, April 1971, reprinted in Robert E. Hicks, Walter J. Klages, and Frederick A. Raffa, eds., *Economics: Myth, Method, or Madness?* (Berkeley, CA: McCutchan, 1971), p. 84.

34. "Giving Till It Hurts: An Interview with Barbara Oakley," *Freeman*, July 29, 2013, http://www.fee.org/the_freeman/detail/giving-till-it-hurts-an-interview-with-barbara-oakley#ixzz2lyHvROD3.

35. An email from David Schmidtz to the author, November 19, 2013. Professor Schmidtz reports that this sentence has made it into several of his lectures, but not in any of his published works to date.

36. Mickey Kaus, "Up from Altruism," *New Republic*, December 15, 1986, p. 18.

37. Bloom, "The Baby in the Well."

CHAPTER 2

1. Central Intelligence Agency, World Factbook, https://www.cia.gov/library/publications/the-world-factbook/. All subsequent calculations are derived from data available here, along with some population estimates from individual national censuses.

2. Office of Management and Budget, 2014 Budget, Historical Table 3.2, "Outlays by Function and Subfunction, 1962–2018." http://www.whitehouse.gov/sites/default/files/omb/budget/fy2014/assets/hist03z2.xls.

3. Ben Crair, "The SCHIP on Bush's Shoulder," *New Republic*, August 21, 2007, http://www.newrepublic.com/blog/the-plank/the-schip-bushs-shoulder.

4. David Goodhart, "Why the Left Is Wrong About Immigration," *Guardian*, March 27, 2013, http://www.guardian.co.uk/books/2013/mar/27/why-left-wrong-mass-immigration#start-of-comments.

5. Ibid.

6. Immanuel Kant, *Observations on the Feeling of the Beautiful and Sublime*, trans. John T. Goldthwait (Berkeley: University of California Press, 1960), p. 59.

7. Elizabeth Anderson, "Social Insurance and Self-Sufficiency," Left 2Right.com, February 5, 2005, http://www-personal.umich.edu/~eandersn/blogpoliticaleconomy.html.

8. Timothy Noah, *The Great Divergence: America's Growing Inequality Crisis and What We Can Do About It* (New York: Bloomsbury Press, 2012), pp. 174–75.

9. Adam Smith, *An Inquiry into the Nature and Causes of the Wealth of Nations by Adam Smith*, ed. Edwin Cannan (London: Methuen, 1904), vol. 2, ch. "Article IV," http://oll.libertyfund.org/title/119/212401.

10. Gordon M. Fisher, "Remembering Mollie Orshansky—The Developer of the Poverty Thresholds," *Social Security Bulletin* 68, no. 3 (2008), http://www.ssa.gov/policy/docs/ssb/v68n3/v68n3p79.html. See also John Cassidy, "Relatively Deprived," *New Yorker*, April 3, 2006.

11. Shawn Fremstad, "Relative Poverty Measures Can Help Paint a More Accurate Picture of Poverty in 21st Century America," CEPR Blog, March 14, 2013, http://www.cepr.net/index.php/blogs/cepr-blog/relative-poverty-measures-can-help-paint-a-more-accurate-picture-of-poverty-in-21st-century-america.

12. Minogue, *The Liberal Mind*.

13. Howard Zinn, "A Kinder, Gentler Patriotism," *Newsday*, April 13, 2003, http://www.commondreams.org/views03/0413-02.htm; Ross Gregory Douthat, *Privilege: Harvard and the Education of the Ruling*

Class (New York: Hyperion, 2005), pp. 204–207.

14. Strobe Talbott, "The Birth of the Global Nation," *Time*, July 20, 1992, pp. 70–71.

15. Ibid.

16. Walter Lippmann, *Isolation and Alliances: An American Speaks to the British* (New York: Little, Brown, 1952), https://www.mtholyoke.edu/acad/intrel/lipp.htm.

17. Charles Krauthammer, "A World Imagined: The Flawed Premises of Liberal Foreign Policy," *New Republic*, March 15, 1999.

18. Peter Schneider, "False Tears over Bosnia," *New York Times*, July 30, 1995, Section 4, p. 15.

19. George McGovern, statement announcing candidacy for the 1972 Democratic presidential nomination, January 18, 1971, http://www.4president.org/speeches/mcgovern1972announcement.htm.

20. George McGovern, "Address Accepting the Presidential Nomination at the Democratic National Convention in Miami Beach, Florida," July 14, 1972, American Presidency Project, http://www.presidency.ucsb.edu/ws/?pid=25967.

21. "Declaration of Sentiments Adopted by the Peace Convention," *Liberator*, September 28, 1838, http://fair-use.org/the-liberator/1838/09/28/declaration-of-sentiments-adopted-by-the-peace-convention#p3.

22. Pierre Manent, "Human Unity Real and Imagined," *First Things*, October 2012, http://www.firstthings.com/article/2012/09/human-unity-real-and-imagined.

23. Walter Russell Mead, *Special Providence: American Foreign Policy and How It Changed the World* (New York: Knopf, 2001), p. 146.

24. Sally Kohn, "White People's Racial Discomfort," *Salon*, August 6, 2013, http://www.salon.com/2013/08/06/white_peoples_racial_discomfort/.

25. Joseph F. Cotto, "Steve Sailer Discusses Genetics' Effect on Intelligence and Society," *Washington Times*, December 27, 2012, http://communities.washingtontimes.com/neighborhood/conscience-realist/2012/dec/27/steve-sailer-economics-human-intelligence/.

26. Matthew Yglesias, "What Would Happen If We Let All the Immigrants In?," *Slate*, January 25, 2013, http://www.slate.com/blogs/moneybox/2013/01/25/what_would_happen_if_we_let_all_the_immigrants_in.html.

27. Ibid.

28. Jeffrey S. Passel, D'Vera Cohn, and Ana Gonzalez-Barera, "Population Decline of Unauthorized Immigrants Stalls, May Have Reversed," Pew Hispanic Center, September 23, 2013, http://www.pewhispanic.org/2013/09/23/population-decline-of-unauthorized-immigrants-stalls-may-have-reversed/.

29. Emily Ryo, "Deciding to Cross: Norms and Economics of Unauthorized Migration," *American Sociological Review* 78 (2013): 586.

30. Joseph H. Carens, "The Case for Amnesty," *Boston Review*, May/June 2009, http://bostonreview.net/BR34.3/carens.php.

31. Ibid.

32. Ibid.

33. Ibid.

34. Ibid.

35. Carol Swain, "Apply Compassion Shown Illegal Immigrants to the Most Vulnerable Citizens," *Boston Review*, May/June 2009, http://bostonreview.net/forum/case-amnesty/apply-compassion-offered-illegal-immigrants-most-vulnerable-citizens-carol-swain.

36. Joseph H. Carens, "Joseph H. Carens Responds," *Boston Review*, May/June 2009, http://bostonreview.net/forum/case-amnesty/joseph-h-carens-responds.

37. Letter to Senator Orrin Hatch, July 9, 1991, http://cis.org/sites/cis.org/files/king-letter.pdf.

38. Christopher Jencks, "Who Should Get In? An Exchange," *New York Review of Books*, May 23, 2002, http://www.nybooks.com/articles/archives/2002/may/23/who-should-get-in-an-exchange/?pagination=false&printpage=true.

39. Mickey Kaus, "Three Sides to Amnesty in a Nutshell," *Daily Caller*, May 8, 2013, http://dailycaller.com/2013/05/08/three-sides-to-

amnesty-in-a-nutshell/.

40. Carens, "Carens Responds."

41. Timothy Egan, "As Idaho Booms, Prisons Fill and Spending on Poor Lags," *New York Times*, April 16, 1998, http://select.nytimes.com/search/restricted/article?res=F30714FF3F 580C758DDDAD0894D0494D81.

42. Deirdre McCloskey, *The Bourgeois Virtues* (Chicago: University of Chicago Press, 2006).

43. Jonathan Cohn, "Blue States Are from Scandinavia, Red States Are from Guatemala," *New Republic*, October 5, 2012, http://www.new republic.com/article/politics/magazine/108185/blue-states-are-scandinavia-red-states-are-guatemala.

44. Calculations based on Census Bureau Table 14, State Population—Rank, Percent Change, and Population Density, 1980 to 2010, http://www.census.gov/compendia/statab/2012/tables/12s0014.pdf.

45. Edward L. Glaeser, "Young Workers Can't Afford Homes in the State," *Boston Globe*, June 14, 2012, http://www.bostonglobe.com/opinion/edito rials/2012/06/14/good-luck-attracting-talent-young-workers-can-afford-homes-massachusetts/Wdxx8pEyWT20khdIMZZkWM/story.html.

46. J. P. Donlon, "2014 Best and Worst States for Business," *Chief Executive*, May 8, 2014, http://chiefexecutive.net/2014-best-worst-states-for-business.

47. Cohn, "Blue States Are from Scandinavia, Red States Are from Guatemala."

48. Suzanne Daley, "Danes Rethink a Welfare State Ample to a Fault," *New York Times*, April 20, 2013, http://www.nytimes.com/2013/04/21/world/europe/danes-rethink-a-welfare-state-ample-to-a-fault.html ?hpw&_r=0.

49. Mark Steyn, "America Must Learn from Our Laziest Woman," *Telegraph*, February 2, 2004, http://www.telegraph.co.uk/comment/personal-view/3602966/America-must-learn-from-our-laziest-woman.html.

50. Daley, "Danes Rethink a Welfare State Ample to a Fault."

51. Frédéric Bastiat, *Selected Essays on Political Economy*, trans. Seymour Cain, 1995, Library of Economics and Liberty, http://www.econlib

.org/library/Bastiat/basEss1.html.

52. Charles Murray, "The Trouble with Taking the Trouble out of Everything," *Wall Street Journal*, March 25, 2009, http://online.wsj.com/article/SB123793074783930483.html.

53. C. S. Lewis, *The Problem of Pain* (New York: Macmillan, 1962), p. 40.

54. Ibid., pp. 40–41.

55. Daley, "Danes Rethink a Welfare State Ample to a Fault."

56. Ross Douthat, "Can We Be Sweden?," *New York Times*, November 21, 2012, http://douthat.blogs.nytimes.com/2012/11/21/can-we-be-sweden.

57. Keith Caulfield, "President Obama's DNC Speech Boosts Springsteen Song Sales by 409%," *Billboard*, September 12, 2012, http://www.billboard.com/biz/articles/news/retail/1083793/president-obamas-dnc-speech-boosts-bruce-springsteen-song-sales-by; Statement by the President on the One-Year Anniversary of Hurricane Sandy, October 29, 2013, http://www.whitehouse.gov/the-press-office/2013/10/29/statement-president-one-year-anniversary-hurricane-sandy.

58. Alexis de Tocqueville, *Democracy in America*, Book I, Chapter 14, http://xroads.virginia.edu/~Hyper/DETOC/1_ch14.htm.

59. Jerry Z. Muller, "Us and Them: The Enduring Power of Ethnic Nationalism," *Foreign Affairs*, March/April 2008.

60. Samuel P. Huntington, *Who Are We? The Challenges to America's National Identity* (New York: Simon & Schuster, 2004), p. 111.

61. Federalist Papers, No. 2, http://avalon.law.yale.edu/18th_century/fed02.asp.

62. John Fonte, "Jack Kemp's Huddled Masses," *National Review*, November 11, 2013, p. 33.

63. Christopher Jencks, "Who Should Get In? Part II," *New York Review of Books*, December 20, 2001, http://www.nybooks.com.ccl.idm.oclc.org/articles/archives/2001/dec/20/who-should-get-in-part-ii/.

64. Ibid.

65. John Lloyd, "Study Paints Bleak Picture of Ethnic Diversity," *Financial Times*, October 8, 2006, http://www.ft.com/intl/cms/s/0/c4ac4a74-

570f-11db-9110-0000779e2340.html?siteedition=uk#axzz2mLtXdfst.

66. Richard Florida, "The Paradox of Diverse Communities," *Atlantic*, November 19, 2013, http://www.theatlanticcities.com/neighbor hoods/2013/11/paradox-diverse-communities/7614/.

67. Lloyd, "Study Paints Bleak Picture of Ethnic Diversity."

68. Goodhart, "Why the Left Is Wrong About Immigration."

CHAPTER 3

1. Quoted in William E. Leuchtenburg, "The Achievement of the New Deal," in Harvard Sitkoff, ed., *Fifty Years Later: The New Deal Evaluated* (Philadelphia: Temple University Press, 1985), pp. 220–21.

2. Barack Obama, "Inaugural Address," January 21, 2013, American Presidency Project, http://www.presidency.ucsb.edu/ws/?pid=102827.

3. David N. Bass, "Pelosi's Children," *American Spectator*, February 6, 2009, http://spectator.org/articles/42179/pelosis-children.

4. William J. Clinton, "Address Before a Joint Session of the Congress on the State of the Union," January 23, 1996, American Presidency Project, http://www.presidency.ucsb.edu/ws/?pid=53091.

5. Mickey Kaus, "The Godmother," *New Republic*, February 15, 1993.

6. Matt Miller, "What Typhoon Haiyan Tells Us About Obamacare," *Washington Post*, November 13, 2013, http://www.washingtonpost .com/opinions/matt-miller-what-typhoon-haiyan-tells-us-about-obamacare/2013/11/13/0438c394-4c08-11e3-be6b-d3d28122e6d4_ story.html.

7. Rheta Childe Dorr, *What Eight Million Women Want* (Boston: Small, Maynard, 1910), retrieved at Project Gutenberg, http://www.guten berg.org/files/12226/12226-h/12226-h.htm#CHAPTER_XI.

8. Hillary Rodham Clinton, *It Takes a Village: And Other Lessons Children Teach Us* (New York: Simon & Schuster, 1996), pp. 11–13.

9. Jean Bethke Elshtain, "Suffer the Little Children," *New Republic*, March 4, 1996.

10. MSNBC promo spot, *Real Clear Politics*, April 9, 2013, http://www .realclearpolitics.com/video/2013/04/08/msnbc_ad_kids_dont_be

long_to_their_parents_its_collective_responsibility.html.

11. Melissa Harris-Perry, "Why Caring for Children Is Not Just a Parent's Job," MSNBC, April 9, 2013, http://www.msnbc.com/melissa-harris-perry/why-caring-children-not-just-parent.

12. Elshtain, "Suffer the Little Children."

13. James Q. Wilson, "Why We Don't Marry," *City Journal*, Winter 2002, http://www.city-journal.org/html/12_1_why_we.html.

14. Joe Klein, "The Original Power Couple," *New Republic*, October 10, 1994, pp. 42–43; Tamara K. Hareven, *Eleanor Roosevelt: An American Conscience* (Chicago: Quadrangle, 1968), pp. 175–80.

15. John O'Sullivan, "What Jackie Did Next," *American Conservative*, January 14, 2008, http://www.theamericanconservative.com/articles/what-jackie-did-next/.

16. James Piereson, "Lincoln and Kennedy: A Tale of Two Assassinations," *Real Clear Politics*, July 27, 2007, http://www.realclearpolitics.com/articles/2007/06/lincoln_and_kennedy_a_tale_of.html.

17. George Packer, "Leaving Dealey Plaza," *New Yorker*, October 15, 2013, http://www.newyorker.com/online/blogs/comment/2013/10/leaving-dealey-plaza.html.

18. Lyndon B. Johnson, "Special Message to the Congress Proposing a Nationwide War on the Sources of Poverty," March 16, 1964, American Presidency Project, http://www.presidency.ucsb.edu/ws/?pid=26109.

19. Arthur M. Schlesinger Jr., *Robert Kennedy and His Times* (Boston: Houghton Mifflin, 1978), p. 824; Steven F. Hayward, *The Age of Reagan: The Conservative Counterrevolution, 1980–1989* (New York: Crown Forum, 2009), p. 115.

20. Schlesinger, *Robert Kennedy and His Times*, pp. 68, 882–83; Jules Witcover, *85 Days: The Last Campaign of Robert Kennedy* (New York: Putnam, 1969), p. 165.

21. Nicholas Lemann, "America Right and Left," *Atlantic*, April 1998, http://www.theatlantic.com/past/docs/issues/98apr/leftrite.htm.

22. David Burnham, "Schlesinger Calls Violence a U.S. Trait," *New York Times*, June 6, 1968, http://partners.nytimes.com/books/00/11/26/

specials/schlesinger-violence.html.

23. Thomas Sowell, *Intellectuals and Race* (New York: Basic Books, 2013), p. 31.

24. Charlotte Perkins Gilman, "A Suggestion on the Negro Problem," *American Journal of Sociology* 14, no. 1 (July 1908): 78–85.

25. David M. Kennedy, *Freedom from Fear: The American People in Depression and War, 1929–1945* (New York: Oxford University Press, 1999), p. 764.

26. Abigail and Stephan Thernstrom, *America in Black and White: One Nation, Indivisible: Race in Modern America* (New York: Simon & Schuster, 1997), p. 104, 564n22.

27. Michael Barone, *Our Country: The Shaping of America from Roosevelt to Reagan* (New York: Free Press, 1990), p. 287.

28. Nicholas Lemann, *The Promised Land: The Great Black Migration and How It Changed America* (New York: Knopf, 1991), pp. 111–12.

29. John F. Kennedy: "Radio and Television Report to the American People on Civil Rights," June 11, 1963, American Presidency Project, http://www.presidency.ucsb.edu/ws/?pid=9271.

30. Quoted in Carl Solberg, *Hubert Humphrey: A Biography* (New York: Norton, 1984), p. 297.

31. Susan Sontag, essay for "What's Happening in America (A Symposium)," *Partisan Review*, Winter 1967, pp. 57–58.

32. Christopher Hitchens, "Susan Sontag: Remembering an Intellectual Heroine," *Slate*, December 29, 2004, http://www.slate.com/articles/news_and_politics/obit/2004/12/susan_sontag.html; Sontag, essay for "What's Happening in America (A Symposium)," p. 58.

33. Stephan Thernstrom, "The Kerner Commission Report Lacks Credibility," Heritage Foundation lecture on the Kerner Commission Report, March 13, 1998, http://www.heritage.org/research/lecture/the-kerner-commission-report.

34. Kaus, "Up from Altruism," p. 18.

35. Jean Bethke Elshtain, "The Hard Questions," *New Republic*, September 30, 1996, p. 29.

36. Glenn C. Loury, "The Return of the Undeserving Poor," *Atlantic*, Feb-

ruary 2001, http://www.theatlantic.com/magazine/archive/2001/02/
the-return-of-the-undeserving-poor/302102/.

37. Franklin D. Roosevelt, "Acceptance Speech for the Renomination for
the Presidency, Philadelphia, Pa.," June 27, 1936, American Presidency Project, http://www.presidency.ucsb.edu/ws/?pid=15314.

38. "Slate Votes," *Slate*, November 5, 2012, http://www.slate.com/arti
cles/news_and_politics/politics/2012/11/slate_votes_2012_why_we_
chose_obama_over_romney_stein_and_johnson.html.

39. Shelby Steele, *White Guilt: How Blacks and Whites Together Destroyed
the Promise of the Civil Rights Era* (New York: HarperCollins, 2006),
pp. 55, 58.

40. John McWhorter, "Don't Ignore Race in Christopher Lane's Murder,"
Time, August 22, 2013, http://ideas.time.com/2013/08/22/viewpoint-
dont-ignore-race-in-christopher-lanes-murder/#ixzz2ck7IBhCB.

41. Alexia Cooper and Erica L. Smith, "Homicide Trends in the United
States, 1980–2008," Bureau of Justice Statistics, U.S. Department of
Justice, November 2011, NCJ 236018, pp. 5, 10, 12, 16.

42. McWhorter, "Don't Ignore Race in Christopher Lane's Murder,"
comment by "fmoolten."

43. Corey Williams, "It's Not My Fault You Paid $250,000 and I Paid
a Buck," Associated Press, February 28, 2011, http://www.nbcnews
.com/id/41810267/ns/us_news-life/#.UcCXE-uE4XX.

44. Ta-Nehisi Coates, "A Rising Tide Lifts Mostly Yachts," *Atlantic*, September 17, 2013, http://www.theatlantic.com/business/
archive/2013/09/a-rising-tide-lifts-mostly-yachts/279769/.

45. Thomas Sowell, *Civil Rights: Rhetoric or Reality?* (New York: William
Morrow, 1984), pp. 20–21.

46. Thomas Sowell, *Intellectuals and Race* (New York: Basic Books, 2013),
pp. 10–18.

47. Nicholas D. Kristof, "A Failed Experiment," *New York Times*, November 21, 2012, http://www.nytimes.com/2012/11/22/opinion/kristof-
a-failed-experiment.html?partner=rssnyt&emc=rss&_r=0.

48. Allison Benedikt, "If You Send Your Kid to Private School, You Are

a Bad Person," *Slate*, August 29, 2013, http://www.slate.com/articles/double_x/doublex/2013/08/private_school_vs_public_school_only_bad_people_send_their_kids_to_private.html.

49. Matthew Yglesias, "It's Time to Tax America's Prep Schools," *Slate*, August 29, 2013, http://www.slate.com/blogs/money-box/2013/08/29/tax_private_schools.html.

50. John Cook, "There's a Simple Solution to the Public Schools Crisis," *Gawker*, September 13, 2012, http://gawker.com/5943005/theres-a-simple-solution-to-the-public-schools-crisis.

51. Al Baker, "Gifted, Talented, and Separated," *New York Times*, January 13, 2013, http://www.nytimes.com/2013/01/13/education/in-one-school-students-are-divided-by-gifted-label-and-race.html?_r=0 .

52. Ibid.

53. Kaus, "Up from Altruism," p. 17.

54. Vincent M. Miles, "Old-Age Retirement Benefits," speech delivered November 16, 1936, http://www.ssa.gov/history/miles.html.

55. J. Douglas Brown, "The American Philosophy of Social Insurance," speech delivered November 28, 1955, http://www.ssa.gov/history/brown2.html.

56. Kaus, "Up from Altruism," p. 18.

57. "Democratic Party Platform of 1972," July 10, 1972, American Presidency Project, http://www.presidency.ucsb.edu/ws/?pid=29605.

58. "Democratic Party Platform of 2004," July 26, 2004, American Presidency Project, http://www.presidency.ucsb.edu/ws/?pid=29613.

59. Joshua Green, "The Angry Middle Class," *Atlantic*, September 23, 2010, http://www.theatlantic.com/politics/archive/2010/09/the-angry-middle-class/63417/.

60. Mark Schmitt, "If Liberals Want to Help the Poor, They Should Focus on the Middle Class," *New Republic*, February 23, 2012, http://www.newrepublic.com/article/politics/100895/foreclosure-middle-class-economy-jobs-housing-crisis.

61. Julia B. Isaacs, Isabel V. Sawhill, and Ron Haskins, *Getting Ahead or Losing Ground: Economic Mobility in America* (Washington, DC:

Brookings Institution, 2008), pp. 15–17, 22.

62. Scott Winship, "Our Misleading Obsession with Growth Rates," *Breakthrough Journal*, Winter 2013, http://thebreakthrough.org/index.php/journal/issue-3/the-affluent-economy/#.

63. Nicholas Lemann, "Stressed Out in Suburbia," *Atlantic*, November 1989, p. 42.

64. Matt Bai, *The Argument: Billionaires, Bloggers, and the Battle to Remake Democratic Politics* (New York: Penguin, 2007), p. 44.

65. Lee Siegel, "Thank You for Sharing," *New Republic*, June 5, 2006, http://www.tnr.com/politics/story.html?id=15d21968-03ba-437e-a5fd-f2712b592b21.

66. Pamela Haag, "Death by Treacle," *American Scholar*, Spring 2012, http://theamericanscholar.org/death-by-treacle/.

67. Lawrence A. Greenfield, "Prison Sentences and Time Served for Violence," U.S. Department of Justice, Office of Justice Programs, April 1995, NCJ-153858.

68. Jean Bethke Elshtain, "Sense and Sensibility," *New Republic*, September 30, 1996, p. 29.

69. Jonathan Haidt, *The Righteous Mind: Why Good People Are Divided by Politics and Religion* (New York: Pantheon, 2012), pp. 85–86.

70. Ibid., p. 91.

71. Garrison Keillor, *Homegrown Democrat: A Few Plain Thoughts from the Heart of America* (New York: Viking, 2004), p. 20.

72. Dan Savage, "Better Dead Than Red," *Portland Mercury*, November 11, 2004, http://www.portlandmercury.com/portland/better-dead-than-red/Content?oid=32491.

73. Jane Smiley, "The Unteachable Ignorance of the Red States," *Slate*, November 4, 2004, http://www.slate.com/articles/news_and_politics/politics/2004/11/why_americans_hate_democratsa_dialogue_8.html.

74. Christopher Lasch, *The Revolt of the Elites and the Betrayal of Democracy* (New York: Norton, 1995).

75. Sohrab Ahmari, "The Crisis of American Self-Government," *Wall*

Street Journal, November 30, 2012, http://online.wsj.com/article/SB 10001424127887323751104578149292503121124.html?mod=WSJ_ Opinion_LEADTop.

76. Walter Russell Mead, "Do Soldiers Drink Tea?," *American Interest*, February 21, 2010, http://www.the-american-interest.com/ wrm/2010/02/21/tea-party-off-the-rails-or-straight-to-the-top/.

77. "How the Race Was Won," *USA Today*, http://usatoday30.usatoday .com/news/graphics/elections-2012/how-race-was-won/index.html.

CHAPTER 4

1. 1988 Democratic Party Platform, American Presidency Project, http://www.presidency.ucsb.edu/ws/index.php?pid=29609.

2. Joe Klein, "Time to Ax Public Programs That Don't Yield Results," *Time*, July 7, 2011, http://www.time.com/time/nation/arti cle/0,8599,2081778,00.html.

3. U.S. Department of Health and Human Services, Press Office, "HHS Accelerates Head Start Quality Improvements and Submits Impact Study on 2002–2003 Head Start Programs," January 13, 2010, http:// www.hhs.gov/news/press/2010pres/01/20100113a.html.

4. Andrew J. Coulson, "Head Start: A Tragic Waste of Money," *New York Post*, January 28, 2010, http://www.nypost.com/p/news/opin ion/opedcolumnists/head_start_tragic_waste_of_money_L7V5d JC333RDC8QT8UEWaO.

5. Lindsey Burke, "Head Start's Sad and Costly Secret—What Washington Doesn't Want You to Know," Heritage Foundation, January 14, 2013, http://www.heritage.org/research/commentary/2013/1/ head-starts-sad-and-costly-secret-what-washington-doesnt-want-you-to-know.

6. See, for example, "Democratic Party Platform of 2000," August 14, 2000, American Presidency Project, http://www.presidency.ucsb .edu/ws/?pid=29612.

7. Barack Obama, "Remarks at the Yeadon Regional Head Start Center in Yeadon, Pennsylvania," November 8, 2011, American Presidency

Project, http://www.presidency.ucsb.edu/ws/?pid=97012.

8.   James Fallows, "Markets Can't Do Everything," *Washington Monthly*, January/February 1996, p. 27.

9.   Alan Wolfe, "Why Conservatives Can't Govern," *Washington Monthly*, July/August 2006, http://www.washingtonmonthly.com/features /2006/0607.wolfe.html.

10. Mark Hemingway, "Mitch the Knife," *National Review*, June 8, 2009.

11. Daniel Shapiro, *Is the Welfare State Justified?* (New York: Cambridge University Press, 2007), p. 5.

12. Joe Klein, "A Feast for Fat Cats, A Project for Liberals," *Time*, June 13, 2011, http://swampland.time.com/2011/06/13/a-feast-for-fat-cats-a-project-for-liberals/.

13. Harry G. Frankfurt, *On Bullshit* (Princeton, NJ: Princeton University Press, 2005), pp. 16, 18, 47.

14. Matthew B. Crawford, "The Case for Working with Your Hands," *New York Times Magazine*, May 24, 2009, http://www.nytimes.com/2009/05/24/ magazine/24labor-t.html?_r=1&hp=&pagewanted=all.

15. Frankfurt, *On Bullshit*, pp. 33–37.

16. Ibid., p. 65.

17. Siegel, "Thank You for Sharing."

18. Daniel J. Boorstin, *The Americans: The National Experience* (New York: Random House, 1965), pp. 296–97.

19. Frankfurt, *On Bullshit*, p. 67.

20. Michael Kelly, "The President's Past," *New York Times Magazine*, July 31, 1994.

21. Obama, "Remarks at the Yeadon Regional Head Start Center."

22. Franklin D. Roosevelt, "Address at Oglethorpe University," May 22, 1932, in *The Public Papers and Addresses of Franklin D. Roosevelt*, vol. 1, *1928–32* (New York: Random House, 1938), p. 639, http://newdeal .feri.org/speeches/1932d.htm.

23. Nathan Glazer, quoted in Daniel Patrick Moynihan, *Maximum Feasible Misunderstanding: Community Action in the War on Poverty* (New York: Free Press, 1969), p. 5.

24. Joe Klein, "Obama's Head Start Reform," *Time*, November 8, 2011, http://swampland.time.com/2011/11/08/obamas-head-start-reform/.

25. E. J. Dionne Jr., "The Noise Around Obamacare," *Washington Post*, November 3, 2013, http://www.washingtonpost.com/opinions/ej -dionne-jr-the-noise-around-obamacare/2013/11/03/1b6f8e6c-4352 -11e3-8b74-d89d714ca4dd_story.html.

26. Franklin Foer, "Obamacare's Threat to Liberalism," *New Republic*, November 24, 2013, http://www.newrepublic.com/article/115695/ obamacare-failure-threat-liberalism.

27. José Ortega y Gasset, *Meditations on Hunting*, trans. Howard B. Wescott (New York: Scribner, 1972), pp. 110–11.

28. "Press Gaggle by Press Secretary Jay Carney," July 22, 2012, American Presidency Project, http://www.presidency.ucsb.edu/ws/?pid=101546.

29. Barack Obama, "The President's News Conference," December 19, 2012, American Presidency Project, http://www.presidency.ucsb.edu/ ws/?pid=102775.

30. Margaret Talbot, "Shots in the Dark," *New Yorker*, April 15, 2013, http://www.newyorker.com/talk/comment/2013/04/15/130415ta- co_talk_talbot.

31. Barack Obama, "Remarks at the Sandy Hook Interfaith Prayer Vig- il in Newtown, Connecticut," December 16, 2012, American Presi- dency Project, http://www.presidency.ucsb.edu/ws/?pid=102767.

32. Barack Obama, "Remarks on Senate Action on Gun Control Leg- islation," April 17, 2013, American Presidency Project, http://www .presidency.ucsb.edu/ws/?pid=103499.

33. Barack Obama, "The President's News Conference," February 9, 2009, American Presidency Project, http://www.presidency.ucsb.edu/ ws/?pid=85728; Michael D. Shear and Anne E. Kornblut, "Obama Paints America's Choice as His Plan or Nothing," *Washington Post*, February 11, 2009, http://articles.washingtonpost.com/2009-02-11/ politics/36818709_1_stimulus-package-george-w-bush-president- obama; Helene Cooper, "Some Obama Enemies Are Made To- tally of Straw," *New York Times*, May 24, 2009, http://www.nytimes

.com/2009/05/24/us/politics/24straw.html.

34. Conor Friedersdorf, "Why 'If We Can Save Just One Child . . .' Is a Bad Argument," *Atlantic*, December 18, 2012, http://www.theat lantic.com/politics/archive/2012/12/why-if-we-can-just-save-one-child-is-a-bad-argument/266379/.

35. Adam Gopnik, "Guns on the Screen: A Failure of the Liberal Imagination?," *New Yorker*, April 11, 2013, http://www.newyorker.com/ online/blogs/comment/2013/04/guns-on-the-screen-a-failure-of-the-liberal-imagination.html.

36. Traffic data from the National Highway Traffic Safety Administration, http://www-fars.nhtsa.dot.gov/People/PeopleAllVictims.aspx. Gun data from National Center for Health Statistics, http://webap pa.cdc.gov/cgi-bin/broker.exe. See also Tom Vanderbilt, "Don't Turn Left!," *Slate*, August 1, 2011, http://www.slate.com/articles/life/ transport/2011/07/dont_turn_left.html.

37. Michael Tomasky, "A Shameful Day in the Senate," *Daily Beast*, April 18, 2013, http://www.thedailybeast.com/articles/2013/04/18/a-shameful-day-in-the-senate.html.

38. Adam Gopnik, "The Cultural Fight for Guns," *New Yorker*, April 4, 2013, http://www.newyorker.com/online/blogs/newsdesk/2013/04/ the-cultural-fight-for-guns.html.

39. Ibid.; Friedersdorf, "Why 'If We Can Save Just One Child . . .' Is a Bad Argument."

40. Sanford Levinson, "The Embarrassing Second Amendment," *Yale Law Journal* 99 (1989): 637–59. See also Randy Barnett, "Constitutional Conventions," *Claremont Review of Books*, Summer 2007, http://www.claremont.org/publications/crb/id.1382/article_detail .asp.

41. Barnett, "Constitutional Conventions"; Jeffrey Goldberg, "The Case for More Guns (and More Gun Control)," *Atlantic*, November 28, 2012, http://www.theatlantic.com/magazine/archive/2012/12/the-case-for-more-guns-and-more-gun-control/309161.

42. Goldberg, "More Guns."

43. Noam Scheiber, "Can We Please Drop the Gun Rights PC-Ness?," *New Republic*, July 23, 2012, http://www.newrepublic.com/blog/plank/105264/can-we-please-drop-the-gun-rights-pc-ness.

44. Joel Mathis, "Maybe Noam Scheiber Should Pipe Down," *Cup o' Joel*, July 25, 2012, http://joelmathis.blogspot.com/2012/07/maybe-noam-schreiber-should-pipe-down.html?q=Scheiber.

45. Goldberg, "More Guns."

46. Nedra Pickler, "Obama Taking Executive Action on Guns," *Real Clear Politics*, April 19, 2013, http://www.realclearpolitics.com/articles/2013/04/19/obama_taking_executive_action_on_guns_118044.html.

47. Julie Pace, "Obama Proposes Firearms Background Check Changes," Associated Press, January 3, 2014, http://news.yahoo.com/obama-proposes-firearm-background-check-changes-180246697--politics.html.

48. David Remnick, "No More Magical Thinking," *New Yorker*, November 19, 2012, http://www.newyorker.com/talk/comment/2012/11/19/121119taco_talk_remnick.

49. John Tierney, "Recycling Is Garbage," *New York Times Magazine*, June 30, 1996; Julian Sanchez, "Fifth Columnist," *Reason*, September 14, 2005, http://reason.com/archives/2005/09/14/fifth-columnist.

50. Tierney, "Recycling Is Garbage"; Sanchez, "Fifth Columnist."

51. Steven F. Hayward, *Index of Leading Environmental Indicators, 2008* (San Francisco: Pacific Research Institute, 2008), pp. 58–61.

52. Michael Shellenberger and Ted Nordhaus, "What Conservatives Can Teach Liberals About Global Warming Policy," NewGeography.com, October 1, 2013, http://www.newgeography.com/content/003963-what-conservatives-can-teach-liberals-about-global-warming-policy.

53. U.S. Energy Information Administration, *Annual Energy Review, 2011*, p. 225, Table 8.2b, http://www.eia.gov/totalenergy/data/annual/pdf/sec8_9.pdf.

54. Megan McArdle, "What Are We Going to Do About Carbon?,"

Daily Beast, June 25, 2013, http://www.thedailybeast.com/arti
cles/2013/06/25/how-we-imagine-carbon-control.html.

55. Michael O'Hare, "Things We Won't Hear in the Big Climate Speech
Tomorrow," *Reality-Based Community*, June 24, 2013, http://www
.samefacts.com/2013/06/politics-and-leadership/things-we-wont-
hear-in-the-big-climate-change-speech-tomorrow/.

56. McArdle, "What Are We Going to Do About Carbon?"

57. O'Hare, "Things We Won't Hear in the Big Climate Speech Tomorrow."

58. Sontag, essay for "What's Happening in America (A Symposium)," p. 58; Paul Watson, "The Beginning of the End for Life as
We Know It on Planet Earth?," Sea Shepherd Conservation Society, May 4, 2007, http://www.seashepherd.org/commentary-and-
editorials/2008/10/30/the-beginning-of-the-end-for-life-as-we-
know-it-on-planet-earth-340.

59. Watson, "The Beginning of the End for Life as We Know It on Planet
Earth?"; Vaclav Smil, "Global Population: Milestones, Hopes, and
Concerns," *Medicine and Global Survival*, October 1998, pp. 105–108.

60. Watson, "The Beginning of the End for Life as We Know It on Planet
Earth?"

61. "The Downside of Diversity," *Economist*, January 21, 2014, http://
www.economist.com/blogs/schumpeter/2014/01/schumpeters-
notebook?fsrc=scn/fb/wl/bl/downsideiveristy.

62. William M. Chace, "Affirmative Inaction," *American Scholar*, Winter
2012, http://theamericanscholar.org/affirmative-inaction.

63. Dahlia Lithwick, "The Legal Fiction of 'Diversity,'" *Slate*, May 16,
2002, http://www.slate.com/articles/news_and_politics/jurispru
dence/2002/05/the_legal_fiction_of_diversity.single.html.

64. Sara Rimer and Karen W. Arenson, "Top Colleges Take More
Blacks, but Which Ones?," *New York Times*, June 24, 2004, http://
www.nytimes.com/2004/06/24/us/top-colleges-take-more-blacks-
but-which-ones.html?pagewanted=all&src=pm.

65. Nicholas Lemann, "Taking Affirmative Action Apart," *New York Times Magazine*, June 11, 1995.

66. Julie Marquis, "Liposuction Doctor Has License Revoked," *Los Angeles Times*, August 26, 1998, http://articles.latimes.com/1998/aug/26/news/mn-16736; Eric Malnic, "Doctor in Landmark Anti-Bias Case Slain," *Los Angeles Times*, August 13, 2002, http://articles.latimes.com/2002/aug/13/local/me-chavis13.

67. Richard Sander and Stuart Taylor Jr., "The Painful Truth About Affirmative Action," *Atlantic*, October 2, 2012, http://www.theatlantic.com/national/archive/2012/10/the-painful-truth-about-affirmative-action/263122/.

68. Balamurali Ambati, "Health Care," blog post, July 25, 2009, http://daylightsmark.blogspot.com/2009/07/health-care-those-who-are-not-liberal.html. See also Carmen DeNavas-Walt, Bernadette D. Proctor, and Jessica C. Smith, U.S. Census Bureau, Current Population Reports, P60-235, *Income, Poverty, and Health Insurance Coverage in the United States: 2007* (Washington, DC: U.S. Government Printing Office, 2008).

69. Virginia Postrel, Dynamist blog, http://www.dynamist.com/weblog/archives/003001.html, http://www.dynamist.com/weblog/archives/003003.html.

70. Barack Obama, "Address Before a Joint Session of the Congress," February 24, 2009, American Presidency Project, http://www.presidency.ucsb.edu/ws/?pid=85753.

71. Sarah Kliff, "Study: Expanding Medicaid Doesn't Reduce ER Trips. It Increases Them," *Washington Post*, January 2, 2014, http://www.washingtonpost.com/blogs/wonkblog/wp/2014/01/02/study-expanding-medicaid-doesnt-reduce-er-trips-it-increases-them.

72. Richard A. Serrano, "High-Tech Border Fence Is Slow Going," *Los Angeles Times*, February 22, 2010, http://articles.latimes.com/2010/feb/22/nation/la-na-border-fence22-2010feb22.

73. Nicholas Kristof, "Prudence or Cruelty?," *New York Times*, November 16, 2013, http://www.nytimes.com/2013/11/17/opinion/sunday/prudence-or-cruelty.html.

74. Nicholas Kristof, "This Is Why We Need Obamacare," *New York Times*, November 2, 2013, http://www.nytimes.com/2013/11/03/opinion/sunday/kristof-this-is-why-we-need-obamacare.html.

75. Peter Schrag, "In California, the Minority Still Rules," *California Progress Report*, July 11, 2011, http://www.californiaprogressreport.com/site/california-minority-still-rules.

76. The expenditure calculations are based on U.S. Census Bureau data on state and local finances (available at http://www.census.gov/govs/estimate/) and state population estimates (http://www.census.gov/popest/data/historical/index.html). The GDP chained price index used to adjust expenditures for inflation is available in Historical Table 10.1 of the *Budget for the U.S. Government in 2013*, http://www.gpo.gov/fdsys/pkg/BUDGET-2013-TAB/xls/BUDGET-2013-TAB-10-1.xls.

77. Andrew Ferguson, "Staggering Idiocy," *Weekly Standard*, October 22, 2012, http://www.weeklystandard.com/articles/staggering-idiocy_654414.html?page=1.

78. Barack Obama, "Address Before a Joint Session of the Congress on the State of the Union," January 25, 2011, American Presidency Project, http://www.presidency.ucsb.edu/ws/?pid=88928.

79. William J. Clinton, "Remarks Announcing the National Performance Review," March 3, 1993, American Presidency Project, http://www.presidency.ucsb.edu/ws/index.php?pid=46291&st=&st1=.

80. Matt Bai, "What Obama Still Hasn't Figured Out About Being President," *Yahoo News*, January 30, 2014, http://news.yahoo.com/what-obama-still-hasn-t-figured-out-about-being-president-221911009.html.

81. U.S. Department of Health and Human Services, "2012 HHS Poverty Guidelines," http://aspe.hhs.gov/poverty/12poverty.shtml.

82. William A. Galston, "Where Left and Right Agree on Inequality," *Wall Street Journal*, January 14, 2014, http://online.wsj.com/news/articles/SB10001424052702304049704579320663685569006?mg=reno64-wsj&url=http%3A%2F%2Fonline.wsj.com%2Farticle%2FSB10001424052702304049704579320663685569006.html.

CHAPTER 5

1. William Graham Sumner, "The Forgotten Man," in *The Forgotten Man and Other Essays,* ed. Albert Galloway Keller (New Haven, CT: Yale University Press, 1918), http://oll.libertyfund.org/title/2396/226423.

2. Franklin D. Roosevelt, "Radio Address from Albany, New York: 'The "Forgotten Man" Speech,'" April 7, 1932, American Presidency Project, http://www.presidency.ucsb.edu/ws/?pid=88408.

3. For a pro-Sumner account of the shift from his to Roosevelt's interpretation of the undeservedly neglected, see Amity Shlaes, *The Forgotten Man: A New History of the Great Depression* (New York: Harper, 2007).

4. Penn Jillette, "I Don't Know, So I'm an Atheist Libertarian," CNN, August 17, 2011, http://www.cnn.com/2011/OPINION/08/16/jillette.atheist.libertarian/index.html.

5. Henry Louis Mencken, *Minority Report: H. L. Mencken's Notebooks* (New York: Knopf, 1956), p. 247.

6. Republican Party Platform of 1936, June 9, 1936, American Presidency Project, http://www.presidency.ucsb.edu/ws/index.php?pid=29639.

7. Friedrich A. von Hayek, *The Road to Serfdom* (1944; reprint, New York: Routledge Classics, 2001), pp. 13–14.

8. William F. Buckley Jr., *Athwart History: Half a Century of Polemics, Animadversions, and Illuminations: A William F. Buckley Jr. Omnibus* (New York: Encounter Books, 2009), p. 20.

9. Ronald Reagan, Farewell Address, January 11, 1989, http://www.reaganlibrary.net/.

10. Michael Duffy and Michael Scherer, "The Role Model: What Obama Sees in Reagan," *Time,* January 27, 2011, http://www.time.com/time/magazine/article/0,9171,2044712-1,00.html.

11. Barack Obama, "Commencement Address at Ohio State University in Columbus, Ohio," May 5, 2013, American Presidency Project, http://www.presidency.ucsb.edu/ws/index.php?pid=103570&st=&st1.

12. Jess Bravin, "Fight Against EPA Orders Heads to Supreme Court," *Wall Street Journal*, January 9, 2012, http://online.wsj.com/article/SB1 00014240529702034369045771490001510886324.html.

13. Jonathan H. Adler, "Sackett Oral Argument," *Volokh Conspiracy*, January 9, 2012, http://www.volokh.com/2012/01/09/sackett-oral-argument/; Lyle Denniston, "A Weak Defense of EPA," SCOTUS Blog, January 9, 2012, http://www.scotusblog.com/2012/01/a-weak-defense-of-epa/.

14. "The Sacketts and the Clean Water Act," *New York Times*, January 9, 2012, p. 18.

15. Ilya Somin, "Unanimous Supreme Court Rules in Favor of Property Owners in Sackett v. EPA," *Volokh Conspiracy*, March 21, 2012, http://www.volokh.com/2012/03/21/unanimous-supreme-court-rules-in-favor-of-property-owners-in-sackett-v-epa.

16. Sarah Conly, "Three Cheers for the Nanny State," *New York Times*, March 24, 2013, http://www.nytimes.com/2013/03/25/opinion/three-cheers-for-the-nanny-state.html?pagewanted=all&_r=1&nl=todaysheadlines&emc=edit_th_20130325&.

17. Ibid.

18. Ben Adler, "Ban the Bats," *American Prospect*, April 24, 2007, http://prospect.org/article/ban-bats.

19. Sarah O. Conly, Bowdoin College faculty biography, http://www.bowdoin.edu/faculty/s/sconly/.

20. C. S. Lewis, *God in the Dock: Essays on Theology and Ethics* (Grand Rapids, MI: Eerdmans, 1970), p. 292.

21. Lionel Trilling, *The Liberal Imagination* (New York: Viking, 1950), p. 221.

22. Patricia Murphy, "The Senate's Last Compassionate Conservative Tries to Help the Jobless," *Daily Beast*, January 7, 2014, http://www.thedailybeast.com/articles/2014/01/07/the-senate-s-last-compassionate-conservative-tries-to-help-the-jobless.html.

23. Elizabeth Harrington, "Mass. Gov. Knocks 'Hard Right' for Wanting to 'Shrink Government, Cut Taxes, Crush Unions,'" *CNS News*,

June 15, 2012, http://cnsnews.com/news/article/mass-gov-knocks-hard-right-wanting-shrink-government-cut-taxes-crush-unions.

24. The video is available at http://www.youtube.com/user/char lottein2012.

25. Steven M. Teles, "The Eternal Return of Compassionate Conservatism," *National Affairs*, Fall 2009, http://www.nationalaffairs .com/publications/detail/the-eternal-return-of-compassionate-conservatism.

26. George Bush, "Inaugural Address," January 20, 1989, American Presidency Project, http://www.presidency.ucsb.edu/ws/?pid=16610.

27. George W. Bush, "Remarks Announcing Candidacy for the Republican Presidential Nomination," June 12, 1999, American Presidency Project, http://www.presidency.ucsb.edu/ws/?pid=77819.

28. George W. Bush, "Address Accepting the Presidential Nomination at the Republican National Convention in Philadelphia," August 3, 2000, American Presidency Project, http://www.presidency.ucsb .edu/ws/?pid=25954.

29. John DiIulio, "John DiIulio's Letter," *Esquire*, October 24, 2002, http://www.esquire.com/features/dilulio.

30. "Births: Final Data for 2011," National Vital Statistics Reports, vol. 62, no. 1, National Center for Health Statistics, U.S. Department of Health and Human Services, http://www.cdc.gov/nchs/data/nvsr/ nvsr62/nvsr62_01.pdf#table16.

31. Josh Mitchell, "About Half of Kids with Single Moms Live in Poverty," *Wall Street Journal*, November 25, 2013, http://blogs.wsj.com/ economics/2013/11/25/about-half-of-kids-with-single-moms-live-in-poverty/.

32. Milton Friedman, *Capitalism and Freedom* (Chicago: University of Chicago Press, 1962), p. 191.

33. Franklin D. Roosevelt, "Campaign Address at Detroit, Michigan," October 2, 1932, American Presidency Project, http://www.presiden cy.ucsb.edu/ws/index.php?pid=88393.

34. Ibid.

35. Ibid.; Leon Wieseltier, "Climates," *New Republic*, August 6, 2007, http://www.tnr.com/columnists/story.html?id=908491de-b0d0-4d2b-8b1e-7bca0fb8bed8&p=1.

36. Computations based on OECD Social Expenditures Database (http://www.oecd.org/social/expenditure.htm) and OECD Factbook 2013 data on gross national income (http://www.oecd-ilibrary.org/econom ics/oecd-factbook-2013/national-income-per-capita_factbook-2013-22-en). Gross national income is a slightly different measure than gross domestic product. As the Factbook explains, "Whereas GDP refers to the income generated by production activities on the economic territory of the country, GNI measures the income generated by the residents of a country, whether earned on the domestic territory or abroad."

37. Alan Wolfe, *Whose Keeper? Social Science and Moral Obligation* (Berkeley: University of California Press, 1989), p. 142.

38. George Lakoff, "The Price of Our Freedom," *Huffington Post*, December 17, 2012, http://www.huffingtonpost.com/george-lakoff/the-price-of-our-freedom_b_2314658.html.

39. Bertrand de Jouvenel, *The Ethics of Redistribution* (1952; reprint, Indianapolis: Liberty Press, 1990), pp. 54–57.

40. Hamill, "Doing Good," p. 39.

41. Joseph Cropsey, "Conservatism and Liberalism," in Robert A. Goldwin, ed., *Left, Right and Center: Essays on Liberalism and Conservatism in the United States* (Chicago: Rand McNally, 1965), p. 54.

42. Robert Kuttner, *Revolt of the Haves: Tax Rebellions and Hard Times* (New York: Simon & Schuster, 1980), p. 103.

43. U.S. Census Bureau, *Public Education Finances: 2011*, G11-ASPEF (Washington, DC: U.S. Government Printing Office, 2013), p. 8.

44. William A. Fischel, "How Judges Are Making Public Schools Worse," *City Journal*, Summer 1998, http://www.city-journal.org/html/8_3_how_judges.html.

45. Richard Rorty, *Contingency, Irony, and Solidarity* (Cambridge: Cambridge University Press, 1989), p. 86.

46. Geoffrey Wheatcroft, "A Terrifying Honesty," *Atlantic*, February 2002, http://www.theatlantic.com/magazine/archive/2002/02/a-terrifying-honesty/302426/.

47. Tod Lindberg, "Left 3.0," *Policy Review*, No. 177, 2013, http://www.hoover.org/publications/policy-review/article/139271.

48. Richard A. Epstein, *How Progressives Rewrote the Constitution* (Washington, DC: Cato Institute, 2006), pp. 5–7. See also U.S. Bureau of the Census, *Historical Statistics of the United States: Colonial Times to 1957* (Washington, DC: U.S. Government Printing Office, 1960), Series D 1-10, Series D 32-46.

49. Peter Beinart, "How Obama Did It," *Daily Beast*, May 21, 2010, http://www.thedailybeast.com/articles/2010/03/21/how-obama-did-it.html.

50. David Brooks, *Bobos in Paradise: The New Upper Class and How They Got There* (New York: Simon & Schuster, 2000), p. 135.

51. Harold Meyerson, "From Japan's Devastation, Our Lisbon Moment?," *Washington Post*, March 15, 2011, http://www.washingtonpost.com/opinions/from-japans-devastation-our-lisbon-moment/2011/03/15/ABPH0yZ_story.html.

52. Friedman, *Capitalism and Freedom*, pp. 191–95.

53. Charles Murray, *In Our Hands: A Plan to Replace the Welfare State* (Washington, DC: American Enterprise Institute, 2006), pp. 10–14, 130–39.

54. William F. Buckley Jr., *Four Reforms: A Guide for the Seventies* (New York: Putnam, 1973).

55. Murray, *In Our Hands*, p. 14.

56. See David T. Beito, *From Mutual Aid to the Welfare State: Fraternal Societies and Social Services, 1890–1967* (Chapel Hill: University of North Carolina Press, 2000).

57. Jonathan Rieder, *Canarsie: The Jews and Italians of Brooklyn Against Liberalism* (Cambridge, MA: Harvard University Press, 1985), p. 6.

58. James W. Ceaser, "True Blue vs. Deep Red: The Ideas That Move American Politics," discussion paper for the Hudson Institute's 2006

Bradley Symposium, p. 16, http://www.bradleyfdn.org/pdfs/framing essay.pdf.

59. Ronald Brownstein, "Population Trends Boosting the Democrats Show No Sign of Slowing," *National Journal*, January 10, 2009, http://www.nationaljournal.com/njmagazine/politicalconnections.php; Ronald Brownstein, "Today's Politics: Coalition of Transformation vs. Coalition of Restoration," *National Journal*, November 21, 2012, http://www.nationaljournal.com/columns/political-connections/today-s-politics-coalition-of-transformation-vs-coalition-of-restoration-20121121.

60. Donat Gallagher, ed., *The Essays, Articles and Reviews of Evelyn Waugh* (Boston: Little, Brown, 1983), pp. 161–62, 634–35.

INDEX

Democratic Party

as party of government, 228

political use of compassion, xvi–xviii

principle constituencies of, 238

Democratic Republic of the Congo (DRC), per capital GDP of, 35

Denmark, social welfare in, 70–72, 75, 216–17

DiIulio, John, 210

Dionne, E. J. Jr., 150–51

Discourse on Inequality (Rousseau), 21–22

diversity. *See* affirmative action

domestic policies, compassion and, 85–137

consequences of lack of self-reliance, 111–18

criticisms of self-reliance, 118–22

culture of victimhood developed, 94–100

dependence versus self-reliance, 91–93

helplessness emphasized, 86–88

liberals' reactions to disagreement with, 132–37

scale of concern and, 88–91

social and political aspects of victimhood, 122–31

U.S. spending on welfare as percentage of GDP, 77

white guilt and black victimhood, 100–111

see also social welfare programs

Don't Think of an Elephant! Know Your Values and Frame the Debate (Lakoff), 9–10

Dorr, Rheta Childe, 89

Douthat, Ross, 49, 75–76

Dukakis, Michael, 208

Dunham, Stanley Ann, xiii–xiv

Ebert, Roger, xvii

economic growth, and liberals' views on social welfare, 66–72

"Economic Mobility Project," of Pew Charitable Trust, 128

Economist, 173

Edelman, Marian Wright, 88, 89, 107–8, 119

education

California and equal finding of all school districts, 220–22

gifted programs, 120–22

private schools, 119–20

see also affirmative action

Edwards, John, 127

Egypt, per capital GDP of, 36

8 Mile (film), 113

Ellis Island immigrants, assimilation and, 79–80, 82

Elshtain, Jean Bethke, 91, 108, 131

Ely, Richard T., 100–101

empathy, defined, 4. *See also* compassion

ABOUT THE AUTHOR

William Voegeli is the author of *Never Enough: America's Limitless Welfare State*, a visiting scholar at the Henry Salvatori Center at Claremont McKenna College, and a contributing senior editor to the *Claremont Review of Books*. His reviews and articles have also appeared in *City Journal*, *Commentary*, *First Things*, *In Character*, the *Los Angeles Times*, the *National Review*, and the *New Criterion*. From 1988 to 2003 he was a program officer at the John M. Olin Foundation. He lives in Claremont, California.